Pembr

Alan James

Mike Robertson

A rock climbing guide to the best areas on the Pembrokeshire Coast

Text, topos, photo-topos, maps Alan James and Mike Robertson
Additional editing Chris Craggs
Cartoons by Alan James

All maps by ROCKFAX. Some maps based on source maps kindly supplied by Collins Maps (www.collins.co.uk).

Printed by Hawthornes, Nottingham
Distributed by Cordee
(Tel: (+int) 44 (0) 145 561 1185)

Published by ROCKFAX Ltd. August 2009

www.rockfax.com

All Rockfax books are printed in the UK.
We only use paper made from wood fibre from sustainable forests and produced according to ISO 14001 environmental standard

ISBN 978-1-873341-12-4

This page: Tim Emmett maintaining three points of contact on his link-up of *Stennis the Menace* and *The Great Elmyra* (E6) - *page 144* - at Stennis Head. Photo: Ian Parnell

Cover: Katie Dominey on *Sea Mist* (HS) - *page 104* - at Saddle Head. Photo: Mike Robertson

Mewsford
Castle/Rusty
Saddle Head
Bosherston Head
Huntsman's Leap
Stennis/Chapel
Trevallen
St. Govan's
Mowing/Stackpole
Mother Carey's

AWESOME WALLS
CLIMBING CENTRE
STOCKPORT
23.5m lead walls, 400sqm bouldering
no membership fees, loyalty card
Awesome (adjective) - so impressive or overwhelming as to inspire a strong feeling of admiration or fear.
(Encarta Dictionary U.K.)
The Engine House, Pear Mill Ind Est, Lower Bredbury
Stockport, SK6 2BP. TEL 0161 494 9949
www.awesomewalls.co.uk
Photo: David SImmonite

Contents

Mark Glaister climbing *Poison Arrow* (E4) - *page 181* - at St Govan's. Photo: Alan James

Moon-rise over Stack Rocks. Photo: Chris Craggs

It's been said that the cliffs of Pembrokeshire are the finest sea cliffs in the world, and I'm inclined to agree. Pembroke epitomises all that our eclectic world of climbing can offer: isolation, wonderment, freedom, space - and a feeling that you're poised on the very edge of nowhere, a place that only the circling gulls and the diving seals can call home. These hinterland qualities, combined with the nuances of the wide-ranging tides, give the region that magical wild-coast flavour. Nowhere else on earth will you discover such a serene oceanic atmosphere coupled with the superb physicality of Pembroke's perfect cliffs, and nowhere else can offer the sheer quantity of its endless tally of routes.

A brief introduction to the cliffs of the region would never be complete without reference to some of the classic areas - the easy-to-navigate, vast walls of Trevallen and St Govan's, the walk-in delights of Stennis Head, and the deep, thrilling chasms of Huntsman's Leap and Stennis Ford. Whilst further into the amazing Range East, we have the grade-friendly Saddle Head, the grand testpieces of The Castle, and the delightful outlying walls and slabs of Mewsford, Crickmail and Flimston Bay, along with all the guaranteed pleasures of Rusty Walls, Misty Walls, Triple Overhang and the atmospheric Hollow Caves Bay. Reaching out eastwards gives yet more excellence: the massive walls of Mowing Word and Stackpole Head provide a bewildering array of challenges, whilst the outlying venue of Mother Carey's is the perfect Tenby-side experience.
In these pages, you'll also find North Pembroke's stunning, south-facing coastline, found close-by to the miniature 'city' of St David's. The rock here is glorious; fine-grained, purple-red sandstone, fast-drying, and significantly more colourful than its limestone counterpart! The angles are more slabby, with a grade average to suit. Carreg-y-Barcud certainly provides the choicest plums, but that's not all the area's sandstone has to offer. The small but beautifully-formed slabs of Porth-Clais, Porth-y-Ffynnon, St Non's Bay, Initiation Slabs and Craig Caerfai provide excellent, mostly well-protected classics - and the majority of these fall into the sub-E1 category. There's possibly no better place to hone your leading skills in Pembrokeshire than on these compact, colourful slabs.

So yes: Pembroke may be the absolute queen of sea cliffs! Experiencing the diversity and charm of Pembroke has never been more accessible than now, and the vast range of routes and grades make it the perfect destination for climbers from all over the world.

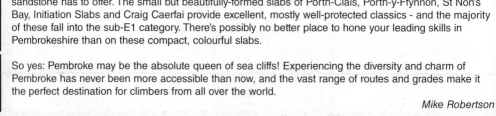

Mike Robertson

Libby Peter climbing the beautiful red wall of *Chinon* (HVS) - *page 46* - on the Velvet Wall at Porth-y-Ffynnon. Photo: Mike Robertson

The 1995 Pembroke Rockfax

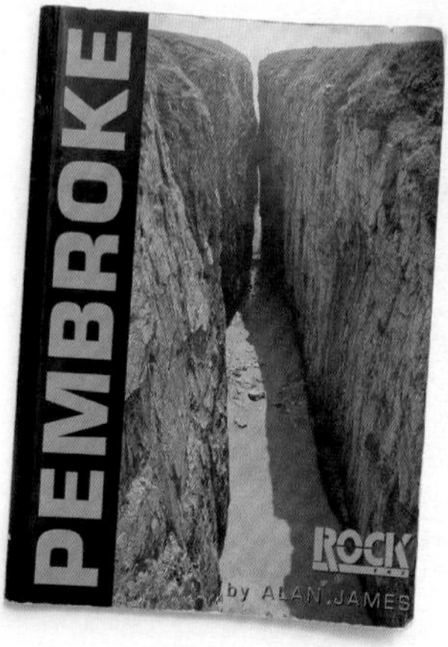

Back in 1995 the 'Pembroke Rockfax' caused something of a stir. Prior to its publication, there hadn't been many privately-produced guidebooks to traditional climbing areas and no-one knew what to make of it - a useful addition to the UK guidebook repertoire, or the 'thin end of the wedge' and the beginning of the end for definitive guidebooks? Whatever the thoughts of the politicians of the time, the detailed topos and precise approach maps were welcomed by those who wished to explore Pembroke. More significantly, it marked a change from guidebooks which stood as a record of what had been climbed, to guidebooks which emphasised the climbing and the routes from the point of view of the reader who was wanting to climb them. It was an important book for Rockfax, one which was key to developing the style with which we now produce all our books, a style which has influenced many of the guidebooks being produced today.

This Guidebook

This 2009 edition of the Pembroke Rockfax is a selective guide which means that it only covers the major sections, of the best cliffs in Pembroke. In general, if we include a buttress, then we will include most of the routes on that buttress even if that means a few lesser routes are listed. The idea is to give climbers a full picture of what is available once they have made the effort to get to the crag, but that does mean including the odd route which isn't a super classic. In total there are 658 routes described in detail which will keep most climbers happy for more than a lifetime's worth of visits.

Route Lines - The photo-topos in this book are big, really big. This has enabled us to mark the route lines on very clearly, showing intricate detail of where the routes go. We have taken great care when adding the route lines but it is inevitable that some may not be exactly right, especially on the more obscure routes and on routes where there is no precise line. If you are unsure then use your own judgement to pick out a line, and let us know via the Rockfax Route Database (**www.rockfax.com**).

There are actually thousands of routes along the Pembrokeshire Coast, including the whole of Range West which isn't covered in this book. For a more complete list of the climbing in Pembroke you should consult the series of guidebooks produced by the Climbers' Club. Their two volume 1995 book is due to be updated in 2010/12 with a series of 5 books. For more information consult the Climbers' Club web site - **www.climbers-club.co.uk**

The information in this book has come from a number of sources with personal experience figuring highly. My collection of old guides has grown considerably over the years and most are filled with scribbles, including a rather tatty copy of the excellent Harber/de Montjoye guide from 1985, a book which was the catalyst for many older climbers to start their love affair/obsession with the sea cliffs of Pembroke. Other information has come from active climbers and there has been a huge amount of feedback submitted to the Rockfax Route Database (**www.rockfax.com**) and the UKClimbing.com Logbook system (**www.ukclimbing.com**).

We would like to acknowledge the effort put in by all those who have worked on documenting the climbing of the Pembrokeshire Coast over the years. This is a vast area with complex access where quick and easy research is hampered by the obvious difficulty of viewing the routes properly. It is an impossible task to document everything with 100% accuracy, but hopefully we can at least record routes in a way that inspires those who want to explore, and provide good information for those who want to climb the classics.

Guidebook Footnote

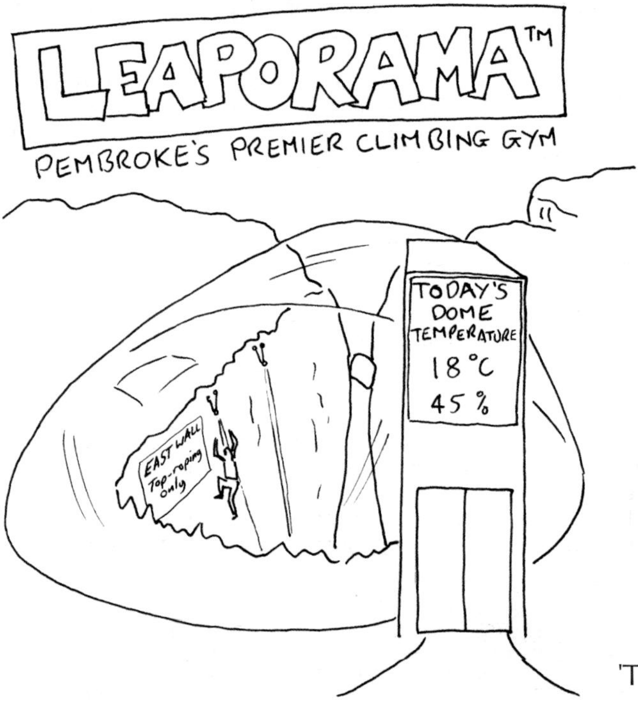

Summer Specials!

Manic Mondays

Come and join in the fun on our Deep Water Solo Specials, as we let the tide in every Monday over the summer!

Cool Wednesdays

Need optimum conditions for your redpoint? Come along and enjoy temperatures of less than 10°C with only 20% humidity!

Weekend Winners

Get 3 routes for the price of two every weekend in August!

Coming Soon
Leporama™ 2
'THE STENNIS SENSATION'

The thick end of the wedge!

Acknowledgements

It's been an absolute pleasure to work once again with Alan on this, my second Rockfax guide, and I owe him a big thanks for this. The project has meant numerous trips to, let's face it, one of the best spots in the known universe, and also prompted my purchase (finally) of a 'proper' inflatable boat and outboard motor - an invaluable tool for all those elusive crag shots! A year or so has passed since these water-borne picture antics were complete, and the colourful end result is now something I think every Pembroke enthusiast will both enjoy and use to the full.

I also owe a huge thanks to many of my climbing pals, without whom this project would have been a great deal more difficult, and infinitely less fun! These folk have all dished the good dirt on all their favourite crags, zawns, bays and caves, and their enthusiasm for this incredible slice of Welsh coastline has been entirely infectious...

So to Julian Lines, for all his invaluable and unfailing assistance with matters both on and off the waves, and also to Dave Pickford, Steve Findlay, Julian Walker, Meilee Rafe, Libby Peter, Gavin Symonds, Sarah Garnett, Simon Tappin and Mark Taylor.

Mike Robertson, July 2009

This book has been a real pleasure to put together. I am grateful to all those who helped with the previous Pembroke guidebooks and those who have given feedback which we have been able to use in this book. Special mention to: Chris Craggs (photos, proofing and route-checking with Colin), Dave Pickford (hard routes and photos), Dave Moore (North Coast), Tim Lounds (great local contact), Jack Geldard (photos, proofing and stalwart member of the Campaign for Real Grades - CamReG), Sherri Davy (advertising), Sophie Milner (bird information), Stefan Doerr, Jordan Buys, Mark Davies, Steve Findlay, Frank Ramsay, Stuart Lade, James McHaffie and Pete Robins.

The photography in this book is probably the best ever seen in a climbing guidebook. In addition to those mentioned above, many thanks to: Ian Parnell, Chad Harrison, Jamie Moss, Patrick Daniel, Sarah Clough, Kev Little, Mike Hutton, Nick Smith, Tim Wilkinson, Mick Ryan, James Marshall, Scott Sadler, Chris Sims, Jon Fullwood, Gareth Hallam and Mark Glaister for their superb contributions.

These days I have far less time to actually author books but Pembroke is one area which I have been reluctant to pass onto someone else. Luckily Mike stepped up and offered his services to update the old information and undertake the huge task of getting a set of quality crag shots from the sea. In terms of coastal sea cliff crag photography, there is no-one better or more dedicated in the world. My thanks to Mike for all his work on the photography and text.

In 1995 I dedicated the book to Hannah and Henriette; this time I'd like to dedicate it to Henriette, Hannah, Sam and Lydia. 14 years ago I accused the baby Hannah of bashing the keyboard with her tiny fists, this time her comment when she looked at a copy of the 1995 book was, "blimey, that looks old-fashioned". How times change!

Alan James, July 2009

Mike and Alan checking lines at St Govan's. Photo: Mick Ryan

Activities Centre

Wet and High Adventures - *page 9*
Somerset. Tel: 07887 737076
www.wetandhigh.co.uk

Accommodation

Thorne Chapel Bunkhouse
- *back flap and page 15*
Thorne, near Bosherston. Tel 01646 661240
www.pembrokerocks.com

Climbing Walls

Awesome Walls - *contents and page 31*
St Alban's Church, Liverpool.
Tel: 0151 298 2422
The Engine House, Stockport.
Tel: 0161 494 9949
www.awesomewalls.co.uk

Boulders - *page 17*
St Catherine's Park, Cardiff.
Tel: 0845 52 118 50
www.boulders-climbing.com

Dynamic Rock - *inside back cover*
16-18 Hebron Road, Swansea.
Tel 01792 845655
www.dynamicrock.co.uk

DR Walls - *page 27*
39 Steps Leeds Road, Otley.
Tel: 0113 284 2369
www.drclimbingwalls.com

Shops

High Sport - *page 7*
51-52 Wyle Cop, Shrewsbury.
Tel 01743 231 649
www.highsports.co.uk

Mountain Intelligence - *back cover*
70 North Street, Leeds.Tel 0113 246 9843
www.mountain-intelligence.co.uk

Other Advertisers

British Mountaineering Council - *page 23*
177-179 Burton Road, Manchester.
Tel: 0161 445 6111
www.thebmc.com

Berghaus - *inside front cover*
Extreme Centre, Sunderland.
Tel: 0191 516 5700
www.berghaus.com

Plas y Brenin - *page 25*
Capel Curig, North Wales.
Tel: 01690 720214
www.pyb.co.uk

Simon Tappin stretching for a runner on *Oratorio* (E3) - *page 95* - at Misty Walls. Photo: Dave Pickford

Pembroke Logistics

Great days on the rock are usually followed by extensive debriefing sessions at the Bosherston Inn.. Photo: Mick Ryan

St. David's
Flimston Bay
Mewsford
Castle/Rusty
Saddle Head
Bosherston Head
Huntsman's Leap
Stennis/Chapel
Trevallen
St. Govan's
Mowing/Stackpole
Mother Carey's

In Emergency

Dial 999 and ask for 'MILFORD HAVEN COASTGUARD'

They have knowledge of the climbing areas and routes and can co-ordinate any rescue efforts.

Mobile Phones

Mobile phone coverage in Pembroke is very poor by modern standards. Many providers don't get a steady signal after you pass St Petrox on the approach to Bosherston, and Bosherston itself is hopeless for older phones, which can be frustrating if you are used to using your mobile to arrange to meet up with people. You can usually get a signal from the top of St Govan's and also at other points from the clifftops in the Range. 999 calls are routed via any available network so you are usually able to find a signal in emergencies but sometimes they are routed via North Devon so please specify 'Milford Haven Coastguard'.

Tourist Information

For more information on accommodation, places to visit, events, walks and weather, then take a look at the following web sites and TI Offices which have far more information than is included here.

www.visitpembrokeshire.com

Pembroke TIC - Tel: 01437 776499
St David's TIC - Tel: 01437 720392
Haverfordwest TIC - Tel: 01437 763110

'Gypsy Colin' in some alternative Pembroke accommodation. Photo: Chris Craggs

Camping

There are lots of campsites all over Pembrokshire, the two sites which are most popular with climbers staying in the south are listed below.

St Petrox - *The Old Rectory, St Petrox, Pembrokeshire, SA71 5EQ.*
Tel: 01646 683980

All facilities and in a convenient position half way between Pembroke and Bosherston. Climbers are always welcome and you can book in advance, there is no pub within walking distance though.

Glebe Campsite - *Glebe Farmhouse, Bosherton, Pembrokeshire, SA71 5DN.*
Tel: 01646 661352

Situated in the village of Bosherston, it has three fields and all facilities. You can turn up late without pre-booking although it does crowded on bank holiday weekends. Great location for the pub.

There are numerous campsites on the St David's peninsula of all standards. There are camping options around the St David's itself, but check the prices before you commit - some of them are expensive.

Caerfai Farm - *St David's, Pembrokeshire, SA62 6QT. Tel: 01437 720548*

A 5 minute walk from St David's and a 20 minutes walk from Carreg-y-Barcud.

Not Camping

There a lots of B&B's in Pembroke, St David's and Tenby. Holiday cottages are also plentiful. For more information, contact one of the TICs listed above or put 'cottages pembrokeshire' into Google.

Thorne Chapel Bunkhouse (see opposite) - Thorne, Merrion, Pembrokeshire, SA71 5EA.
Tel: 01646 661240

Bunkhouse (for 10) and house (for 4) for rental, plus 3 gypsy caravans (for 2 each - see photo above). Fully catered or self-catering. Only 5km from Bosherston. **www.pembrokerocks.com**

Thorne Chapel
Bunkhouse
Three miles
from 3000 routes:
and some great beaches......
Bunkhouse
Gypsy Caravans
Self Catering
Half Board
Transport
Five minutes drive from
St Govan's Head
www.pembrokerocks.com
Tel: 01646 661240

Pubs

Pubs and pub talk are integral to climbing and it is important to know where the best places are to hang out after a tiring day at the crag. There are many more pubs than listed below but these tend to be of most interest to climbers.

St Govan's Inn - Bosherston, Pembrokeshire. Tel: (01646) 661311
Real ales and a full menu. THE pub for post-crag anaylsis.
Swanlake Inn - Jameston, Manorbier, Pembrokeshire. Tel: (01834) 871262
The Armstrong Arms - Jasons Corner, Stackpole, Pembrokeshire. Tel: (01646) 672324
The Salutation - On the road from Pembroke to Castlemartin.
Farmer's Arms - Goat Street, St David's. The best pub for Barcud. Good food and an outside terrace.

Cafes

Around here, cafe means pots of tea and toasted tea cakes while greasy full set breakfasts are hard to find. The following two are the ones best situated for the climbing areas:
The Olde Worlde Cafe (Ma Weston's) - The legendary cafe situated next to the pub in Bosherston.
Jones Cafe - In St David's. 8am opening, with great grub and coffee.

Climbing Gear

There are a couple of shops which have a small stock of climbing gear. Pembroke Outdoors is situated on the main street in Pembroke Dock - **www.pembsoutdoors.co.uk**. There is also a small outdoor gear shop in St David's that carries some basic stock.

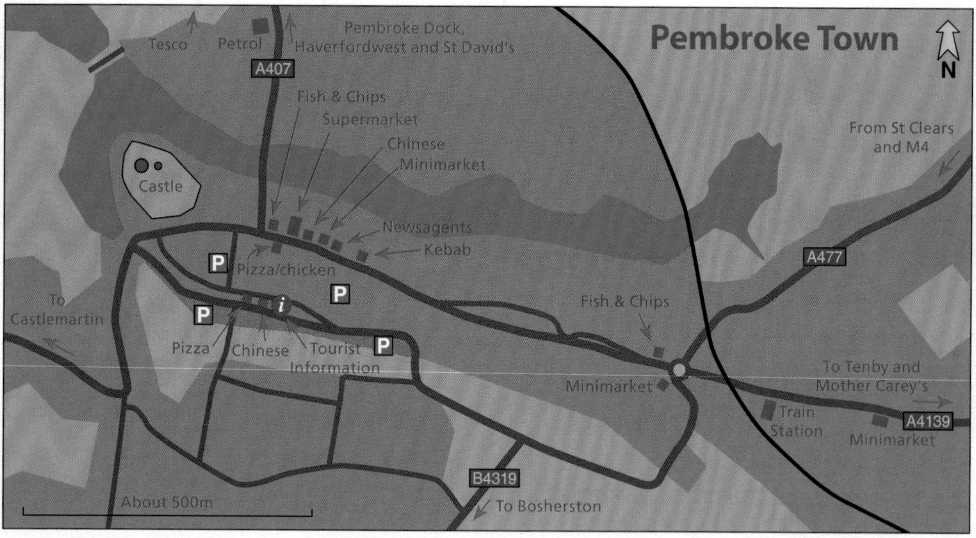

Food Supplies

There are three late-opening Minimarkets, one on the way into Pembroke, one on the main street, and the final one is on the road to Tenby. For more choice (and better prices) try the supermarket on the main street. For big shops head towards Pembroke Dock and you can't miss the monster Tescos. St David's has a small Minimarket.

Take-aways

All climbing areas need their take aways, there should be lots of them, with lots of different choices of food and they should all be open early on Sunday evenings, so that you can grab a bite before the long drive home. Pembroke is quite good on this latter point and has a good spread of Fish & Chips, Chinese, Indian, pizzas, chicken and burgers - see map above.

boulders
BECAUSE IT'S RAINING AGAIN
Over 120 lines of climbing
Cafe, equipment shop and changing rooms
Bouldering comps every month
New routes every week
North
Swansea
Bristol
M4
M4
J30
J29
A48(M)
Eastern Ave
A48
CARDIFF
A4232
boulders
Ridiculously massive bouldering!
For more info on events; lectures & comps check out our website
0845 52 118 50
WWW.BOULDERS-CLIMBING.COM

Freshwater West beach's aspect almost guarantees great sunsets. Photo Chris Craggs

Whether you want them for a rest day or to take the whole family to, beaches are an important aspect of climbing in Pembroke, mind you, I have yet to meet a climber who has the ability of lazing on a beach all day without getting itchy fingers. Luckily there are beaches in Pembroke which have been thoughtfully provided with small bouldering areas, interesting places to explore or some great surfing. These beaches are indicated on the maps on page 232.

St David's

The entire region is a mecca for surfing, kayaking and coasteering - the coastline is one of the most stunning you'll find anywhere (and I mean, anywhere), just drive to the car park at Caerfai Bay and take a look at the view. Along with Freshwater West, the two main beaches near St David's are the best surfing beaches in South Wales - Newgale Sands and Whitesand Bay beach. Newgale is passed on the drive from Pembroke town.

Broad Haven Beach

This is the delightful beach which you cross on the way to Mowing Word. There is some good bouldering on the far side of the beach, just above a small stream. Also worthwhile is the girdle traverse of Star Rock which is the large pointed stack on the right-hand side (looking out) of the beach. Approach it by turning left after the pub in Bosherston and following this road to the National Trust car park (pay) at the end. The beach is below.

Barafundel Beach

This beach is crossed on the Stackpole Quay car park approach to Mowing Word and Stackpole. The sideline entertainment for hyperactive climbers is not as good as Broad Haven, but it is a very pretty beach. Approach it by driving through Stackpole (see map on page 194) and turning right to Stackpole Quay parking (pay). The beach is about 1km south along the coast path.

St Govan's East Beach

A small nearly-secret beach situated just north of St Govan's East. It is reached from the St Govan's car park by heading towards the headland but branching left when above Trevallen down a small valley.

Flimston Bay Beach

An amazingly atmospheric place at the Stack Rocks end of Range East. You pass over the top of it on the way to Flimston Slab and Crystal Slabs but getting to the beach itself is a bit tricky so don't set off with all your deck chairs and wind breaks. It is a superb place for a barbecue since there is masses of driftwood and there are sections which never get covered at high tide. Approach from the Stack Rock's car park and walk east along the coast path for about 1km. When you see the beach, which can be identified by the two isolated pinnacles, scramble down a steep gully on the west (right looking out) side of the bay.

Freshwater West Beach

A large beach which is superb for surfing, but it can be a bit bleak and it is always windy. Approach by driving to Castlemartin, follow the road towards Angle and park on the right, after 2km.

St. David's
Flimston Bay
Mewsford
Castle/Rusty
Saddle Head
Bosherston Head
Huntsman's Leap
Stennis/Chapel
Trevallen
St. Govan's
Mowing/Stackpole
Mother Carey's

Pembroke Climbing

Mike Weeks starting the run out on *Boat to Naxos* (E7) - *page 125* - on the West Wall of Huntsman's Leap. Photo: Ian Parnell

St. David's
Flimston Bay
Mewsford
Castle/Rusty
Saddle Head
Bosherston Head
Huntsman's Leap
Stennis/Chapel
Trevallen
St. Govan's
Mowing/Stackpole
Mother Carey's

St. David's
Flimston Bay
Mewsford
Castle/Rusty
Saddle Head
Bosherston Head
Huntsman's Leap
Stennis/Chapel
Trevallen
St. Govan's
Mowing/Stackpole
Mother Carey's

Photo: Ian Parnell

Climbing in Pembroke is fraught with complex access arrangements; if it isn't the MOD firing then it may be a bird restriction. Even once you have got past those two then you still have to get the tides right; it is a wonder that any climbing gets done at all! Over the years though climbers have got used to these stringent requirements and, with a bit of good planning, there is usually plenty to climb. What it does mean is that week-long trips are probably only worth planning later in the year, after August 1 when the bird restrictions have lifted, otherwise you could find yourself spending 5 days at Mother Carey's.
Most of these agreements have come about because of patient negotiation by the BMC and others fighting for the climbers' right of access to this wonderful area. These rights have been hard-earned so please respect this effort by sticking to the agreed restrictions as described in this guide and on the BMC Regional Access Database (RAD) - **www.thebmc.co.uk/bmccrag/**
If you do encounter access problems, contact the **BMC** at ***The British Mountaineering Council, 177-179 Burton Road, West Didsbury, Manchester, M20 2BB***.

Range East Restrictions

The MOD use Range East to practice firing. The main area which is affected includes all the cliffs from Flimston Bay (page 64) up to, and including, Chapel Point (page 152). The MOD usually plan to close the Range for 5 days mid-week but never at weekends or on bank holidays. They have often finished firing by around 3 or 4pm and then you can nip in for a quick route.
When firing is taking place there is supposed to be a red flag flying, however there is often still a red flag flying when access is allowed. When Range East is shut, there is always someone on the gate by St Govan's car park, or by the cattle grid above Bullslaughter Bay when only half Range East is shut.
On some occasions the road from Bosherston to St Govan's car park is also closed. When this is the case, all of Range East and Trevallen, St Govan's and St Govan's East are inaccessible.
During August MOD activity is much reduced and they usually only close the Stack Rocks end of Range East up to Bullslaughter Bay. This allows access to all crags from St Govan's car park up to and including Mewsford (page 70). For much of August, the whole of Range East is open all the time.
Notification of when firing is to take place is shown on the notice boards outside Mrs. Weston's Cafe in Bosherston and at the notice boards by St Govan's and Stack Rocks car parks. The firing times are also posted one month in advance on **www.pembrokeshireranges.com**.
It is worth noting that the MOD don't use up all their allocated firing days and sometimes the Range will be open even though the schedule suggested it would be closed.

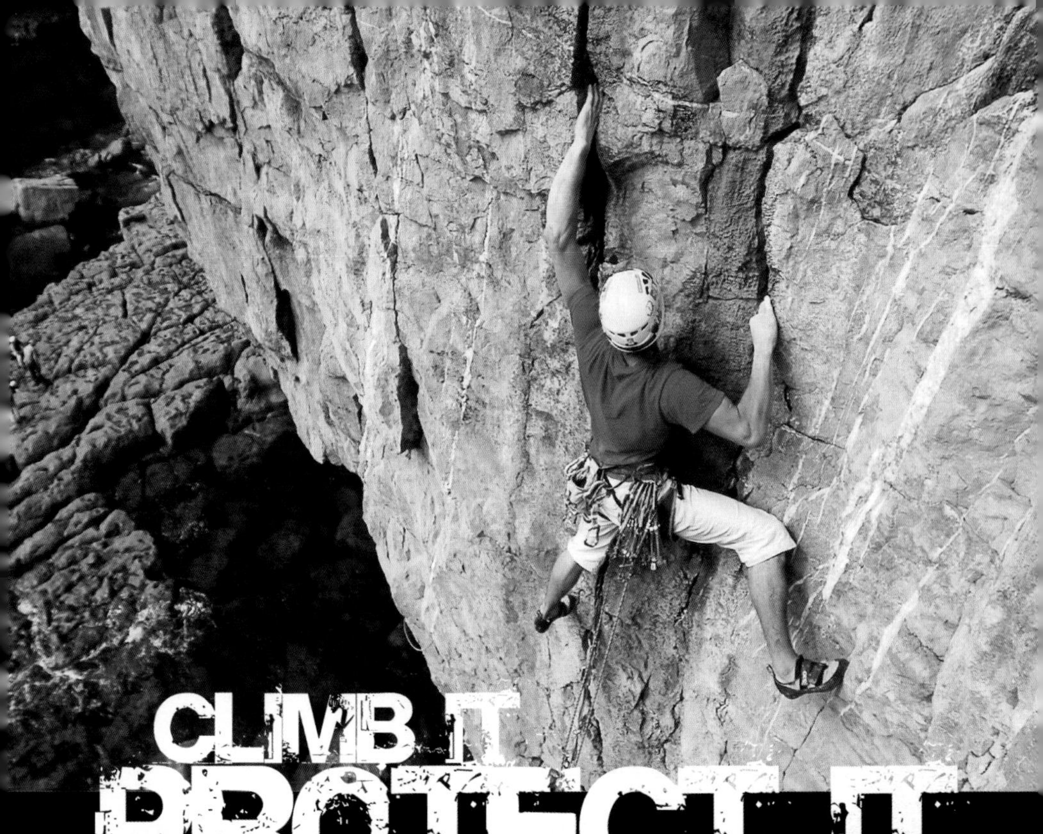
CLIMB IT
PROTECT IT

St. David's | Flimston Bay | Mewsford | Castle/Rusty | Saddle Head | Bosherston Head | Huntsman's Leap | Stennis/Chapel | Trevallen | St. Govan's | Mowing/Stackpole | Mother Carey's

No climbing to the left of this sign in the restricted season. The number refers to the areas on the PCNPA map at the access points. Photo: Chris Craggs

All wild birds and their eggs are protected by law under the Wildlife and Conservation Act 1981. The bird nesting restrictions on the cliffs in this guide are voluntary and are a result of careful negotiation between the B.M.C. and the R.S.P.B. These restrictions aim to protect the rarer birds. A crag which has obvious and plentiful nests may have no ban because the species there are deemed to be common enough to fend for themselves. Those which need the protection of a ban include guillemot, chough, peregrine, kittiwake and razorbill.

Just because you can't see birds nesting on a banned cliff or route doesn't mean the ban can be ignored. Some birds, such as chough, nest in deep crevices so they could well be there even though you can't see them. Others, such as peregrine, have such exacting requirements for a nest site that only a few spots may be appropriate. They return to these year after year, or after a gap of many years or even generations.

Disturbance of the rarer birds can have serious consequences. Peregrines are unlikely to nest anywhere if there is a climber near their chosen site. Guillemots place their eggs on their feet to incubate them and if they are disturbed suddenly, the egg may well end up in the sea.

You may look at the acres of rock around you and think "but they've got all that to nest on"! However some birds like their personal space. For example, a Peregrine generally won't nest within 800m of another peregrine.

Please remember that habitat is very precious. Respect all bird nesting restrictions.

Climbing Restrictions

"Now, where can I get some red paint from?"

Each year the Pembrokeshire Coast National Park (**www.pcnpa.org.uk**) produce a free leaflet with a detailed map which gives definitive and up-to-date information about the bird restrictions which do change from year to year. You can download this leaflet from the BMC site (**www.thebmc.co.uk**) and the PCNPA site but you need to search for it. The leaflet should always be available from the notice boards by St Govan's and Stack Rocks car parks, plus various other locations familiar to climbers - the toilet at the Bosherston campsite for example.

Clifftop markers (inverted bucketfuls of concrete, painted red) have also been placed on all the areas where there is a bird restriction. On the top of these markers there is a number, which refers to the leaflet, and an arrow, which refers to the direction from the marker in which the restriction applies.

At the time of writing the cliffs with restrictions in this guidebook are listed below.

Area	No climbing from 1 March to 1 August
Chapel Point	All routes
Trevallen	3 routes only, *Gypsy Lane*, *Romany*, *Breaking the Habit*
Mowing Word	Most routes except a few on the East Face
Stackpole	All routes in this book
Mother Carey's	3 routes only, *Star Gate*, *Warp Factor*, *Hyperspace*

Tides are a very important consideration when climbing in Pembroke since the access to, or escape from, most of the cliffs, is affected by the tides. The area has one of the largest tidal ranges in the World with tides swings as big as 7 to 8 metres being common, keep in mind that the average tidal range over most of the oceans is less than a metre! Understanding more about tides can be a great help in making the most out of your visit.

About Tides

Throughout one lunar month there are two *spring* or high-range tides, and two *neap* or low-range tides. *Spring* tides occur during the full and new moons, when the sun and moon are in line and the combined gravitational pull causes the highest tides, which then ebb to the lowest level. During *spring* tides the low tides will always fall towards the middle of the day.

During the first and third quarters of the moon, when the sun's and moon's attractional forces are at right angles, we experience the lower *neap* high tides and the higher low tides. *Neap* tides will always be low at either end of the day with the high tide occurring in the middle. By knowing the phases of the moon you can pretty roughly work out what kinds of tide you are going to get. Local tide tables (displayed on the notice boards at the entrance to the Range, and available from the Climbers' Club web site - **www.climbers-club.co.uk**) will give you precise times and levels of high and low tide.

From high tide to low tide takes approximately 6 hours, which means that there are two high tides and two low tides in every 24 hour period. The average time for the tide to turn around is actually slightly longer than 6 hours. This means that each day the high and low tide times are between 30 and 80 minutes later than the previous day.

In Pembroke *spring* tide swings range from a massive 8.5m (spring and autumn) to usually at least 6.5m (summer and winter), and *neap* tide swings range from around 2.5m (spring and autumn) to 4.5m (summer and winter).

Important Considerations

1) During the middle hours between low and high tide, the sea comes in MUCH faster and areas of flat rock and boulder beach can disappear rapidly and escape routes can be cut off. This means that you may have spent a few hours at the crag and not noticed much tide movement when suddenly there is water lapping around your ankles. This is significantly more pronounced during *spring* tides.

2) The smaller fall to low *neap* tides may give much less access than low spring tides to certain cliffs. For example, *Blue Sky* at Saddle Head, the routes in the mouth of The Leap, and The Space Face at Mother Carey's are all inaccessible from below during low *neap* tides.

3) The lower level of high *neap* tides may allow access to certain routes which are cut off in high *spring* tides.

4) Persistent and strong onshore winds can prolong or even slightly raise high tide levels as can a high swell from some distant ocean storm.

← High tide → Each topo is marked with an approximate high tide level using the indicator to the left. These are roughly aligned to high *spring* tide levels hence there could be accessible ledges below them during *neap* high tides. The sea could also reach higher levels than these indicators when it is rough.

A suggested rack for Pembroke	
Small-to medium wires	Take at least 2 sets, maybe three, of the smaller sizes. These are your bread and butter runners on most routes and a good selection is essential.
Larger wires and hexes	One set with some variety.
Slings	A good selection of slings including some with thin tape for threads and spikes. Take untied cord for replacing threads on the harder routes.
Camming devices	A few of the middle sizes will be useful but there are fewer solid camming placements than in other UK areas areas, hexes tend to sit much better in the convoluted and knobbly cracks here. Take some smaller technical cams for the harder routes. Very large cams will be dead-weight except on certain obvious routes with wide cracks.
Microwires	These are essential on (mostly hard) routes which tackle the very compact grey rock - Misty Wall, Keelhaul Wall, Trevallen. Take plenty since you tend to place lots of them and they weigh virtually nothing.
Quickdraws	Take 12 to 16 quickdraws depending on the length of the pitch, and how much gear you usually place. The pitches are long and the lines weave so make sure you have some long quickdraws to extend your placements and reduce rope drag which can be a big problem on the long pitches.

Fixed Gear

A top-notch Pembroke peg.

Pegs - Over the years many of the harder routes put up in Pembroke have been climbed using pegs for protection on the first ascent. Most of these pegs should now be regarded as untrustworthy and **NO NEW PEGS SHOULD BE ADDED TO THE CLIFFS IN PEMBROKE**, this includes stainless steel pegs. For routes that still have pegs in them the slow process of re-climbing them without relying on the pegs as key runners is ongoing. Some of the routes in Huntsman's Leap have been re-climbed and given new grades, others have been found to be the same grade. Many other routes with pegs have not been re-climbed and they are currently something of an unknown. We have listed such routes with their grades in brackets and commented in the descriptions about the state of the fixed gear. In all cases these routes will need re-climbing by someone up to the challenge to provide a new grade assessment which assumes the peg(s) are worthless. It would be great if climbers could adopt the quest to eliminate pegs from Pembroke in the same way that those of the 1970s and 1980s sought after free ascents of old aid routes.

Threads - There are a lot of threads in Pembroke and they can be found on routes across the whole grade range. Threads tend to be more accepted than pegs since they use a natural feature without damaging the rock, and they are replaceable, however some climbers are also of the opinion that threads too should be removed. When you get to a thread, pull it around so that you can examine all of it and leave a different section in the rock. If you decide to replace a thread, remove all the old ones since one brand new thread is a lot better than 5 manky ones of different lengths.

Stuck Wire - The last form of fixed gear is the accursed stuck wire. These little tinkers loiter around crux moves and see a lot of air time. Don't trust them and get them out if you can.

It is now clear that bolts don't have any place in Pembroke, a fact which has been universally accepted by climbers of all ages and abilities.

Climbing Ropes

The normal practice for leading routes is to use double 50m x 9mm ropes. This will enable you to follow the weaving lines with limited rope drag.

Rope Buckets - One of the problems when at the cliff bases can be keeping your rope dry and away from rock pools or the sea. A useful tool for routes where you abseil in to a hanging stance is a rope bucket. You can feed your twinned 9mm ropes into the bucket before you abseil down and clip the bucket onto the belay. If you have done it right then the ropes will feed easily out of the bucket as the leader climbs.

Abseil Ropes

An abseil rope is virtually essential for Pembroke to reach the base of most of the cliffs and it is hardly ever possible to abseil on your climbing ropes due to the belays being set well back from the edge. A single rope of 50m is the minimum requirement but preferably 60m if you have one. Sport climbing single ropes that are no longer supple enough to lead climb on make good ab ropes usually but make sure they are still trustworthy, obviously!

Many of the abseils are made of stakes hammered into the ground. There are now a lot of solid stakes in Pembroke but also a few old ones which are somewhat less inspiring - the photo above show both generations of Pembroke stake. Use your own judgement when abseiling and always back-up a belay if you are unsure.

Often when you arrive at your crag you may well find an ab rope in place. In such circumstances it is accepted practice to use ropes that are in place rather than clutter up belays with an extra rope.

Helmets and Loose Rock

Many routes in Pembroke have loose rock on them, especially on their final sections. Always wear a helmet since rock can be dislodged at any time, and always put an extra runner in before you do the last moves, no matter how easy it looks. Test every hold and be especially careful early in the season, or on days after heavy rain. When belaying keep out of the fall zone when your leader is finishing a pitch.

Other Gear

Prussik Loops - A prussik loop is useful for protecting you when you abseil and having 2 is invaluable if you fall off when seconding a steep route, although make sure you know how to use them if you suspect you might struggle - learning 'on the job' is not much fun!

Threads - If you are climbing harder routes then loose untied tape or cord is useful for replacing threads.

Abseil Rope Protectors - These are useful for the clifftop edges particularly if the rope is going to see a lot of traffic ie. if you are first to arrive at St Govan's or the Leap.

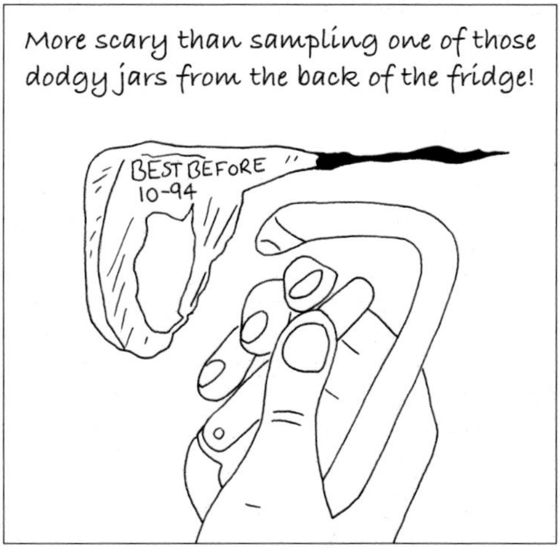
More scary than sampling one of those dodgy jars from the back of the fridge!
BEST BEFORE
10-94

The routes in this book are graded using the British Traditional Grading system. Some of the harder routes are given a sport grade in their descriptions, which is becoming more common these days amongst hard climbers. This doesn't mean that the routes are 'sport routes', it is just used to give another impression of the overall difficulty of the route.

British Trad Grade

1) Adjectival grade (Diff, VDiff, Severe, Hard Severe (HS), Very Severe (VS), Hard Very Severe (HVS), E1 and upwards)
How well protected a route is, how sustained and a general indication of the level of difficulty of the whole route.
2) Technical grade (4a, 4b, 4c,..... to 7b)
The difficulty of the hardest single move.

More information on grades:
www.rockfax.com/publications/grades.html

Deep Water Solo Grades

A few routes in this book can be done as deep water solos - places like the East Face of the Castle and Blind Bay near Mother Carey's have such routes. They have mostly been given a Sport Grade and an S grade within their descriptions. The simple S Grade consists of a 0, 1, 2 or 3. S0 gives relative safety, with S3 offering considerable possibility of injury in the event of a fall. The routes in this book that are mentioned as possible deep water solos are almost all very hard and a degree of experience is essential if you intend to climb them un-roped. You will also need to pay particular attention to the tides since DWS in Pembroke requires high spring tides in most areas.

ROUTE GRADES

BRITISH TRAD GRADE

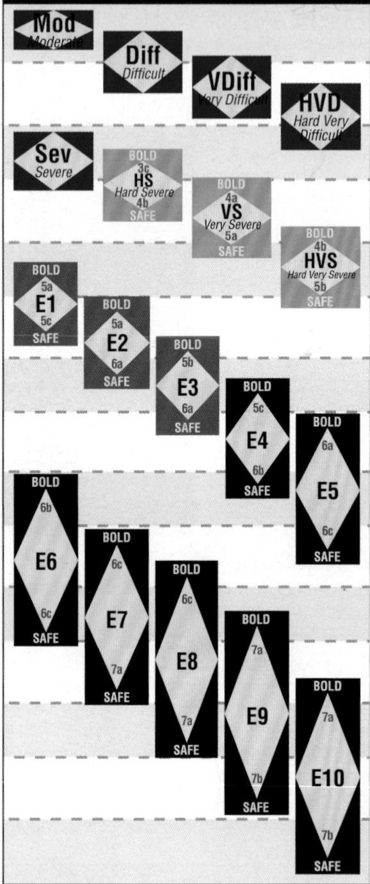

Sport Grade	UIAA	USA
1	I	5.1
2	II	5.2
2+	III	5.3
3-	III+	5.4
3	IV / IV+	5.5
3+	V-	5.6
4	V	5.7
4+	V+	5.8
5	VI-	5.9
5+	VI	5.10a
6a	VI+	5.10b
6a+	VII-	5.10c
6b	VII	5.10d
6b+	VII+	5.11a
6c		5.11b
6c+	VIII-	5.11c
7a	VIII	5.11d
7a+	VIII+	5.12a
7b	IX-	5.12b
7b+		5.12c
7c	IX	5.12d
7c+	IX+	5.13a
8a	X-	5.13b
8a+	X	5.13c
8b		5.13d
8b+	X+	5.14a
8c	XI-	5.14b
8c+	XI	5.14c
9a	XI+	5.14d
9a+		5.15a

Colour Coding

The routes are all given a colour-coded dot corresponding to a grade band.

● **Green Routes** - Everything at grade **Severe** and under. Good routes to start on especially on the St David's crags, Flimston Bay and Saddle Head, with a few classics at Mother Carey's as well.

● **Orange Routes** - **HS** to **HVS** inclusive. General ticking routes for those with more experience, a large range of excellent routes is available across this band.

● **Red Routes** - **E1** to **E3** inclusive. Routes for the experienced and keen climber. Anyone operating at this level can expect to enjoy some of the best sea cliff climbing in the world here in Pembroke.

● **Black Routes** - **E4** and above - the hard stuff! At this grade there is probably no where better for climbers to onsight hard trad routes.

This graded list was compiled by careful analysis of the grade voting on the Rockfax Route Database combined with the experience of a number of different climbers operating at different grades. As ever, the upper end of the list is more open to conjecture though we have sought a consensus wherever possible. If you think there are errors in the graded list, or you disagree strongly with it, then please let us know via the voting on the Route Database on the web site - **www.rockfax.com**

E9

Stars	Route	Page
***	The Big Issue	112

E8

Stars	Route	Page
***	San Simian	98
***	Chupacabra	125
***	Point Blank	150
Top 50	Nothing to Fear	124

E7

Stars	Route	Page
***	The Black Lagoon	124
***	Boat to Naxos	125
Top 50	Terminal Twilight	124
***	Always the Sun	204
***	From a Distance	150
Top 50	The Great White	224

E6

Stars	Route	Page
***	Stennis the Menace/The Great Elmyra	144
***	Ghost Train	151
**	Boss Hogg	161
Top 50	Souls	125
***	Fireball XL5	223
***	Grezelda, Grezelda	96
**	The Pulsebeat	131
Top 50	Orange Robe Burning	161
***	Hunter-Killer	124

E5

Stars	Route	Page
***	Woeful	124
**	Snake Charmer	127
***	Chasing Shade	87
Top 50	Yellow Pearls	161
**	John Wayne	178
***	Grey English Morning	144
Top 50	Barbarella	161
***	Beat Surrender	214
Top 50	Get Some In	182
***	Just Klingon	223
***	White Heat	224
***	Circus Circus	93
***	Heat of the Moment	87
Top 50	Darkness at Noon	124
***	Dogs of Hoare	167
**	Fitzcarraldo	130
***	Ships that Pass in the Night	167
Top 50	The Minotaur	126
Top 50	Mean Feat	59

E4

Stars	Route	Page
**	Head Hunter	126
***	Hyperspace	222
**	Just Another Day	128
***	Mother Night	223
*	Moving Away from the Pulsebeat	131
***	Wallbanger	67
*	Let Him Babble On	178
Top 50	Tangerine Dream	185
***	Out for the Count	86
Top 50	Under the Influence	86
**	Body Language	190
**	Flash	142
Top 50	The Fascist and Me	165
**	Scorch the Earth	128
***	Witch Hunt	124
***	Suspense	151
**	The Rising Tide	181
Top 50	Bloody Sunday	128
**	Over the Hill	86
***	Downward Bound	87
Top 50	Brave New World	188
**	Meet the Monster Tonight	133
*	Charisma	178
Top 50	Trevallen Pillar	167
*	Poisoned Arrow	181
Top 50	Star Wars	119

E3

Stars	Route	Page
Top 50	Test Case	179
***	Alien World/Blind Vision	215
Top 50	Pleasure Dome	144
***	Plane Sailing	206
Top 50	Sunlover	160
**	Merchant of Stennis	147
***	Heaven's Door	205
Top 50	Swordfish	206
Top 50	Kitten Claws	59
Top 50	Zeppelin	217
**	Billy Spragg	59
**	Forbidden Fruits	191
**	Strap-Up	131
Top 50	Ghost Ship	110
Top 50	Star Gate	220
***	Space Cadet	179
***	Gravy Train	99
**	Howling Gale	191
***	Play Misty for Me	94
**	Oratorio	95
**	The Voyage Out	72
*	Range Rider	185
**	Deep Throat	77
**	Quiet Waters Direct	130
**	Wraith	217
***	Mysteries	151

E2.5

Stars	Route	Page
Top 50	The Butcher	176

Barry Durston on the impressive *Chupacabra* (E8) - *page 125* - in Huntsman's Leap. Photo: Ian Parnell

E2

Stars	Route	Page
*	Dire Straits	142
**	Ivory Tower	113
***	Puritan	208
***	Charenton Crack	200
**	Mythical Monster	132
**	Hidden Secrets	188
*	Anyone for Stennis	144
***	Deranged	184
**	War Crime	183
***	Super Galactic Hammy	99
***	Keelhaul	111
Top 50	Silver Shadow	206
Top 50	Brazen Buttress	219
**	Intensive Scare	111
Top 50	Chimes of Freedom	197
Top 50	First Blood	190
**	Herod	219
Top 50	Deep Space	220
**	Depraved	184
**	The Honey Monster	133
**	Ricochet	181
Top 50	Bon Voyage	94
**	Sunsmoke	217
*	Vice is Nice	176
Top 50	Daydreams	73
**	Ultravox	155
**	Grey English Wimpout	144
*	Enter the Goat	162
Top 50	Preposterous Tales	115
**	The Beast from the Undergrowth	131

E1

Stars	Route	Page
Top 50	The Strait Gate	217
**	Baker's Door	111
***	Surprise Attack	72
**	Be Clever	58
Top 50	Lucky Strike	93
**	Shape-Up	130
*	Kraken	179
***	Wishful Thinking	89
**	War Games	183
***	Sealhunt	199
***	Cool for Cats	143
**	Hangover '77	183
**	Ultravixens	155
**	Solidarity	92
**	Beyond the Azimuth	60
*	But Incest is Best	176
Top 50	Manzoku	143
**	B-Team Buttress	75
Top 50	Rock Idol	217
*	Piggy's Crack	178
Top 50	The Arrow	181
**	Snozwanger	197
*	Calisto	191
**	Sinecure	57
***	Too Much Pressure	86
*	New Morning	198
Top 50	Heart of Darkness/New Morning	199

HVS

Stars	Route	Page
**	Blowin' in the Wind	197
**	The Hole	162
***	Sunny Corner	114
***	Galactic Glory	99
**	Joyous Gard	217
**	Tactitian	183
**	Ethos	56
**	Cupids Bow	181
**	Dreamboat Annie	42
*	The Loosener	176
*	Stennis Pillar	144
***	Pigs on the Wing	77
**	Front Line	174
Top 50	Army Dreamers	175
***	Inner Space	220
**	Hercules	142
**	Galactic Co-ordinator	76
Top 50	Riders on the Storm	140
***	Heart of Darkness	198
**	Bludgeon	147
***	Welcome to the Cruise	76
*	Crystal Edge	66
*	Tinker Tailor	75

VS

Stars	Route	Page
*	Flanker	180
Top 50	Armorican	53
*	Chieftain	176
*	Crystal Arete	66
**	Aero	75
*	Crithmum	217
**	Gone with the Wimp	113
**	Pink 'Un	104
*	The Gadfly	66
*	Limbo	142
*	Razzle Dazzle	66
**	Sea Groove	225
**	The Meridian	217
*	No Hands	104
Top 50	Blue Sky	102

HS

Stars	Route	Page
**	Stennis Arete	147
Top 50	Diedre Sud	198
Top 50	Myola	139
***	Bow-Shaped Corner	65
Top 50	Bow-Shaped Slab	65
*	Nameless Wall	104
**	Sea Mist	104

Severe

Stars	Route	Page
**	Sheer Delight	80
**	Red Wall	43
*	Flake-Quake	104
Top 50	Threadneedle Street	218
**	The Cracks	217

VDiff

Stars	Route	Page
**	Flimston Slab	65
Top 50	Flimston Crack	65
**	The Crack	45

St. David's
Flimston Bay
Mewsford
Castle/Rusty
Saddle Head
Bosherston Head
Huntsman's Leap
Stennis/Chapel
Trevallen
St. Govan's
Mowing/Stackpole
Mother Carey's

Julie Mair leading one of the best routes in the St David's area; *Armorican* (VS) - *page 53* - at Craig Caefai. Photo: Sarah Clough

Pembroke Crags	Routes	up to Sev	HS to HVS	E1 to E3	E4 and up
St David's Port Clais, Porth-y-Ffynon, Initiation Slabs, Craig Caerfai, Carreg-y-Barcud	92	19 ✓✓✓	36 ✓✓✓	25 ✓✓	12 ✓✓
Flimston Bay Flimston Slab, Bow-Shaped Slab, Crystal Slab, Mosaic Wall	19	3 ✓✓	10 ✓✓✓	3 ✓	3 ✓
Mewsford Mewsford, Crickmail Point, Triple Overhang, Blockhouse to Bullslaughter	34	2 ✓	20 ✓✓	9 ✓✓	3 ✓
Castle/Rusty The Castle, Rusty Walls, Misty Walls, Hollow Caves Bay	73	2 ✗	7 ✓	30 ✓✓✓	34 ✓✓✓
Saddle Head	21	8 ✓✓	10 ✓✓✓	3 ✓	- ✗
Bosherston Head	40	- ✗	9 ✓✓	16 ✓✓✓	15 ✓✓✓
Huntsman's Leap	46	- ✗	- ✗	9 ✓✓	37 ✓✓✓
Stennis/Chapel Stennis Head, Stennis Ford, Chapel Point	62	4 ✓	15 ✓✓✓	26 ✓✓✓	17 ✓✓✓
Trevallen	44	- ✗	3 ✓	12 ✓✓	29 ✓✓✓
St Govan's St Govan's, St Govan's East	100	3 ✗	22 ✓✓	40 ✓✓✓	35 ✓✓✓
Mowing/Stackpole Mowing Word, Stackpole	58	- ✗	13 ✓✓	30 ✓✓✓	15 ✓✓✓
Mother Carey's	48	2 ✓✓	6 ✓✓✓	18 ✓✓✓	22 ✓✓✓

Quality and range of routes in different grade bands: ✓✓✓ - Excellent ✓✓ - Good ✓ - Okay ✗ - Not worth a visit

Approach	Sun	Tides	Abseil	Birds	Range	Summary	Page	
5 to 20 min	Lots of sun	Tidal	Abseil in			A series of fine south-facing slabby cliffs that run along the coast to the south west of St David's. The area features more lower grade routes than most cliffs in Pembroke and access is generally unrestricted.	38	St. David's
20 min	Lots of sun		Abseil in		Mid-week	Three isolated slabs with plenty of low-to-mid grades routes, and one hard wall. A distant location and a dramatic setting.	62	Flimston Bay
20 to 30 min	Lots of sun	Tidal	Abseil in		Mid-week not August	The furthest crag from the parking is well worth the walk. Mostly two pitch routes with steep starts and slabbier upper sections. Very atmospheric setting and two classics to keep you busy.	68	Mewsford
20 min	Lots of sun	Tidal	Abseil in		Mid-week not August	Four compact venues each with a cluster of classics and its own character and conditions. The best routes tend to be in the mid and higher grades. Some tidal sections but plenty to do still.	82	Castle/Rusty
15 min	Lots of sun	Tidal			Mid-week not August	The best venue in south Pembroke for green and orange spot climbers. Many great routes on superb rock. It can get a bit busy at times. Tides only effect the starts of some routes.	100	Saddle Head
10 min	Lots of sun	Tidal	Abseil in		Mid-week not August	A huge headland offering great variety from VS upwards. Thin slabs, overhanging walls and exposed ribs, plus an outrageous caving expedition. A few tidal routes only.	106	Bosherston Head
8 min	Not much sun	Tidal	Abseil in		Mid-week not August	The deep and narrow zawn is an iconic Pembroke landmark, thought by many to be one of the finest crags in the country. At E4 and above there is little to rival it. The base is tidal and the condition of the rock can vary dramatically.	120	Huntsman's Leap
2 to 10 min	Lots of sun	Tidal	Abseil in	Chapel only 1 Mar-1 Aug	Mid-week not August	An extensive headland and zawn, plus a less extensive cliff with a few good routes (and a restriction). The walk-in approach and non-tidal ledge make it one of the easiest places to get to and consequently very popular.	134	Stennis/Chapel
5 min	Lots of sun	Tidal	Abseil in	3 routes 1 Mar-1 Aug	Occasional not August	A magnificent crag packed with stunning hard routes on some great rock formations. Less to offer in the mid-grades and nothing easy. Half of it is tidal, plus a small section has restrictions.	156	Trevallen
8 to 10 min	Lots of sun	Tidal	Abseil in		Occasional not August	The most popular crag in Pembroke with loads of quality routes at VS and above. Only a few routes affected by the tide. Plenty to keep you going for many visits. Also includes the quieter East crag with its good red and black spot routes.	170	St. Govan's
25 min	Lots of sun	Tidal	Abseil in	1 Mar-1 Aug		Two superb crags associated with late summer and autumn due to the restrictions. One is friendly and approachable with plenty in the orange and red spot grades, the other is huge and imposing and not for the faint-hearted.	192	Mowing/Stackpole
10 min	Lots of sun	Tidal	Abseil in	3 routes 1 Mar-1 Aug		A superb and varied location with classic routes from Severe to E7! Great lines and exposure, plus plenty to do when the tide is in. Situated away from the main areas and virtually free of any restrictions.	210	Mother Carey's

Shaded means that only some of the routes are tidal / require an abseil / are restricted

St. David's
Flimston Bay
Mewsford
Castle/Rusty
Saddle Head
Bosherston Head
Huntsman's Leap
Stennis/Chapel
Trevallen
St. Govan's
Mowing/Stackpole
Mother Carey's

St David's

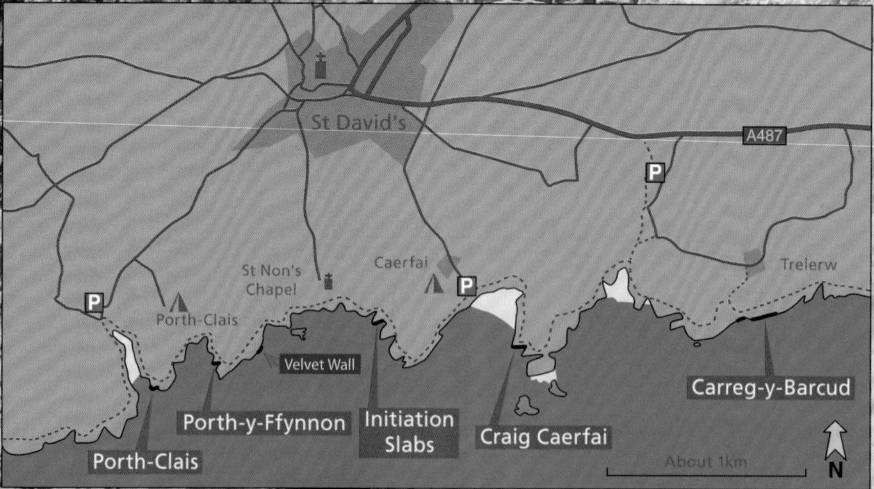

Sam Loveday (climbing) and James Humble (belaying) on *Ethos* (HVS) - *page 56* - at Carreg-y-Barcud. Photo: Chad Harrison

	No star	1 star	2 star	3 star
Mod to S	-	3	2	-
HS to HVS	-	6	2	-
E1 to E3	-	-	-	-
E4 and up	-	-	-	-

St. David's
Flimston Bay
Mewsford
Castle/Rusty
Saddle Head
Bosherston Head
Huntsman's Leap
Stennis/Chapel
Trevallen
St. Govan's
Moving/Stackpole
Mother Carey's

The twin-crag setup of Porth-Clais is an inviting spot, with the two compact purple faces offering a choice of cracks, slabs and aretes. The main buttress provides the bulk of the routes, with *Porth-Clais Crack* and *Dreamboat Annie* proving to be worthy adversaries. Over on the taller right slab, the classic tick is undoubtedly the superb *Red Wall*.

Approach

From the main square in St David's, follow the downhill road signposted to 'Porth-Clais 1.5 miles'. This road takes you all the way down to the picturesque Porth-Clais harbour, which appears on your left. Parking here is in a (pay) National Trust car park. From the car park, follow the footpath along the left side of the harbour, bearing left up the slope on the smaller, coastal footpath. Some 500m along this, the path curves left at the end of the estuary; look for a small track on the right, heading down through gorse, which immediately gives way to the top of the crag - about 5 minutes from the car.

Conditions and Tides

The rock here is fast drying and very clean. All routes are easily approachable at low tide, with the base of the crag gained via an easy scramble down on the east side. At higher tides, the left-hand buttress is best approached on its western edge, via the ridge or a short abseil down Harbour Crack.
Note that the belays here are a combination of stakes and other gear; it's easy to pre-arrange this before your ascent.

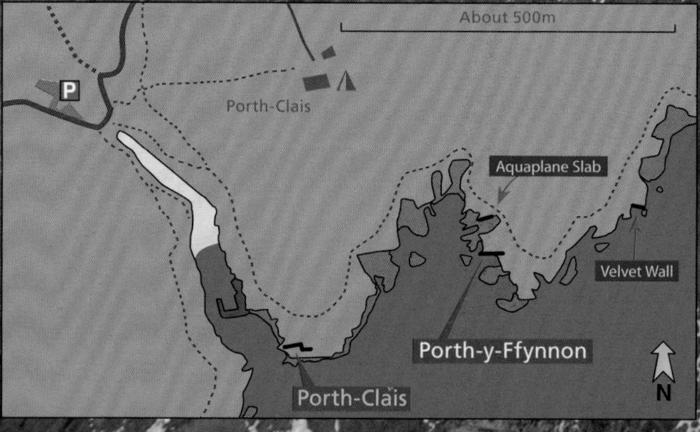

Libby Peter balancing up *Dreamboat Annie* (E1) - page 42 - Porth-Clais. Photo: Mike Robertson

St. David's
Flimston Bay
Mewsford
Castle/Rusty
Saddle Head
Bosherston Head
Huntsman's Leap
Stennis/Chapel
Trevallen
St. Govan's
Mowing/Stackpole
Mother Carey's

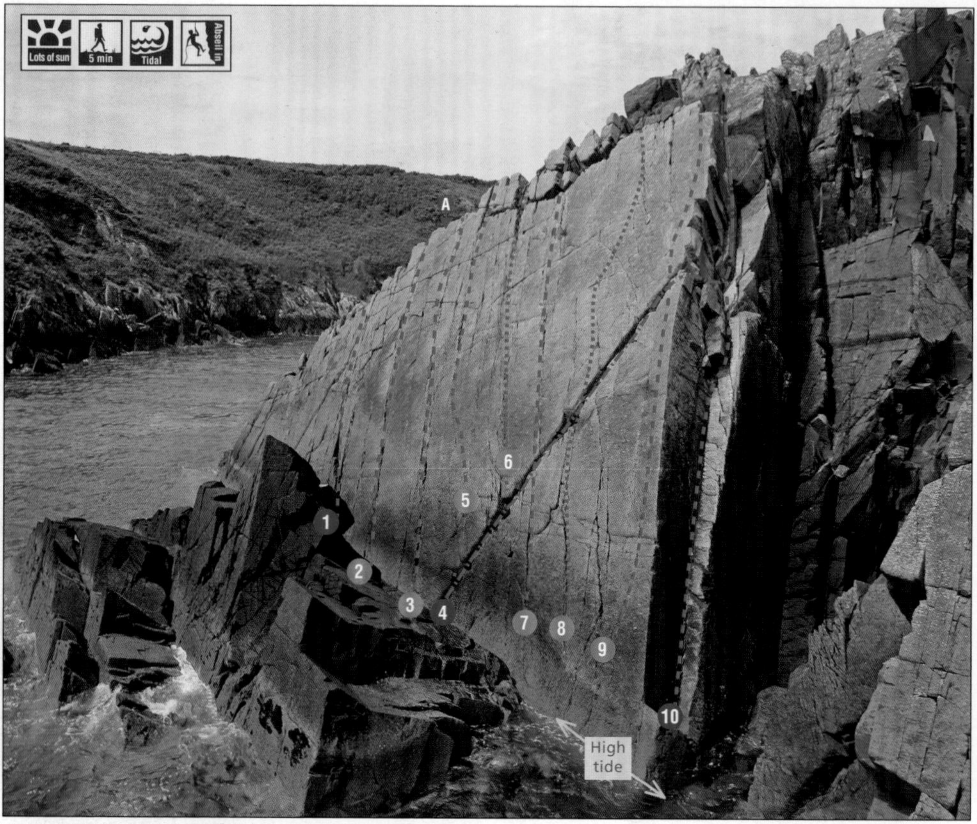

Dreamboat Annie

A fine triangular slab with a neat series of diagonal cracks and a beautiful clean right-hand arete.
Approach - Abseil down the wall to the non-tidal block - not advisable in rough seas.

1 Harbour Crack . . . . 1 ☐ **VDiff**
9m. The wide crack 7m from the left edge of the slab provides a good intro to the area.
FA. B.Royle 5.75

2 Glaze Crack. . . . . 1 ☐ **HS 4b**
11m. A good line. The straight crack has some technical moves.
FA. Derek Carnell 1975

3 Porth-Clais Crack. . . . . . 1 ☐ **HS 4b**
12m. Start a metre or so left of the base of *Diagonal Crack*, and climb the thin crack in the centre of the slab. A gem.
FA. Colin Mortlock 1967

4 Diagonal Crack . . . . 2 ☐ **Sev 4a**
16m. Delightful. Follow the steady diagonal crack all the way to the arete, then step right and finish up a tricky angular groove.
FA. Barry Webb 1967

5 Vegetable Rights . . . . 1 ☐ **VS 4c**
12m. Climb the slab past some pockets, then move left to a crack.
FA. Jules McKim 31.7.84

6 Frieze. . . . . 1 ☐ **VS 4c**
13m. Another good one. Start up *Diagonal Crack*, breaking out leftwards to climb the spidery cracks to the top.
FA. A.Webster 1975

7 All Lines Engaged . . . . 1 ☐ **HS 4b**
14m. Climb to the diagonal break and follow the thin crack.
FA. Tim Leach 6.77

8 Sea Rider . . . . 2 ☐ **VS 4c**
14m. The cracks 2m left of the arete are followed thoughout.
FA. A.Webster 5.75

9 Dreamboat Annie. . . 2 ☐ **HVS 5a**
14m. A brilliant but testing bit of balancy climbing. High in the grade and be prepared for small, spaced protection. Traverse rightwards to the arete, and climb it on its left side.
Photo on page 41.
FA. Al Evans 8.78

10 Inset . . . . 1 ☐ **Sev 4a**
15m. The tight groove right of the *Dreamboat Annie* arete is good, it maybe a little easier for short, narrow folk?
FA. Nat Allen 5.74

The gloomy groove to the right of Inset is taken by a poor loose route **Ship of Fools, HS** *- not recommended.*

Red Wall

The next routes are found on the crag's taller right-hand section; note that crossing the gap between the crag's two halves is tide-dependent! The belays at the top of the wall prove to be quite subtle; a recce is advised.
Approach - Scramble down ledges to the east of the slab or traverse in from *Dreamboat Annie* - best avoided in rough seas.

Lots of sun | 5 min | Tidal

11 Red Adair . . . **Sev 4a**
14m. The left arete. Start on the left side of the arete, thereafter moving rightwards, to finish on the arete direct.
FA. Tim Leach 6.77

12 Red Wall **Sev 4a**
14m. A miniature classic. Cross the chimney to climb the well-featured slab just left of centre, with good holds and good pro all the way. Low in the grade.
FA. Colin Mortlock 1967

13 Red Wall Right-Hand . . . . . . **HS 4b**
14m. The right edge of the slab gives some great moves. Finish on the right edge of the slab.
FA. Nat Allen 5.75

Porth-y-Ffynnon

	No star	1 star	2 star	3 star
Mod to S	-	3	1	-
HS to HVS	-	3	1	-
E1 to E3	-	2	1	-
E4 and up	-	-	-	-

Some 500m east of the cliffs of Porth-Clais are the excellent paired slabs of Porth-y-Ffynnon. The show-piece here is certainly the distinctive, main slab, with routes such as *The Crack* and *Grab the Slab*; it's quite an eclectic affair, rising from small crozzled ledges just above the sea, and featuring a double-angle purple sheet of rock, a high ramp-line, and one or two approach choices. The narrower, grey Aquaplane slab does, however, provide some extra spice.

Approach See map on page 40

The two slabs are visually located with ease from the approach footpath, especially if you're walking east-wards - they're both set into the eastern side of a deep craggy bay, and they're both found pretty much right under the main coast path. It's possible to view the Aquaplane slab easily from above, as it's found on one wall of a narrow zawn; the main slab can be viewed by deviating southwards from the coastpath and looking back across it. The slabs are a 10 minute walk from the parking at Porth-Clais.

Conditions and Tides

The rock is usually excellent here, with the typical friction and fast-drying properties you'd expect from the region. The more sheltered *Aquaplane* slab should be accessible in all but large tides and high seas, with the main slab requiring a little more tide planning, depending on your chosen route.

Aquaplane Slab

Approach - There is one abseil/belay stake in place above the slab. Please don't belay on the fence post since this will trip up walkers. Abseil down to the boulders in the zawn to gain the base of the routes.

1 Purple People Eater . 1 star **HVS 5a**
20m. The twin cracks just left of the centre of the slab. Take care with the finish; a short (2m) tail from your abseil rope could prove useful here.
FA. Al Evans 8.78

2 Aquaplane . . . . 1 star **E1 5b**
20m. The thin crack right of centre. The best of the pair, with excellent, clean climbing and great moves. That short exit rope is handy once more.
FA. Paul Donnithorne 5.87

Main Slab

Approach - The top of the main slab has a massive block that was installed by tractor - thus solving the belay problem permanently! In practice, this single block arrangement does mean you'll need to think about some deviations to keep your ropes in line with your route.
If the sea is calm, any abseil will gain the lower ledges; choose the most comfortable place for you and your ropes. If the sea is a little bumpy, it is usually possible to belay slightly higher up the cliff. A scramble descent is also possible down broken ground to the right

3 Apex Arete . . . . ☆1 ☐ **VDiff**
14m. The slabby arete has great positions!
FA. Nat Allen 5.72

4 Brown Slab . . . . ☆1 ☐ **HS 4b**
14m. The centre of the weirdly-patterned slab feels a bit 'out there'. The rock might be a touch friable in places.
FA. B.Black 29.5.72

5 Slab Recess . . . . ☆1 ☐ **Sev 4a**
15m. The striking corner/groove is followed all the way.
FA. Derek Carnell 12.4.74

Lots of sun | 10 min | Tidal | Abseil in

6 The Crack . . . . ☆2 ☐ **VDiff**
15m. A great little route, and the purest line here.
FA. D.Hadlum 9.68

7 Grab the Slab . . . . . ☆1 ☐ **E1 5b**
15m. The excellent, blank-ish slab some 3m right of *The Crack* is often top-roped. Take small pro for the lead.
FA. Paul Donnithorne 21.1.87

8 Cracked Wall. . . . . ☆1 ☐ **VS 4c**
16m. A pleasant wander. Disjointed cracks take you up to *Rising Damp*; nip leftwards along this, then climb the spidery cracks above to the top. A **Direct Start** just to the left is **4b**.
FA. S.Hadlum 9.68

9 Rising Damp . . . . ☆1 ☐ **Diff**
16m. A terrific line. The leftwards-rising rampline is adhered to all the way.
FA. D.Hadlum 9.68

Velvet Wall

The last crag to be detailed accessed from the Porth-Clais car park is the surprising Velvet Wall. A textured, purple seaside cliff, and completely hidden despite being just metres below the coastpath. The only downside is the scale of it - if it were somewhat wider (and higher), we'd have more to go at! The colours are outrageous, the crozzly pockets are heaven to the touch, and the two plum-vertical routes are quite brilliant. So: small, but perfectly formed.

Approach - Walk 150m east of the Ffynnon Slabs to three craters in the coastal path. At the third/biggest one, follow a vague grassy path down and eastwards, along a prominent line of calcite-white blocks (these blocks will be more obvious once you've dropped down the slope a few metres). This short slope will bring the Velvet Wall into view, where a short scramble is required to reach the base (low tide). It's also possible to scramble to the top of the routes, via the upper slope; two stakes in place.

Conditions and Tides - Normal tides should not be a problem here, but avoid rough seas and huge tides. The rock is fast-drying, but the corner of *Shiraz* might hold the damp a little longer than its sister route after rain.

10 Shiraz 2 **E1 5b**

14m. Beautiful climbing, and on sculpted, jagged pockets and edges. Climb the lower ramp, then the pocketed wall above, with a tough move to gain the upper break. Finish direct to block belays a little higher.
FA. B.Wilkinson 2.9.92

11 Chinon . . . . 2 **HVS 5a**

14m. Exposed, highly enjoyable arete climbing. Pull rightwards from the start of *Shiraz* to gain the arete, and follow it to the top; belay on blocks. It's also possible to start to the right of the arete at a short crack at the same grade. *Photo on page 3.*
FA. B.Wilkinson 4.9.92

	No star	★1	★2	★3
Mod to S	3	1	1	-
HS to HVS	-	3	2	-
E1 to E3	-	-	-	-
E4 and up	-	-	-	-

The Initiation Slabs are typical North Pembroke - surrounded by other craglets and by grass, usually quiet and sublimely idyllic. It's true to say that folk would visit the crag to take a picnic - it's just one of those spots. The routes aren't too bad either! The slabs are solid, offering good climbing and situated in a secluded bay, with one of the prettiest walk-ins known to man. So…

Approach See map on page 51

The best parking spot for the Initiation Slabs is the St Non's Chapel car park. You'll find this by taking the Porth-Clais road down/out of St David's, then look for a sign marked St Non's Chapel 1/4 mile (this road is more like 3/4 mile, but whatever). Follow this road down to a free car park by the St Non's Retreat. Walk down the path (past the ruins) to gain the coastal path at the very rustic St Non's Well. Turn left/east, and follow the path around firstly St Non's Bay, then the gloriously architectural Lunar Bay. The Initiation Slabs are found in the smaller, slotted bay beyond this - about 700m from your car. It is recommended to go to the far side and look back at the crag (from the grassy knoll) for a general scope of the routes. That done, return to the coast path and detour along the ridge/top of the crag itself, where you should see at least three abseil stakes in place.

Conditions and Tides

The crag is fast-drying, and is usually in good condition. It would be best to avoid heavy seas, and you'd better aim for a low-ish tide situation, whilst you're about it. If you have the chance, aim for a big low, when you might even be able to belay right off the pebble beach!

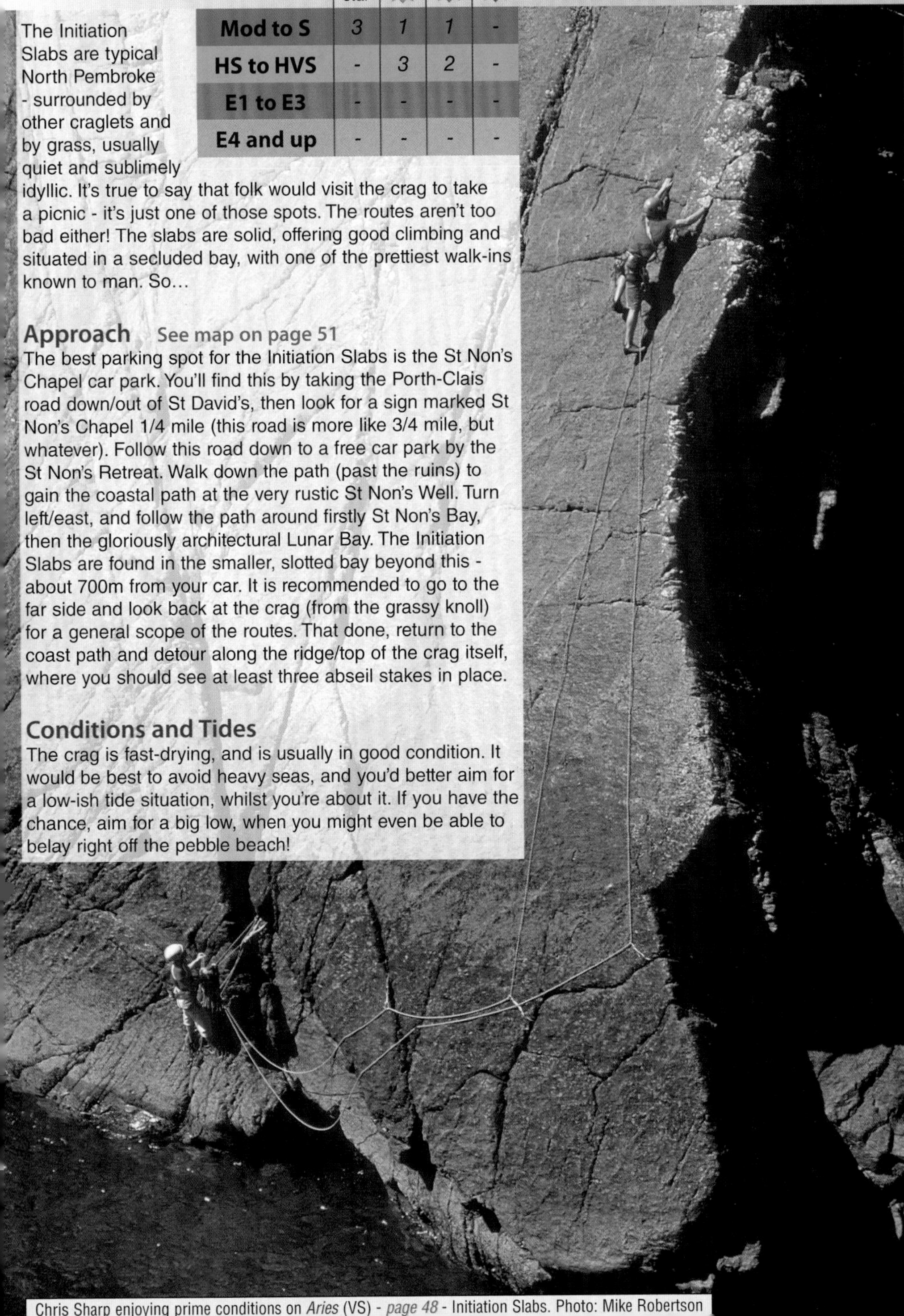

Chris Sharp enjoying prime conditions on *Aries* (VS) - *page 48* - Initiation Slabs. Photo: Mike Robertson

St. David's
Flimston Bay
Mewsford
Castle/Rusty
Saddle Head
Bosherston Head
Huntsman's Leap
Stennis/Chapel
Trevallen
St. Govan's
Mowing/Stackpole
Mother Carey's

St. David's

Flimston Bay

Mewsford

Castle/Rusty

Saddle Head

Bosherston Head

Huntsman's Leap

Stennis/Chapel

Trevallen

St. Govan's

Mowing/Stackpole

Mother Carey's

Initiation Slabs

Approach - The wide slab is split well to the left of centre by a deep slot/cave and right of centre by a grass-filled groove. Abseil in from one of the belay stakes to the base of the slabs, the central niche is the best stance for most of the routes.

The first routes are on the pillar left of the cave. Ledges at its base are accessed by a short abseil.

❶ Cormorant Front . . . . ☐ **VDiff**
12m. The wall in the centre of the buttress is fun.
FA. Derek Carnell 2.5.81

❷ The Gerbil. . . . . . . ☼1 🌊 🔅 ☐ **HVS 5a**
13m. The steep arete on the right side of the smaller buttress responds well to a dws approach! Traverse in low from the left, then climb steeply leftwards on undercuts to gain the arete. The crux is low down, but take a decent tide along with you. **(S1)**
FA. Mike Robertson 7.07

❸ Aquarian. . . . . ☼1 👤 ☐ **VDiff**
15m. Great stuff. The double crackline right of the cave is followed up to the top recess; step right to an 'out-there' finish.
FA. Derek Carnell 2.5.81

❹ Capricorn . . . . ☼1 👤 ☐ **HS 4b**
17m. Traverse 4m leftwards from the recess, and climb the fine crackline to the top. A **Direct Start** is easier when the tide allows.
FA. Derek Carnell 18.10.80

❺ Gemini . . . . ☼2 👤 ☐ **VDiff**
17m. A great line, exposed, and at a steady grade. Follow the diagonal crack all the way to the ridge.
FA. Derek Carnell 18.10.80

❻ Versary Slab . . . . 🔅 ☐ **Sev 4a**
17m. Follow *Gemini* for about 6m, then pull rightwards to gain the cracked slab. Climb this to the top.
FA. Derek Carnell 18.10.80

❼ Aries . . . . ☼2 🔅 🐏 ☐ **VS 4c**
19m. Just brilliant; the best route here. Great climbing, great positions, and good rock. The lower traverse (crux) takes you to the base of a soaring arete; follow this, on its left side, to an exposed finale. *Photo on page 47.*
FA. Derek Carnell 29.5.81

❽ Vanishing Crack. . . . . ☐ **Sev 4a**
18m. Abseil down the crusty corner to gain this line. From the good ledge at the base of the corner, break out rightwards to a crack system; follow this to a ramp, then drift left to the top.
FA. Derek Carnell 29.5.81

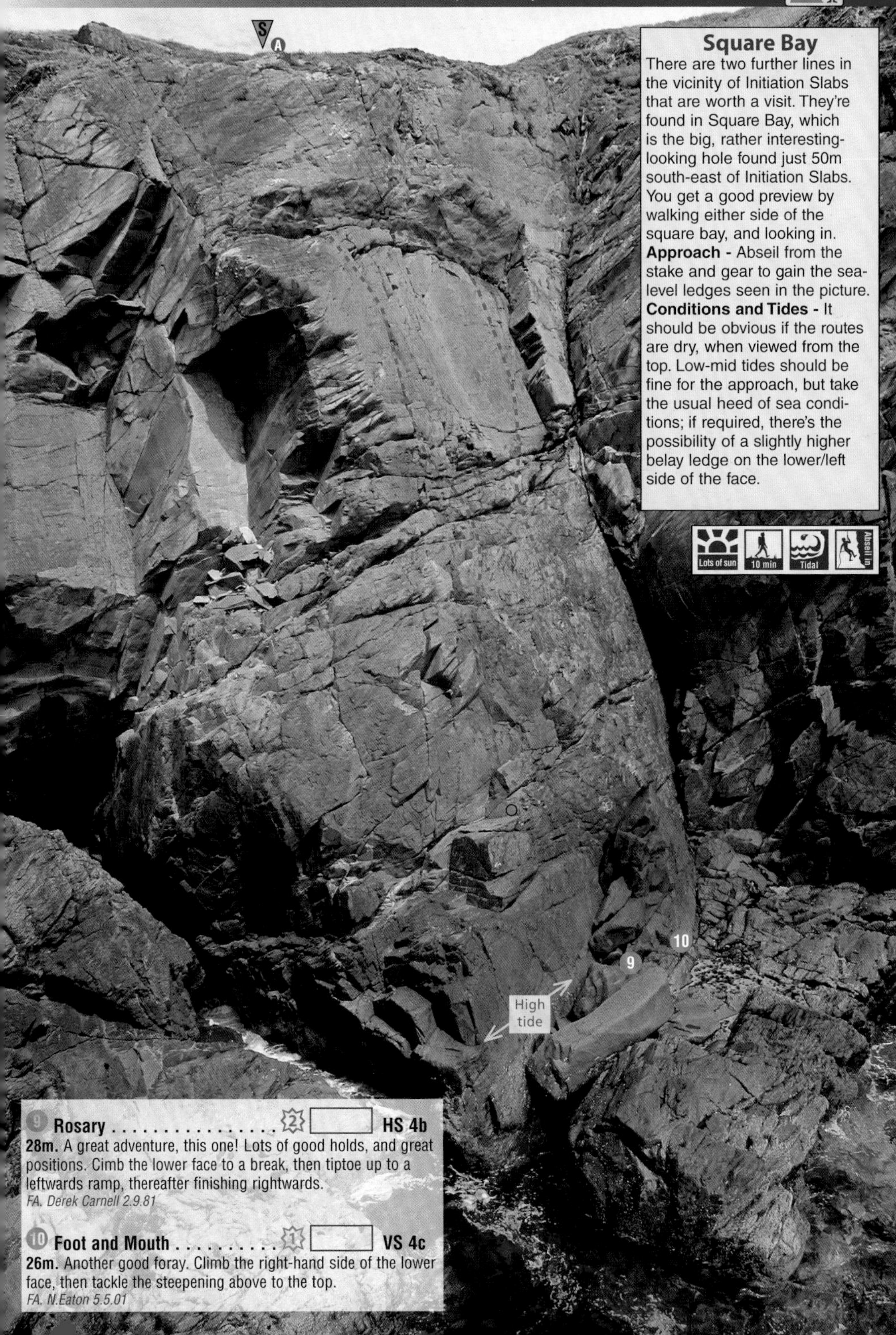

Square Bay

There are two further lines in the vicinity of Initiation Slabs that are worth a visit. They're found in Square Bay, which is the big, rather interesting-looking hole found just 50m south-east of Initiation Slabs. You get a good preview by walking either side of the square bay, and looking in.

Approach - Abseil from the stake and gear to gain the sea-level ledges seen in the picture.

Conditions and Tides - It should be obvious if the routes are dry, when viewed from the top. Low-mid tides should be fine for the approach, but take the usual heed of sea conditions; if required, there's the possibility of a slightly higher belay ledge on the lower/left side of the face.

Lots of sun | 10 min | Tidal | Abseil in

9 Rosary . . . . 2 ☐ **HS 4b**

28m. A great adventure, this one! Lots of good holds, and great positions. Cimb the lower face to a break, then tiptoe up to a leftwards ramp, thereafter finishing rightwards.

FA. Derek Carnell 2.9.81

10 Foot and Mouth . . . . 1 ☐ **VS 4c**

26m. Another good foray. Climb the right-hand side of the lower face, then tackle the steepening above to the top.

FA. N.Eaton 5.5.01

Armorican (VS) - *page 53* - Craig Caerfai. Photo: Nick Smith

Another excellent sandstone slab, and with a good choice of grades. The rock here is well-supplied with edges and cracks, and the most alluring ticks are probably *Caerfai Crack* and *Armorican*. The crag is a two-fold affair, with the easier lines on the higher-positioned left-hand end; the taller, darker slab on the right provides the longer and more adventurous forays into the Extreme grades plus a classic VS.

	No star	1	2	3
Mod to S	-	2	-	-
HS to HVS	1	6	-	1
E1 to E3	-	2	2	-
E4 and up	-	-	-	-

Approach

Drive up the hill to the edge of St David's (heading east), then take the first right to Caerfai Bay. Follow this road (past two rather expensive campsites) to reach the free car park at the end (the view here is absolutely STUNNING). Walk south-east on the coastal path; at around 600m, you'll reach a bend in the path and the top of the two-part slab, where five or so abseil stakes will be evident. It's possible to scramble into the crag from the left-hand side (looking in) utilising slabs and a ramp system - to locate this, first trend rightwards (north), then swing back southwards to gain the crag base. An alternative is an abseil down the crag's centre.

Conditions and Tides

The rock is generally dry here and it should be very obvious when it's not. The first five routes start high up, and should be accessible in all but the roughest seas, whilst the second five routes need calmer seas and lower tides for their approach.

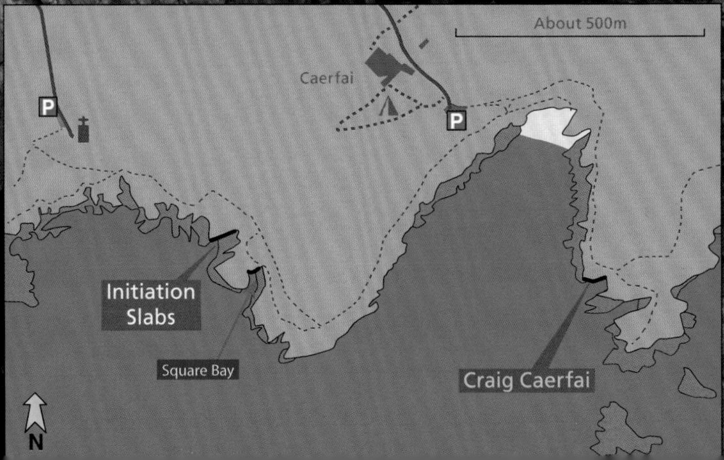

Main Slab

The slab is split in two with the easier routes including *Caerfai Crack* on the left-hand section, and the harder and thinner climbing on the clean right-hand slab. Bring plenty of microwires with you.

Approach and Tides - Both sections are easily approached at low tides either by abseiling or reversing down *White Corner* for the confident. *Orogeny* and *American* should be accessible from the slanted approach ramp, at all but the highest tides. The finishes of these routes are all shared, to a degree; take a little care with the rock in the last few metres.

1 Mildred Mindwarp . . . . 1 star HS 4b
15m. The left arete of the slab, heading to a rightwards-trending finishing crack.
FA. Steve Quinton 14.9.92

2 White Wall . . . . 1 star HS 4b
16m. The left-hand side of the wall brings you to the twin-cracks finish just to the right of *Mildred Mindwarp*.
FA. Nat Allen 30.5.78

3 Nameless . . . . 1 star VS 4c
18m. This one feels a little steeper. Climb the slab to a slot, trend left to better holds in a horizontal break, then climb the crack.

4 Unknown Sentry. . . . . 1 star HVS 5a
18m. The line direct past the sentry box. Never claimed but frequently climbed.

5 The Byrn. . . . . 1 star VS 4c
20m. The clean slab/wall left of *Caerfai Crack* has some testing moves. Climb the wall, moving gradually leftwards to gain the horizontal break. Finish more easily.
FA. Elfyn Jones 6.2.86

6 Caerfai Crack . . . . 1 star HS 4b
20m. An alluring feature. Climb the lower slab to gain the most pronounced crack, and follow it to the top. Low in grade.
FA. Nat Allen 31.5.78

7 White Corner. . . . . 1 star Diff
25m. The left-hand corner gives a pleasant easier route.
FA. Nat Allen 5.8.77

8 Submarine Slab. . . . . VS 4b
25m. Climb the narrow slab between the two corners and pull right over the steeper section onto a nice finishing slab.
FA. D.Pleydell 15.6.94

9 Scorch Groove. . . . . 1 star Diff
25m. The right-hand groove is also good.
FA. Derek Carnell 30.5.78

10 Orogeny **E2 5b**
25m. An exhilarating line. Climb the thin crack, then make tricky moves up and leftwards, to gain the prominent arete. Finish cautiously up this to a loose exit.
FA. Elfyn Jones 6.2.86

11 Armorican . . . . Top 50 **VS 4c**
25m. Brilliant; the crag's best route. Sprint up the lower crack, than ease your pace for the lengthy wobble up the balder slab above. Cross the overlap (right of the small notch) with confidence, and teeter up the final slab to the top. *Photo on pages 35 and 50.*
FA. Nat Allen 23.7.78

12 Age Gap **E2 5b**
28m. Climb the right-trending crack (thin on gear) to a convergence with *Age Concern*, step right then dive up the slab above, past a peg runner. Climb direct to the overlap, and cross this to gain the upper slab.
FA. Steve Quinton 15.5.91

13 Age Concern **E3 5c**
28m. Fine climbing, this is the original start. Follow the leftwards slash, then step right to the peg runner. Finish as for *Age Gap*.
FA. Martin Wilson 3.86

14 Uncertain Smile. **E2 5b**
32m. A circuitous wander up the right side of the big slab; top entertainment! Start a little right of the lower triangular recess. Climb the left-trending crack, then break out slightly right, to gain and pass a horizontal break. Keep moving up and right, until it's possible to climb direct to the overlap above. Complete your foray by climbing diagonally leftwards all the way to a junction with the previous routes.
FA. R.Jones 9.8.84

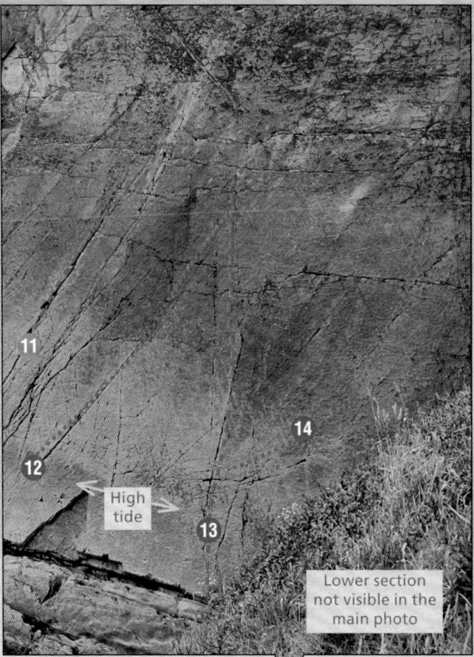

	No star	1 star	2 stars	3 stars
Mod to S	1	2	-	-
HS to HVS	5	2	2	-
E1 to E3	2	7	7	2
E4 and up	3	3	4	2

Carreg-y-Barcud is undoubtedly North Pembroke's finest sheet of sandstone; its purple/brown walls and slabs are taller and more impressive than the region's other venues, and are home to some brilliant, high-quality routes. The rock here is a compact sandstone, which has formed into huge uniform slabs covered in tiny edges and thin cracks. The Main Wall of Carreg-y-Barcud is the largest slab in the area and has a superb selection of trad routes from E1 upwards.
The climbing is mostly very sustained and technical but if you have strong calves you will be able to take all day over the moves. Most of the routes follow thin cracks which are wide enough for wires but not for your fingers. In places the cracks run out which gives bolder sections and there is little in the way of fixed protection. Indeed routes climbed in the past with bolt runners have all had these removed, any new bolts will also be removed. There are some pegs but these are likely to be untrustworthy so take great care before you place any reliance on them. The lesser climbed routes of all grades may have the odd loose hold so take care.

Conditions and Tides

Both walls face due south and catch all the sun that's going. They are reasonably quick to dry and don't suffer too badly from seepage. If there is any moisture around then the routes will be unclimbable. It is not unknown for there to be good weather here when it is dull and wet on South Pembroke although it would be foolish to regard this as a bad weather venue and the drive to find out isn't trivial. The base of the cliff is tidal but a convenient ledge runs under the right-hand side of the main face allowing access at high tide. For the rest of the routes choose a mid-to-low tide. In rough seas it can be a bit too exciting here. Note: the abseil-less scramble in approach is not useable at high tide.

Approach

Approaching from Haverfordwest locate the second turning to Trelerw (not signposted but halfway down a steep dip.) Turn left and after 30m there is a large grassy area on the right, park here. Walk down the road to Trelerw (5 to 10 mins walk). Once in the village turn down a small lane towards the coast path. Join this and head east (left, looking out) for a short distance until a vague path leads down the hill side to the crag top gearing up spot.

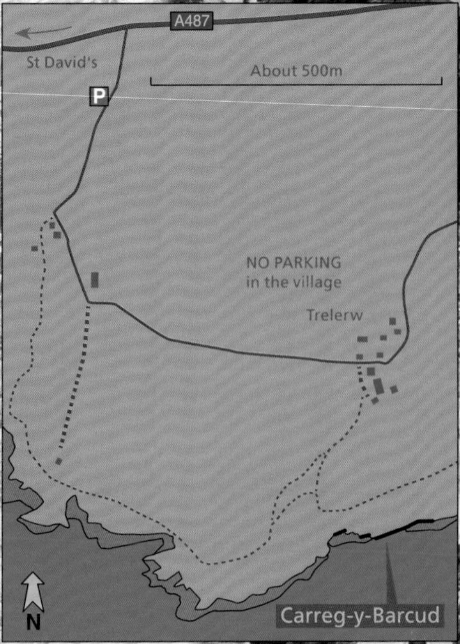

Martin Hoather following *Ethos* (HVS) - page 56 - Carreg-y-Barcud. Photo: Nick Smith

St. David's
Flimston Bay
Mewsford
Castle/Rusty
Saddle Head
Bosherston Head
Huntsman's Leap
Stennis/Chapel
Trevallen
St. Govan's
Mowing/Stackpole
Mother Carey's

Grey Face

The far left-hand side (looking in) of Carreg-y-Barcud has several bays with some striking corners and walls.

Approach - It can be approached by abseil from a stake passed on the approach walk (see map) however it is also easily reached along the cliff-base platform.

1 Ethos . . . . HVS 5a

30m. A fine crack climb which is well worth seeking out. Start up the lower wall at a vertical sentry-box of a crack. Climb the lower crack to a large ledge (optional stance if the sea threatens). The substance of the climb is the fine slanting crack above, follow this throughout and belay well back on a stake.

Photo on pages 38 and 54.

FA. Mike Harber 9.6.85

2 The Woodentops E2 5b

27m. The cracked slab to the right of *Ethos*. Take plenty of cams. Climb the thin crackline up the slab, moving leftwards near the top to join the mother route and avoid the crud cornice.

FA. Giles Barker 9.85

3 Mombasa E1 5b

27m. The soaring groove-line over to the right provides this mini adventure. Climb the groove, passing a couple of roofs en-route.

FA. Gary Lewis 3.5.87

Yellow Wall

To the left of the Main Face is a fine little bay with an impressive back wall.

Approach - The usual approach is to abseil directly down the wall from a stake at the top. Alternatively, it can be reached by scrambling along ledges below the Main Face and turning the corner to a wide platform. Originally bolt runners were placed of some of the bolder routes here. These were subsequently removed as they were not needed.

4 Yellow Edge .... 1 star **HS 4b**

25m. Start left of the recess and climb leftwards to the arete. Climb the right-hand side of the arete to a ledge, then move round to left and finish up a groove.

FA. Luke Dawe 30.4.83

5 Pass the Parkin on the Left-hand Side .... 1 star **E3 5c**

22m. An eliminate up the wall left of *Sinecure*, keeping right of the final arete to tackle the bold face.

FA. Gary Lewis 29.9.85

6 Sinecure .... 2 star **E1 5b**

22m. The most popular route at Barcud, and with good reason. Start just left of the recess and climb leftwards up flakes to a break below the headwall. The thin cracks above lead to the top.

Photo on page 61.

FA. Gary Lewis 25.5.85

7 The Hypocrite ..... 2 star **E3 6a**

22m. A fine hard slab route direct up the wall. The finish is thin and feels bold, unless you find the runner off to the right!

FA. Chris Parkin 9.6.85

8 Smirnoff **E3 5c**

22m. Tackle the right-hand side of the wall. A touch bold low down, though protection improves a bit with height.

FA. Gary Lewis 1.6.85

9 Octopus **E3 5b**

22m. Follow the groove on the right-hand side of the slab via the ledge on the left. It originally started from the chimney at about the same grade.

FA. Gary Lewis 2.6.85

10 Granny Basher........... **HVS 4c**

22m. The chimney is usually a greasy struggle.

FA. Luke Dawe 17.7.84

11 Gentlemen's Corner .... **VS 4c**

22m. The corner in its entirety.

FA. Mike Harber 30.4.83

12 Agent Orange .... **VS 4c**

22m. The crack in the wall just left of the edge.

FA. Luke Dawe 1984

Lots of sun | 20 min | Tidal | Abseil in

St. David's | Flimston Bay | Mewsford | Castle/Rusty | Saddle Head | Bosherston Head | Huntsman's Leap | Stennis/Chapel | Trevallen | St. Govan's | Mowing/Stackpole | Mother Carey's

St. David's
Flimston Bay
Mewsford
Castle/Rusty
Saddle Head
Bosherston Head
Huntsman's Leap
Stennis/Chapel
Trevallen
St. Govan's
Mowing/Stackpole
Mother Carey's

Main Face

The finest climbing at Carreg-y-Barcud is on the huge main slab. The routes here tend to be sustained and technical with the well protected ones following thin cracks and the bold ones plugging the gaps in between. The majestic central section of the Main Wall gives some of the classic sea-cliff slab-ticks in Britain. Take plenty of small wires and make sure your calf muscles are well warmed up.

Approach - The most common approach is direct by abseil from the block at the top of the wall, above *Mean Feet*. Before chucking your rope down have a look to see that there is no-one on the main routes! At low tide it is possible to scramble down via ledges on the far right (looking in) and walk along the sea-washed ledges below the face.

1 Left Edge . . . . **VDiff**
18m. Interesting climbing up the edge of the slab which also provides an easy escape route.
FA. Mike Harber (solo) 30.4.83

2 My Back Pages **E1 5b**
18m. The thin wall right of the arete.
FA. Jules McKim 1987

3 Metamorphosis . . . . **HS 4b**
18m. A justifiably popular route up the line of cracks six metres to the right of the arete.
FA. Jules McKim 17.7.84

The slab to the right is supposed to be climbable anywhere at about E3 - though the vague cracks at least give the odd runner and some idea about a line to follow.

4 Be Careful **E1 5a**
18m. A thin crack system is the first discernable line.
FA. Haydn Griffiths 1.6.85

5 Be-bop-a-lula **E1 5a**
18m. Head up the slab to pass the left-hand side of the flake above the mid-height break.
FA. Steve Quinton 23.5.91

6 Be Reckless **E2 5b**
18m. This time climb to and past the right-hand side of the flake above the break.
FA. Steve Quinton 23.5.91

7 Be Brave **E1 5b**
18m. A good route. Thin cracks lead to the break, then trend left.
FA. Haydn Griffiths 1.6.85

8 Beeline **E1 5b**
18m. Excellent thin climbing following vague cracks to right.
FA. Jules McKim 1987

9 Starling by the Seaside . . **E2 5b**
18m. More good climbing, thin and fairly bold.
FA. Elfyn Jones 9.5.87

10 Be Clever **E1 5c**
18m. Great climbing with a very thin but well protected crux to finish. This is the line to the left of the prominent square pocket in the slanting break.
FA. Haydn Griffiths 8.6.85

11 The Great Valerio. E1 5a
40m. Brilliant; one the crag's strongest lines. Low in the grade. Climbing with your hands in the break provides the best protection, feet in the break is less strenuous and much more scary! Climb up to the square pocket, then follow the rising break all the way to *Left Edge*, and finish up this.
FA. Haydn Griffiths 8.6.85

12 Snap Crackle 'n' Splash . E4 5c
18m. Bold climbing past the square pocket and up the wall above.
FA. Elfyn Jones (solo) 8.87

13 A Head in the Clouds E4 5c
24m. Bold climbing up the thin cracks just right of the hole with a testing move to reach the break.
FA. Steve Quinton 14.4.87

14 Kitten Claws . . . . . . Top 50 E3 5c
24m. The classic of the crag with superb sustained climbing and just enough gear. High in the grade. Start up the thin cracks three metres right of the square hole. Step right when the going gets tough and move up to a ledge. Finish more easily above.
FA. Gary Lewis 8.6.85

15 Commoner's Rights . E6 6a
24m. A bold eliminate up the blank piece of slab between *Mean Feat* and *Kitten Claws*. The crux is protected only by a skyhook.
FA. Dave Moore 28.07.99

16 Mean Feat . . . . Top 50 E5 6a
24m. Another majestic slab route with extremely sustained and fingery climbing. Start at the first crack right of *Kitten Claws*. Climb this to join *Billy Spragg*, then step right to follow the continuation crack and then directly up the wall above.
FA. Chris Parkin (bolt) 1985. FA. Steve Monks (bolt free) 27.5.90

17 Thrift E6 6b
24m. More superb climbing starting at the 'non-line' to the left of the point where the diagonal break reaches the ledges Climb straight up passing a thrift plant en route. The gear is spaced but good, the climbing sustained but positive.
FA. Steve Quinton 1999

18 Billy Spragg E3 6a
30m. A good route but it gets lost higher up. Follow the diagonal crack to the main break. Traverse left and finish up *Kitten Claws*.
FA. Haydn Griffiths 29.9.85

19 All or Nothing E6 6c
25m. Break out right from *Billy Spragg* and go! Desperate.
FA. Pat Littlejohn 19.5.86

20 Daddy Cool . E8 6b
20m. A very serious route but it avoids the direct challenge high up. Climb the protectionless slab direct by increasingly thin moves to the break. Clip a peg out right then move right and join *Sledgehammer* for its second crux which leads to the next break. Now move left and finish direct more easily.
FA. Dave Pickford 4.05

21 Sledgehamer. . . E6 6b
20m. Direct up the blank right-hand side of the slab.
FA. Paul Donnithorne (bolts) 12.5.87. FA. Elfyn Jones (bolt free) 1994

22 Naddyn. E5 6a
18m. The bold wall left of the corner has some chipped holds. Gear can be placed from the corner to protect the crux.
FA. Elfyn Jones 14.4.87

Lots of sun | 20 min | Tidal | Abseil in

St. David's
Flimston Bay
Mewsford
Castle/Rusty
Saddle Head
Bosherston Head
Huntsman's Leap
Stennis/Chapel
Trevallen
St. Govan's
Mowing/Stackpole
Mother Carey's

Main Face - Right

The right-hand side of the Main Face at Barcud presents a trio of left-facing stepped grooves separated by blank walls. This area gives a set of hard routes interspersed with easy routes up the grooves, and even some mid-grade offerings following the occasional crack.
Approach - Either abseil down the Main Face, or scramble down ledges on the right-hand side (looking in) of the crag.

23 First Corner . . . . VDiff
15m. The stepped corners is easy enough, and pleasant too.
FA. Reece Williams 30.4.83

24 First Corner Direct . . . . . VS 4c
22m. The cracks in the face round to the right are worthwhile.

25 I'm Not Addicted... . . . . E6 6a
22m. Very bold, blank and loose. Skyhooks may help protect.
FA. Lyndsey Foulkes (bolts) 1995. FA. Mark Higgs (bolt free) 1995

26 Beyond the Beyond . E5 6b
18m. The left-hand of two diagonal cracks. The crux is at the top and the whole affair is harder for the short.
FA. Steve Quinton 8.6.86

27 Beyond the Azimuth E1 5b
16m. A great route up the right-hand crack. Use the crack first for your hands and then for your feet.
FA. Jules McKim 16.7.84

28 Double Corner . . . . Sev 4a
15m. The three corners! Use the right arete when it gets tough.
FA. Mike Harber 16.7.84

29 Rust Never Sleeps E3 5b
18m. The bold wall. Once had 3 bolts and now has none.
FA. A.Williams (bolts) 1988. FA. Steve Monks (bolt free) 27.5.90

30 Stingray E2 5c
18m. A good route up the central crackline. The **6b** direct start is by-passed at this grade by starting from the ledge on the right
FA. Gary Lewis 26.5.85

31 Gilded Moments E5 6a
18m. Another cleaned up ex-bolt route. Bold and sustained.
FA. Paul Donnithorne (bolts) 1988. FA. Steve Monks (bolt free) 27.5.90

32 Just Fits . . . . HVS 4c
18m. The wide crack in the third of the corners is the wrong size for most folks.
FA. S.Robinson 30.4.83

33 Shelf Life E3 5b
18m. The stepped arete has a bold upper section.
FA. J.Ball 7.5.88

34 The Fermenting Telescope . . . . HVS 5a
18m. The two tiered cracks round right from *Just Fits.*
FA. Luke Dawe 17.7.84

Lots of sun | 20 min | Tidal | Abseil in

Max Adamson leading the fingery classic of *Sinecure* (E1 5b) - *page 57* - Carreg-y-Barcud. Photo: Nick Smith

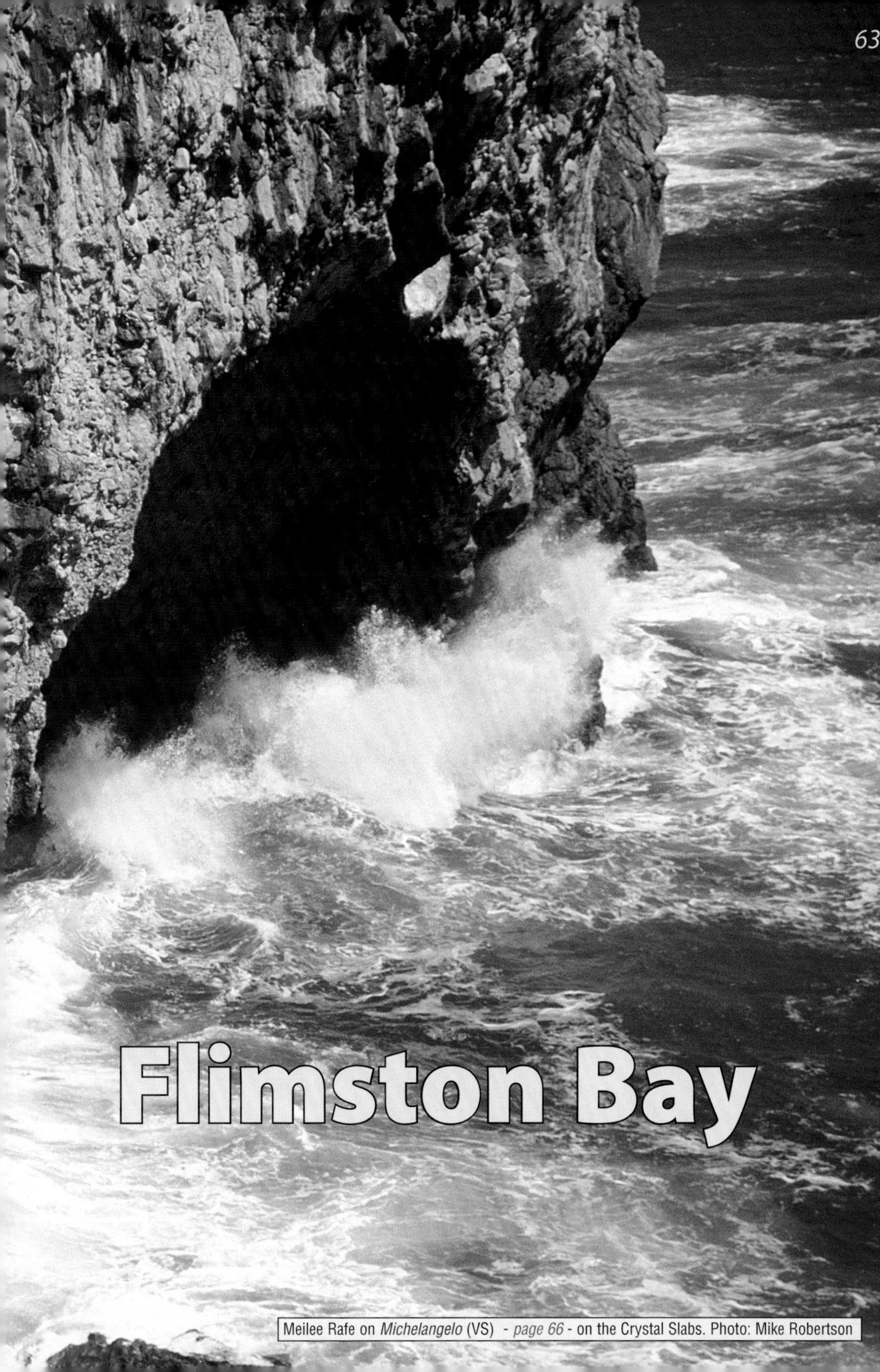

Flimston Bay

Meilee Rafe on *Michelangelo* (VS) - *page 66* - on the Crystal Slabs. Photo: Mike Robertson

	No star	1 star	2 stars	3 stars
Mod to S	-	1	1	1
HS to HVS	-	7	1	2
E1 to E3	-	-	2	1
E4 and up	-	2	-	1

Regarded as a bit of an outpost from the more popular Pembroke haunts, Flimston Bay offers plenty of decent routes including many at a useful grade. There is climbing all over the area but for most visitors, much of this will be too hard or too esoteric. The four walls covered in this section include three easy-angled slabs, and one hard-angled wall. The two narrow slabs of *Flimston Crack* and *Bow-Shaped Slab* give the full sea cliff experience at a grade that most can manage. The most popular area is the accessible Crystal Slabs - heaven for those into slabby VSs. Adding another dimension to the area is the unique Mosaic Wall - heaven for people who are into well-protected savagely-strenuous crack climbs of E3 and above ..... and I know there are a lot of you out there!

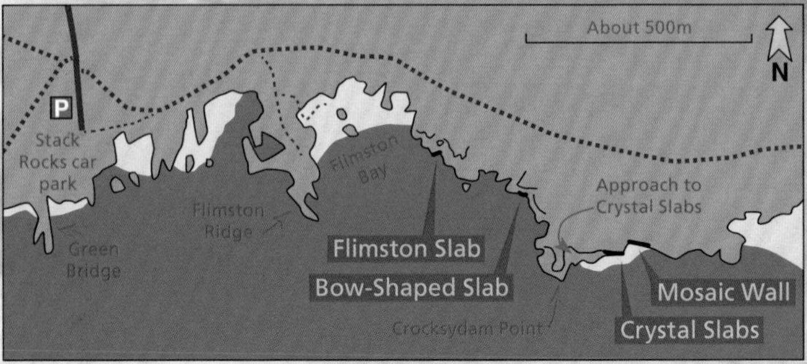

Approach

The best approach is from Stack Rocks car park which is situated at the border between Range East and Range West. To get there, drive along the Castlemartin road from the St Petrox to Bosherston road. 200m after you pass two Chieftain tanks with their barrels pointing skyward, turn left into the Range. The car park is at the end of this road. From the car park, walk east along the coast path past some spectacular scenery and a lot of bird watchers. Flimston Bay is reached after about 1km. See the individual route pages for detailed approaches from here.

Conditions and Tides

None of the routes in these four areas are tidal but the approaches to Bow-Shaped Slab and Mosaic Wall can be affected at high tide. All four areas face south and get all the afternoon sun that is going. Flimston Slab and Bow-Shaped Slab are both shaded from the morning sun by their steep side walls. These are also useful areas to consider if it is very windy since they all offer relatively sheltered conditions, however they are not places to be in rough seas. Mosaic Wall is almost continuously overhanging and may give dry climbing in light rain.

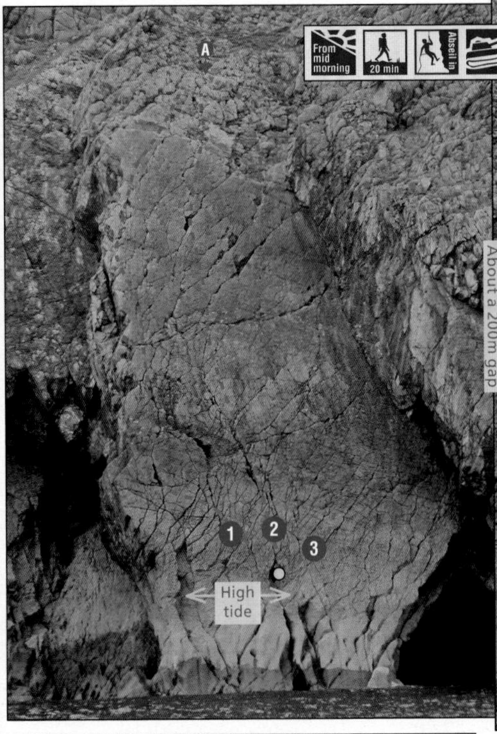

About a 200m gap

Flimston Slab

A delightful narrow slab in this impressive bay.
Approach - From the coast path, bear diagonally right towards the cliff edge. Find a blunt pinnacle with a small col on its landward side. Head down a gentle grass slope to the right of this pinnacle which leads across the top of Flimston Slab. Abseil down the slab.

1 Brass in Pocket . . . . ☆1 ☐ **Sev 4a**
40m. This route follows the slab's left edge. The only tricky section is the very last bit. Start from the ledge in the centre of the slab and climb across to the arete. Follow this to the top.
FA. Jim Curran 7.4.80

2 Flimston Slab . . . . ☆2 ☐ **VDiff**
40m. A reasonably direct line, however don't worry if you stray off route, just enjoy the position. Start from the ledge in the centre of the face and climb up a crack to a diagonal break. Roughly follow the left-hand crack above then transfer to a wider crack which is followed to the top.
FA. Colin Mortlock 28.5.67

3 Flimston Crack . . . . Top 50 ☐ **VDiff**
40m. A delightful pitch on which you can wander anywhere you like. It is a curiously-named pitch since it doesn't really follow any single crack. Starting from the ledge, climb diagonally rightwards up a crack. Then make a series of moves upwards crossing several more cracks (and runner placements). Eventually you arrive at a wider diagonal crack leading to the top.
FA. Colin Mortlock 28.5.67

Bow-Shaped Slab

A similar but slightly blanker slab in the same bay.
Approach - From the coast path head right roughly along the top of the cliffs. When almost level with the headland of Crocksydam Point, walk back rightwards down a grass slope and scramble across to the top of the slab.
High to mid tide - Abseil down the corner to the left (looking in) of the slab and traverse across to ledges beneath the routes.
Low tide - Scramble easily down a slope to the right (looking in) of the slab. Then traverse around onto the slab.

4 Inset Slab . . . . ☆2 ☐ **HS 4b**
40m. At the bottom of the slab is a smaller inset slab, start under this. Climb the mini-slab then pull awkwardly onto the main one. Follow the left edge of this then head for the top, avoiding moving left. Less continuous than the others here but worth doing.
FA. Jim Perrin 21.5.70

5 Bow-Shaped Slab . . . . Top 50 ☐ **HS 4a**
42m. A Pembroke favourite which gives good climbing; it can get a bit congested on Bank Holiday weekends. Start below the centre of the slab. Climb the slab to where it steepens. Move up rightwards up some cracks then climb straight to the top.
FA. Jim Perrin 21.5.70

6 Bow-Shaped Corner . . . . ☆3 ☐ **HS 4b**
44m. A popular climb up a big line, following the corner on the right of the slab throughout.
FA. S.Williams 28.5.67

St. David's | Flimston Bay | Mewsford | Castle/Rusty | Saddle Head | Bosherston Head | Huntsman's Leap | Stennis/Chapel | Trevallen | St. Govan's | Mowing/Stackpole | Mother Carey's

Crystal Slabs

A pleasant and popular slab but with some loose rock.
Approach - From the coast path, walk towards the headland of Crocksydam Point. Keep slightly left and locate a path down the steep rocky slope. At the base of the slope the path can be clearly seen. Start scrambling down above and left (looking out) of this. Follow the lower path leftwards to the non-tidal blocks under the slab.

There are two routes up the loose corners left of the main slab, neither is recommended.

1 The Gadfly .... VS 4c

40m. This almost-popular route follows a devious line up the main slab. Start below the second crack right of the corner. Climb the crack for 12m then switch to the crack on the left. Follow this over the bulge and then move left again to yet another crack. Follow this one to the top.
Variation, VS 4c - Climb direct up the first crack right of the corner to join the original, then step left below the bulge and climb straight up to the finishing crack.
FA. Dave Cook 5.4.80

2 Sixth Crack .... VS 4c

40m. Now it has got confusing since the first ascensionist of this route started numbering from the right! Start at the same crack as *The Gadfly* but climb it without deviation all the way to the top.
FA. Tim Daniells 6.4.80

3 Razzle Dazzle .... VS 4c

40m. The other popular route on the slab is the central line. Start below the middle of the slab and climb the crack to the bulge, pull through this using twin cracks. Finish direct, or traverse left to join and finish up *Sixth Crack*.
FA. Ken Wilson 4.4.80

4 The Crucifix.......... VS 4c

40m. The next crack right of *Razzle Dazzle* has a square niche at the bottom. Climb the crack all the way over the bulge and continue for about 5m. Then trend leftwards across the wall heading for the left-hand side of the upper ramp.
FA. Paul Carling 17.4.81

5 Michelangelo .... VS 4c

40m. Past a crack which hasn't got a route up it, but which has probably been climbed, is the last crack before the edge. Climb it! Continue straight up to the upper ledge and belay. Then climb the short wall at the back of the ledge, or traverse off leftwards. It is also common to saunter leftwards in *The Crucifix* lower down.
Photo on page 62.
FA. Jim Perrin 4.4.80

6 Crystal Edge ...... HVS 5a

40m. Start next to the wide chimney at the bottom right-hand corner of the slab. Climb the slab to the left of this then follow the arete above with a hard move past the overlap. Join and finish up *Michelangelo*. Low in the grade but quite serious.
FA. S.Whimster 4.80

7 Crystal Arete .... VS 4c

35m. A 'one-move-wonder' route up the narrow side slab. Start from a ledge 10m up on the arete.
1) 4c, 30m. Climb the right-hand side of the slab to a break. Step up left and follow the centre of the slab to the top overlap. Pull through this by a crack in its centre and belay on the ledge above.
2) 4a, 5m. Finish up the short wall at the back of the ledge.
FA. Brian Wyvill 5.4.80. It was once home to a magnificent 'sea cabbage' which was a useful hold on the upper section. Sadly this has now disappeared.

Lots of sun | 20 min

Warning
Unlike much of Pembroke, the rock here is potentially loose even on the popular climbs. There have been several accidents - CARE IS REQUIRED.

8 Paint by Numbers 1 E4 6a

Start just right of the big flake in front of the wall.

1) 6a, 35m. Climb up to the roof, move left then pull over slightly rightwards. Haul up on spaced slots and cracks to a ledge. Climb the centre of the wall above (thread) to a belay in a cave.

2) 5b, 10m. Swing immediately rightwards onto the slab. Climb this straight up to a loose finish.

FA. Paul Donnithorne, Emma Alsford 28.5.95

9 Mural Landscape 2 E3 5c

Easier than it looks. The start below the centre of the small cave - usually marked by some threads.

1) 5c, 30m. Climb straight over the roof then follow the crack (past threads) to a ledge at the base of a wide chimney. Step right and climb the wall just right of the chimney until forced into it at its top. Move up right to belay on a ledge just left of *Rollerwall.*

2) 5c, 15m. Step back left and climb directly up the wall above (peg on the first ascent).

FA. Paul Donnithorne, Carl Ryan 28.5.95

10 Rollerwall........... 2 E3 5c

This route gives some wonderfully steep crack climbing up the left hand side of the tallest section of the wall. Right of the large block in front of the face is a cave. Start below a crack in the right-hand side of the cave.

1) 5c, 30m. Climb the crack out of the cave to a horizontal scoop. Continue up cracks above to an easing in angle and good stance.

2) 5b, 15m. Follow a diagonal crack rightwards to a spike in a recess. Climb straight over the bulge above.

FA. Steve Lewis, Gary Lewis 11.5.80

11 Public Anenome 1 E5 6b

45m. A hard left-hand start to *Bristol Cream.* Start just right of *Rollerwall* and climb a diagonal crack to reach the break on *Bristol Cream.* Finish up this.

FA. Paul Pritchard 1993

12 Bristol Cream 3 E6 6b

45m. A route for which the word strenuous is nowhere near big enough. The climbing is extremely sustained and difficult. Start from a block beneath the crack of *Wallbanger.* Move left then make some hard moves straight up, past a shallow horizontal scoop to a break. Move left and pull up on pockets (non-crucial peg to the left) and then make a hard reach up left to a thin crack. Trend up and rightwards across the wall, on blind pockets, to a thin crack. This leads, past a thread, to the easier upper wall and the spike on *Rollerwall.* Finish as for this.

FA. Martin Crocker 25.5.87

13 Wallbanger.......... 3 E4 5c

A superb and unusual route which is by far the most popular on the wall. It is actually considerably more strenuous than it looks, mainly because the cracks aren't the correct width for good jams. Start at the lower right-hand side of the wall, three metres left of a wide chimney with a large wedge of solid rock in it.

1) 5c, 25m. Climb up steep juggy rock to the base of the crack laced wall. Pull into the crack and paddle your way up it with a slight leftwards detour where it gets tricky. Continue to the blocky recess to belay. A powerful pitch that will feel 6a if at all damp.

2) 5b, 20m. Move up to a ledge on the left then climb straight up the cracks above. After 6m move left to a spike in a recess (on *Rollerwall*). Finish by passing the bulge above on its left.

FA. Pat Littlejohn 23.3.80

Mosaic Wall

This witheringly steep wall gives a complete contrast to the adjacent slabs. Bring your turbo-charger here.

Approach - From underneath Crystal Slabs, continue past the right edge of the slabs and scramble across boulders to reach the wall. There is a small inlet here which can get cut off in rough seas or very high spring tides. If this is the case you can still abseil in.

Mewsford

Crickmail

Triple Overhang

Blockhouse to Sitting Bull

Ruth Taylor completing the amazing traverse of *Welcome to the Cruise* (HVS) - *page 76* - on Triple Overhang. Photo: Mike Robertson

St. David's
Flimston Bay
Mewsford
Castle/Rusty
Saddle Head
Bosherston Head
Huntsman's Leap
Stennis/Chapel
Trevallen
St. Govan's
Mowing/Stackpole
Mother Carey's

	No star	1 star	2 stars	3 stars
Mod to S	-	-	-	-
HS to HVS	-	-	-	-
E1 to E3	-	1	3	1
E4 and up	-	2	-	1

One of the problems with Mewsford is the huge number of brilliant routes that you walk past on the approach - you really need to want to go there! So how can I convince you?
Well, here goes ....
Mewsford has a great set of routes in the E1 to E3 range that take brilliant and complex lines up a magnificent face of rock. The climbing starts strenuously but eases as you get higher and the exposure increases. All the routes listed here are worth doing but Daydreams and Surprise Attack are uber-classics!

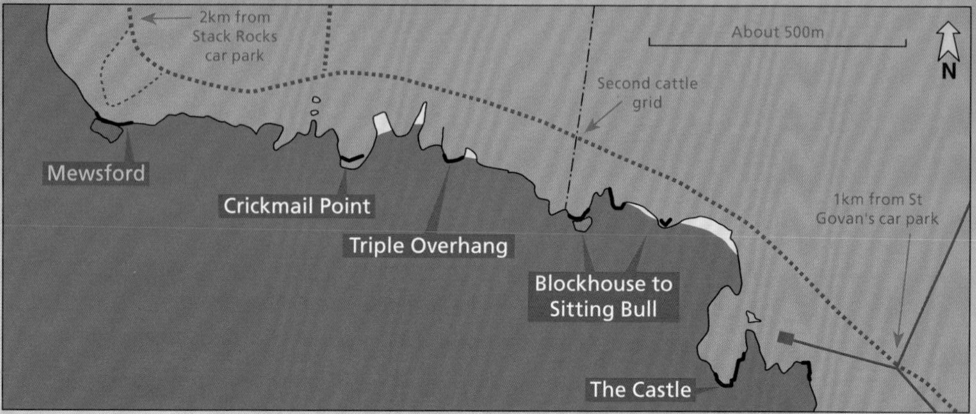

So now you are convinced, here is how to get there .....

Approach

From St Govan's car park - Walk for about 1¾km west, along the coast path, to the second cattle grid. Continue, past the headland of Crickmail Point, and veer left towards a mound of earth which is above the crag. The huge tilted block at the base of the crag is also an obvious feature.
From Stack Rocks car park - Walk for about 2km east, along the coast path, to approach the mound from the other side.
For those with 60m abseil ropes, the best line is down the steep wall right (looking out) of the main face. Belay on the concrete blocks at the top and skirt the edge of the rickety fence. Traditionally, for those with shorter ropes, people have abseiled down *Surprise Attack*, and this is an option since there are good belays a little way down the cliff to make a second 50m abseil from, but this is not desirable for those who are already climbing *Surprise Attack*. A better option is to use a second rope to reach the crag edge by the rickety fence and make a 50m abseil from here.

Tides

The most obvious feature of Mewsford is the large tilted block underneath the cliff. The highest point of the block is non-tidal but unfortunately the section below the face drops below the high tide line. This channel is covered for about two hours at high tide and slightly longer for the section below *Daydreams*.

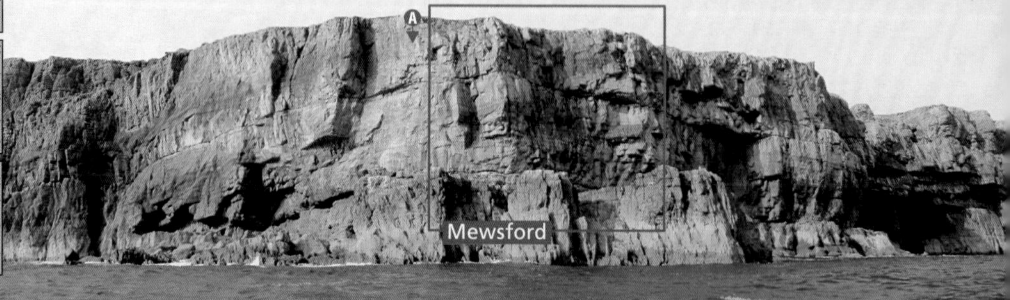

Conditions

If the wind is blowing anywhere then it will be blowing at Mewsford and often, when St Govan's and Trevallen are sun-traps, it is still freezing at Mewsford. However, it does have a very favourable aspect and the routes themselves are more sheltered than the top and bottom of the cliff. The greasy starts are not usually a problem since, with the exception of *Daydreams*, they are the easiest bits of most of the routes. The very top section is a curious band of stuck together pebbles which are a bit friable, so take care when finishing, as is always the case in Pembroke.

Suzie Wilson on the testing second pitch of *Daydreams* (E2) - *page 73* - at Mewsford. Photo: Jack Geldard

The groove left of the upper groove of Surprise Attack is **Let Me Down Easy, E5 6b**.

1 Surprise Attack 3 E1 5c

The most popular line here follows the long grooveline which is gained by a steep and impressive start. The climbing is a bit unbalanced but the line and situation more than make up for this. Start below and right of the main grooveline.

1) 5a, 15m. Pull up and traverse left, then climb direct to the stance. All easier than it looks.

2) 5c, 32m. A technical little move up the slab above (micro-wires) gains the main groove. Follow this, trending leftwards at the top. A fine pitch.

FA. Steve Lewis, Charlie Heard 10.10.79

2 Nearly a Whisper...... 2 E3 6a

This interesting route follows the right-hand wall of the *Surprise Attack* corner finishing in a good position on the large blunt arete.

1) 5b, 12m. Climb straight up from the starting block of *Surprise Attack*, via a groove, to a belay on the break.

2) 6a, 32m. Climb boldly straight up above the stance to a point 5m below the roof. Traverse left to a crack and pull through the roof just right of *Surprise Attack*. Tiptoe rightwards above the roof and climb a thin flake crack on the left-hand side of the arete. From the next break move up the arete above to the top.

FA. Gary Gibson, Matt Ward 6.4.85

3 The Lure of the Sea . 2 E5 6a

A variation pitch based on the big rounded arete right of *Surprise Attack*. Start as for *Nearly a Whisper* to the belay.

2) 6a, 32m. Climb straight up to a good hold below the right-hand side of the roof. Swing boldly up rightwards through the bulges into a fine hanging groove. Climb the groove and rejoin *Nearly a Whisper* to finish.

FA. Gary Gibson 3.7.85

4 The Shining.......... 2 E4 6a

The last route to use the start of *Surprise Attack* to break through the initial roofs is a hard and technical climb up the big wall just right of the rounded arete.

1) 5b, 18m. Step right from the first break on *Surprise Attack* and then climb over a bulge to a crack. Pull up rightwards to belay on a ledge (shared with *The Voyage Out*).

2) 6a, 30m. Step left and climb an open groove for 10m until you can move up and right to better holds. Gain a line of holds above which leads up and left to the base of a steep groove. Follow this to a ledge then climb a crack above to the top.

FA. Pat Littlejohn, Lyndsey Foulkes 23.4.84

5 The Voyage Out....... 2 E3 6a

A good route which follows a slanting groove in the big wall. The start of the second pitch has a bold and technical move that is much harder than the rest of the route. Start below a crack which runs from right to left through the initial bulges.

1) 5a, 20m. Climb the butch crack and flake to the break - more strenuous than it looks. Traverse left to belay on a ledge below the slanting groove.

2) 6a, 30m. Make a very thin move up and right into the groove using a hidden crimp (poor wire) and establish yourself in the groove. Move up then left around a bulge at the top. Continue up the wall and slabby groove above to the left-hand end of the large roof. Finish straight up easy cracks.

FA. Jim Perrin, Jim Curran 15.4.80

Direct through the belay of Voyage Out is **Try to Imagine Drowning, E5 6a**.

6 Somnambulist........... 1 E2 5c

48m. A long pitch which tackles the wall directly above the start of *The Voyage Out*. It can be climbed in one pitch on 50m ropes. From the break on *The Voyage Out*, climb a groove above past a roof onto a slab. Climb this to the roof to join and finish up *The Voyage Out*. Stretch your ropes to the belay.

FA. Andy Parkin 4.80

The next two routes are both popular challenges. There are a number of harder routes which weave around them. Direct up the upper wall is **By Popular Demand, E4 6a**. *Taking a parallel but lower line to Daydreams is* **Nightmare on Lily Street, E5 6b, 5c, 5b**. *On the right is* **Chartered Courses E5 5b, 6a, 6a**.

7 Lateral Bearings . . . . . . 2 ☐ **E2 5c**

A superb direct climb up the wall which provides an excellent alternative to *Daydreams*. Since there is often a party on *Daydreams*, it is best started from the left.

1) 5b, 15m. Traverse right from the break on *The Voyage Out* to belay on the ledge (shared with *Daydreams*).

2) 5c, 32m. Follow the groove of *Daydreams* until level with a roof on the right. Step left and climb straight up the open grooves above to a large thread in the break below the roof. Move left again and make some powerful pulls through the roof on large undercuts. Climb the bubbly wall, past a couple of holes, to the top.

FA. Gary Gibson, Hazel Gibson 8.6.86

8 Daydreams . . . . Top 50 ☐ **E2 5b**

One of the great Pembroke classics. It follows a cunning line up the wall weaving in and out of the steep bits. Start at the right-hand end of the block under the face, below a steep groove which leads to a ledge on the left. *Photo page 71.*

1) 5b, 20m. Climb the groove and wall above the ledge to the break. Traverse left for 10m to belay on a ledge below the longest of several grooves in the wall above.

2) 5b, 15m. Climb the groove, passing left of two roofs, onto a slab and belay. Often found to be the hardest pitch.

3) 5b, 15m. Climb up to a corner on the right-hand side of the large roof. Follow this then move leftwards around the roofs to finish up another corner. These last two pitches can be run together.

FA. Ben Wintringham, Marion Wintringham, Jim Perrin 7.4.80

	No star	1	2	3
Mod to S	-	1	-	-
HS to HVS	2	4	1	-
E1 to E3	-	-	1	-
E4 and up	-	-	-	-

St. David's
Flimston Bay
Mewsford
Castle/Rusty
Saddle Head
Bosherston Head
Huntsman's Leap
Stennis/Chapel
Trevallen
St. Govan's
Mowing/Stackpole
Mother Carey's

The south-facing aspect of Crickmail's compact exposed walls provide the visitor with a good number of quality 20m+ routes, including classics such as the ever-popular *Aero* (VS), and *B-Team Buttress* (E1). It's a long-ish walk-in, as it falls roughly halfway between the two possible car parks, but it is well worth the effort, especially if you extend your time in the area by nipping across to Mewsford, or Triple Overhang. The previous guide book implied high numbers of sheep suicides on this cliff; the intervening years have seen a marked decrease in this malodorous activity.

Simon Dale on the super crack of *B-Team Buttress* (E1) - *opposite* - Crickmail Point. Photo: Mike Hutton

Approach See map on page 70

From St Govan's car park - Walk for about 1¾ km, west along the coast path, to the second cattle grid. Continue for about 500m then head left along the headland.
From Stack Rocks car park - Walk for about a 2km east along the coast path to Mewsford where there is a mound of earth. Continue for about 300m then head right along the headland. From here gear-up and then make a short 15m abseil down the south face to a good ledge. The climbing is towards the west (left looking in) end of the ledge.

Conditions and Tides

Since all of the climbing is perched high above the sea, Crickmail Point doesn't suffer from any of the slimy rock of other areas. Its height and position on a headland don't give much shelter in windy conditions, but it will dry quickly. It is south facing and gets all of the available sunshine.

1 Snap, Popple and Crack . . . . . . VS 4b
25m. Start below the crack to the left of a large block. Climb the crack to a niche. Pull steeply out of this to a break. Move left and climb the wide cracks to the top.
FA. C.Curle 27.10.79

2 Crunchy . . . . VS 4b
25m. A better route than its neighbour. Climb a groove up rightwards to reach a two wide cracks. Follow these to finish.
FA. Steve Lewis 3.6.79

3 Catch . . . . VS 4b
25m. Start below the corner on the right of the block. Climb this then step right to a crack which leads to a wide finishing groove.
FA. Mike Harber 3.6.79

Lots of sun | 25 min | Abseil in

4 B-Team Buttress E1 5b
25m. An old favourite. It gives good crack and wall climbing on wonderful rock. Start below the cracks 3m right of the block. Climb the cracks to a break. Move up then left to a hidden flake hold and pull back right and up to another crack. Finish direct.
Photo opposite.
FA. Mick Learoyd 27.10.79

5 Aero. . . . . VS 5a
25m. Another popular classic. Start roughly in the centre of the wall by a small cave. Climb the cracks, past a small overlap, to a break continue up the crack above into a finishing groove.
FA. Mick Learoyd 3.6.79

6 Tinker Tailor . . . . HVS 5a
25m. The crack right of *Aero* gives a similar pitch but the move past the overlap is a touch harder. From the overlap continue up the wall to a niche and finish up the right-hand of two cracks.
FA. M.Price 27.10.79

7 Marathon . . . . HVS 5a
25m. This route has a good lower section with a hard move around a roof. Start below a leftwards leaning ramp. Climb the ramp and groove above to a roof. Pull steeply around this to gain an easier groove which leads to the top.
FA. Mick Learoyd 10.6.79

8 The Jogger . . . . HVS 5a
25m. Start at the left-hand side of the main cave. Pull up onto a small ledge above the undercut base on the left. Follow a crack above which leads to a groove and the top.
FA. Bill Lounds 27.8.84

9 Slipway . . . . Sev 4a
25m. The groove below the abseil is pleasant.
FA. Mike Harber 2.6.79

Triple Overhang

	No star	1-star	2-star	3-star
Mod to S	-	-	-	-
HS to HVS	-	-	1	2
E1 to E3	-	-	1	-
E4 and up	-	-	-	-

This fine, outstanding buttress (in every sense of the word) is a delight, and home to a clutch of excellent multi-pitch up-and-sideways jaunts, such as the very exposed excursion of *Welcome to the Cruise* (HVS) and, if you add that elusive two-pitch classic, *Deep Throat* (E3), you'll have more than enough to throw yourself at for a day (and possibly the night too…). The buttress is hard to view from the coast path, meaning knowledge is only gained after committing to an approach, although the photo to the right helps. Maximum adventure found right here - dust off your abseil rope and get on board.

Access - Currently none of the routes listed here on Triple Overhang are restricted although please only use an abseil approach during the nesting season from 1 March to 1 August. In the past there have been restrictions here so check the BMC Access database if you are unsure (see page 23).

Conditions and Tides

The buttress faces south and gets all the available sun. It is possible to do all the routes at any state of the tide, however *Deep Throat* is easiest, and most escapable, at dead low tide. *Galactic Co-ordinator* can be started on easy-angled rock above the high tide level. *Deep Throat* is often damp, but the nature of the climbing means that this shouldn't be much of a problem, particularly if you've got long legs.

Approach

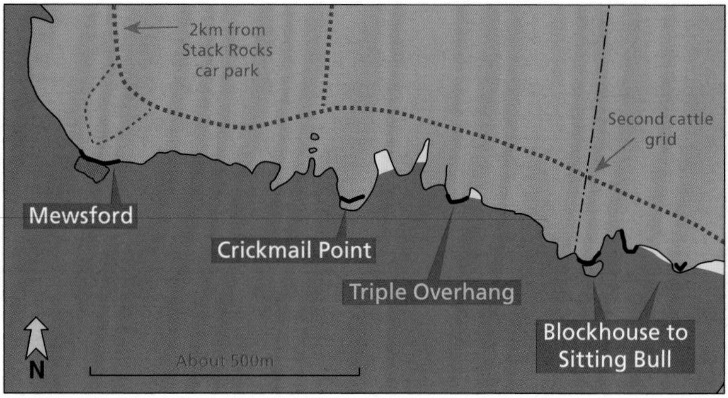

Triple Overhang is a touch nearer St Govan's car park than Stack Rocks car park.

From St Govan's car park - Walk for about 1¾ km west along the coast path to the second cattle grid. Continue for 150m then head left along the headland.

From Stack Rocks car park - Walk for about 2km east along the coast path to Mewsford where there is a mound of earth. Continue for about 400m then head right along the headland.

Approach (Routes 1 to 3) - Abseil direct down the groove of *Galactic Co-ordinator* to a small ledge at its base. Outside the nesting season you can scramble down easy rock to the left (looking in) of the buttress to reach this same point.

Approach (Deep Throat) - Make a spectacular free-hanging abseil to a non-tidal ledge at the base of the route. You will need to swing and place the odd runner to gain this ledge, but at low tide you will be able to scramble up to it. Outside the nesting season you can scramble down easy rock to the left (looking in) of the buttress and take an awkward high traverse line to the same point, or an easier low tide line. You can also abseil down for *Galactic Co-ordinator* and traverse across at any time of year although avoid rough seas.

1 Galactic Co-ordinator . . . . . . 2-star **HVS 5a**
A superb route which follows the groove which runs up the left-hand side of the main overhangs and then blasts out to an exposed position on the front edge of the buttress. Start below the long tapering groove.
1) 4c, 30m. Climb a steep wall into the main groove and follow this to a large ledge to the left of the main roofs.
2) 5a, 15m. Climb diagonally right across the wall, past a flake, to a niche. Move right again to the arete then pull up into a larger niche and finish up a steep crack.
FA. Steve Lewis, Charlie Heard 17.6.79

2 Welcome to the Cruise . . 3-star **HVS 5a**
18m. The first wacky traverse that doesn't really go anywhere, but is so exposed that you can't fail to enjoy it. Start on the high belay ledge as for *Pigs on the Wing*. Follow *Galactic Co-ordinator* to the arete and continue traversing along a break, under a small roof. Follow this to the crack of *Deep Throat* and finish up this.
Photo on page 68.
FA. Steve Lewis 20.10.79

3 Pigs on the Wing . . . HVS 5a

This breath-taking traverse follows the lower line below the main roof. The climbing is never very difficult and the positions are amazing. Start from the belay ledge at the end of the first pitch of *Galactic Co-ordinator*, reached by either doing this pitch or by scrambling easily down from the top.

1) 4c, 15m. Swing around the arete onto the main face and follow the break below the roof to a wild stance on an arete.

2) 5a, 15m. Continue traversing along the break, past the crack of *Deep Throat*, to a large ledge. Scramble off easily.

FA. Charlie Heard, Steve Lewis 17.6.79

4 Deep Throat . . . E3 5c

An atmospheric route which follows the wide crack on the right-hand side (looking in) of the buttress. The bridging moves required on the route are a lot easier for tall people.

1) 5c, 25m. Climb the corner-crack and chimney to a break in the first roof. Move up to a rest then chimney out to a spike on the arete. Swing (or bridge if you are lanky) to a ledge up and right.

2) 5a, 25m. Climb the crack above, over the other two roofs.

FA. Charlie Heard, Steve Lewis 16.6.79

Lots of sun | 25 min

Blockhouse to Sitting Bull

	No star	1	2	3
Mod to S	-	-	1	-
HS to HVS	2	6	2	-
E1 to E3	-	1	1	-
E4 and up	-	-	-	-

St. David's
Flimston Bay
Mewsford
Castle/Rusty
Saddle Head
Bosherston Head
Huntsman's Leap
Stennis/Chapel
Trevallen
St. Govan's
Mowing/Stackpole
Mother Carey's

Between the jutting headland of the Castle, and the prow of Triple Overhang, are a series of bays giving a mixture of solid buttresses and overhanging rubble and choss. Although there is nothing outstanding here, one or two routes are well worth investigating especially if you want to escape the crowds. Blockhouse Buttress is an impressive formation with a tidy little set of slab and crack routes up its front face, turning to easy scrambling for the upper 15m or so. The well-named *Sheer Delight* is the pick of the bunch giving easy climbing up a wonderful solid pillar of rock. Space Buttress offers a complex set of roofs and horizontal bands of jugs with the routes tending to take intricate lines in an attempt to stick on the big holds and avoid the nasty steep pulls around the roofs (they are not always successful in this). The final section described is the protruding *Jolly Sensible Arete* - the most famous tick on Sitting Bull Buttress - not the greatest route in Pembroke, but a popular one nevertheless.

Conditions and Tides

The area faces south getting plenty of sun. It is exposed to any big seas hence best avoided in rough conditions. Blockhouse Buttress has a huge slanting block under it (a mini version of the platform below Mewsford). Although this stays above the tide, the channel between the platform and the face is cut off at high tide. Space Buttress requires mid-to-low tide for all the routes. *Jolly Sensible Arete* itself can be climbed at any state of tide, however the easy lower pitch needs mid-to-low tide.

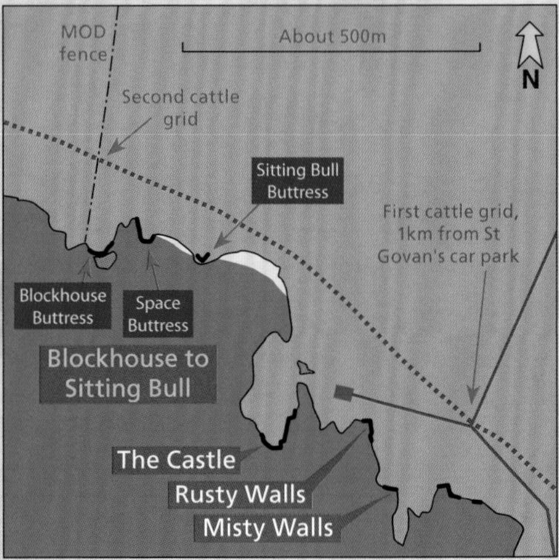

Approach

Approach from St Govan's car park. Walk for about 1½ km west along the coast path but break left toward the cliff edge before the second cattle grid, and just after you pass the Castle area and the second MOD building. The three buttresses are on the section of cliff to the east of the MOD fence.

Ray Harris on *Planet Waves* (E2) - *page 81* - on Space Buttress. Photo: Kevin Little

St. David's
Flimston Bay
Mewsford
Castle/Rusty
Saddle Head
Bosherston Head
Huntsman's Leap
Stennis/Chapel
Trevallen
St. Govan's
Mowing/Stackpole
Mother Carey's

Sheer Delight

Approach and Tides - Abseil from large blocks on the left (looking out) of the buttress from mid-to-low tides.

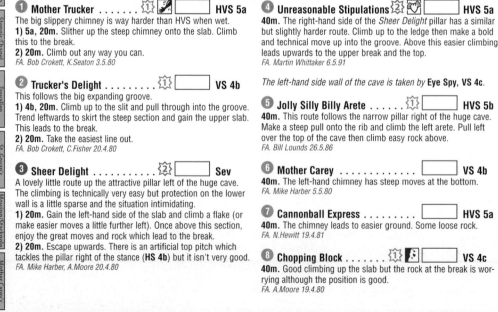

1 Mother Trucker .... HVS 5a

The big slippery chimney is way harder than HVS when wet.
1) 5a, 20m. Slither up the steep chimney onto the slab. Climb this to the break.
2) 20m. Climb out any way you can.
FA. Bob Crokett, K.Seaton 3.5.80

2 Trucker's Delight .... VS 4b

This follows the big expanding groove.
1) 4b, 20m. Climb up to the slit and pull through into the groove. Trend leftwards to skirt the steep section and gain the upper slab. This leads to the break.
2) 20m. Take the easiest line out.
FA. Bob Crokett, C.Fisher 20.4.80

3 Sheer Delight .... Sev

A lovely little route up the attractive pillar left of the huge cave. The climbing is technically very easy but protection on the lower wall is a little sparse and the situation intimidating.
1) 20m. Gain the left-hand side of the slab and climb a flake (or make easier moves a little further left). Once above this section, enjoy the great moves and rock which lead to the break.
2) 20m. Escape upwards. There is an artificial top pitch which tackles the pillar right of the stance (**HS 4b**) but it isn't very good.
FA. Mike Harber, A.Moore 20.4.80

4 Unreasonable Stipulations HVS 5a

40m. The right-hand side of the *Sheer Delight* pillar has a similar but slightly harder route. Climb up to the ledge then make a bold and technical move up into the groove. Above this easier climbing leads upwards to the upper break and the top.
FA. Martin Whittaker 6.5.91

The left-hand side wall of the cave is taken by **Eye Spy, VS 4c**.

5 Jolly Silly Billy Arete ...... HVS 5b

40m. This route follows the narrow pillar right of the huge cave. Make a steep pull onto the rib and climb the left arete. Pull left over the top of the cave then climb easy rock above.
FA. Bill Lounds 26.5.86

6 Mother Carey .... VS 4b

40m. The left-hand chimney has steep moves at the bottom.
FA. Mike Harber 5.5.80

7 Cannonball Express .... HVS 5a

40m. The chimney leads to easier ground. Some loose rock.
FA. N.Hewitt 19.4.81

8 Chopping Block .... VS 4c

40m. Good climbing up the slab but the rock at the break is worrying although the position is good.
FA. A.Moore 19.4.80

Space Buttress

Approach and Tides - Abseil directly down the west face to tidal ledges at the base. You can scramble round to reach the start of *Space*.

9 Rising Damp . . . . 1 **HVS 5a**
A good rising traverse across the prominent breaks. Start on the lower left corner of the face.
1) 5a, 20m. Climb up to the breakline, then follow it rightwards to belay below a flake.
2) 4b, 18m. The break leads right to a belay in the groove.
3) 4c, 18m. Move rightwards movement under the roof until you can step around the corner onto the front face.
4) 15m. Get out of there!
FA. Chris Jackson, Bill Wintrip 5.5.80

10 Planet Waves 2 **E2 5b**
A secluded route that takes a good line up the clean face.
Photo on page 79.
1) 5b, 20m. Weave up the lower wall to a notch in the main overhang. Pull over right onto the wall above then climb to the break. Move left to belay below a flake.
2) 5b, 20m. Move back right along the break then pull up left onto the wall. Trend right to gain a crack which leads to the upper break. Move right here then pull up and finish direct.
FA. (P1) Steve Monks 19.8.84. FA. (P2) Pat Littlejohn 11.5.80

11 Space . . . . 2 **HVS 5a**
The right-hand side of the buttress has this amenable adventure.
1) 4c, 15m. Climb direct to reach the horizontal breaks. Move left to belay in a corner.
2) 4c, 25m. Climb the steep groove above to a breakline. Move left to some ledges then back right onto a slab, and to the top.
FA. Dick Renshaw, John Mothersele 25.6.79

The next two routes are on Sitting Bull Buttress.

12 Running Bear . . . . 1 **HS 4b**
The central crack of the buttress gives a good pitch at the grade.
1) 4b, 12m. The lower crack in the slab.
2) 4b, 15m. The continuation crack to the groove.
FA. A.Davies, C.Curle 4.5.80

13 Jolly Sensible Arete 1 **E1 5a**
15m. The short arete on the left of *Running Bear* has been much-photographed over the years. Climb it on its right-hand side.
FA. Nick Dixon, Andy Popp 4.84

Sitting Bull Buttress

Approach and Tides - Abseil directly down the buttress to tidal ledges at the base. You can stop at the half-height ledge to do *Jolly Sensible* in any tide.

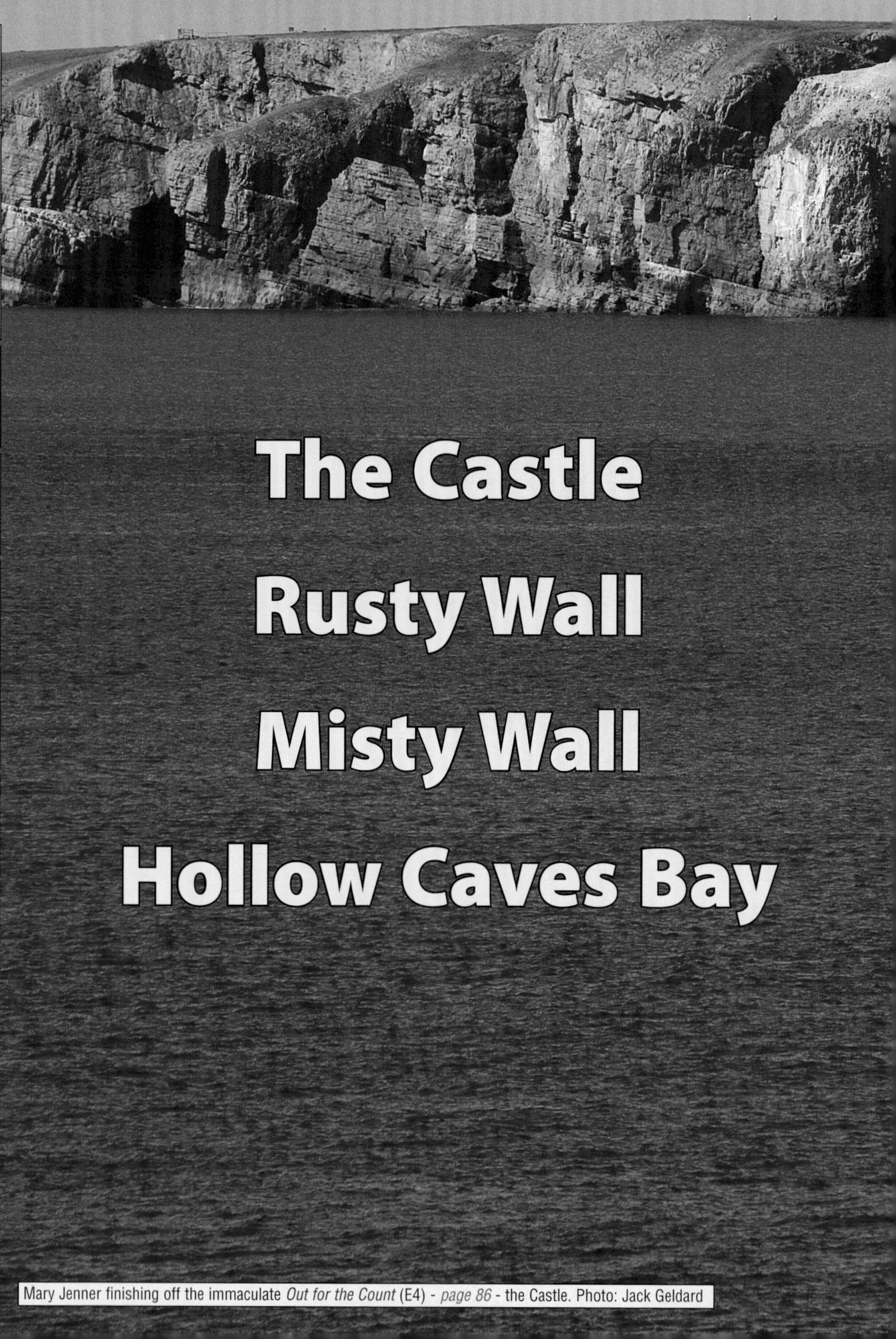

The Castle
Rusty Wall
Misty Wall
Hollow Caves Bay

Mary Jenner finishing off the immaculate *Out for the Count* (E4) - *page 86* - the Castle. Photo: Jack Geldard

	No star	1	2	3
Mod to S	-	1	-	-
HS to HVS	1	5	-	-
E1 to E3	2	3	2	2
E4 and up	-	1	6	6

The headland of The Castle is a bastion; a shapely disarming profusion of cracks, grooves and aretes. Its classics are many and varied, and usually on perfect compact rock; testpieces include the brilliant *Too Much Pressure* (E1), *Vista* (E2), and *Out for the Count* (E4). In the past the South Face was traditionally undergraded which earned the crag a fearsome reputation. Even after the upgrades these cracks in the E4/5 category still pack a punch and are no soft options.

The East Face is somewhat more enigmatic, offering a diverse region of bizarre corners, leaning faces and aretes. Here, classics include the superb *Wishful Thinking* (E1) and *Critical Masses* (E4), but you will need to invest considerable time in unlocking its secrets and accessing its tucked-away lower belay ledges. A further complication is the lack of simple belays blocks on the upper slope - be inventive!

Deep Water Solos - Most recently, the East Face has seen many of its routes ascended in DWS style, as a big tide will bring the security of deep water below many of the routes - the cruxes can be as low as 6m above the ocean. See the route descriptions for S grades and further info.

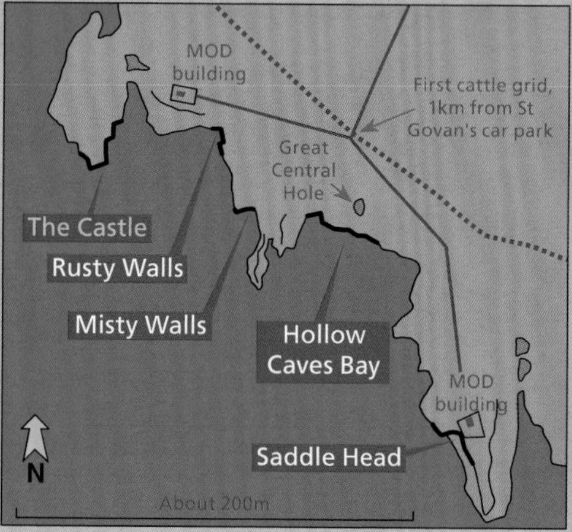

Approach

From St Govan's car park, walk west on the coast path for about 1km (15 minutes). Just after you have passed the second MOD building, there is a natural arch. Turn left and walk out along the headland to its end. The main wall is underneath a large tooth-shaped block on the cliff edge. This block doubles as one of the World's better abseil anchors.

Conditions and Tides

This is another one of those slippery grey rock places, the only difference is that here there are loads of cracks for your gear. As usual things can be greasy in the mornings, particularly on the right-hand wall. The main walls face south, receiving plenty of afternoon sun. The East Face only gets the morning sun and the West Face is a pleasant late afternoon and evening crag. As with most jutting headlands, this one can be windy and cold - avoid it in rough seas.

The Castle is affected by tides although some routes are still possible, especially the deep water solos mentioned above. There is a small ledge beneath *Too Much Pressure* which usually stays dry but will get a good soaking in rough seas. As the tide goes out the ledges below the routes are steadily revealed, with everything being accessible from about 2 hours after high tide.

Ed Brown chasing shade on *Heat of the Moment* (E5) - *page 87* - the Castle. Photo: Jack Geldard

St. David's | Flimston Bay | Mewsford | Castle/Rusty | Saddle Head | Bosherston Head | Huntsman's Leap | Stennis/Chapel | Trevallen | St. Govan's | Mowing/Stackpole | Mother Carey's

1 Too Little . . . . ☆1 ☐ **VS 4c**
16m. Nice climbing up the cracks in the left wall of the open corner. Trend left towards the arete then follow the cracks direct.
FA. R.Crockett 10.5.1980

2 Seulement . . . . ☆1 ☐ **HVS 5a**
18m. The open groove leads to an overhang, move right to outflank this then continue with a sense of urgency!
FA. R.Crockett 9.5.1980

3 Rizla . . . . ☆1 ☐ **HVS 5a**
20m. Steep rugged cracks up the wall to the right give the line.
FA. R.Crockett 9.5.1980

4 Atmospheric Tent . . . . . . ☆1 ☐ **HVS 5a**
20m. Climb a steep crack to where a slippery jam and technical move gain the easier hanging groove.
FA. M.Chapman 18.4.81

5 Atmospheric Tent Direct . ☆1 ☐ **E1 5c**
20m. The leaning crack in the wall is approached easily and gives a short tussle. Finish up the groove or across the right wall for a more independent experience.
FA. S.Blackman 1984

6 Abseil Groove . . . . ☆1 ☐ **Sev 4a**
16m. Meander up to the groove and saunter up it. Used as a descent by the competent.

7 Davy Crocket . . . . ☆1 ☐ **HVS 5a**
18m. In the wall right of *Abseil Groove*, is a another rough crack line. Gain this from the right and climb it to a steepening 5m below the top. Either traverse right to the arete and finish up this, or climb direct up the wall above.
FA. Alec Sharpe 28.6.80

8 Acropolis . . . . ☐ **E3 5c**
20m. The left arete of the wall is a bit bold and not too popular. Start on its lef side by a flake then switch to the right higher up.
FA. Gary Gibson 29.5.83

9 Too Much Pressure . . . . ☆3 ☐ **E1 5a**
20m. A superb route beneath the prominent tooth at the top of the cliff, sustained and but low in the grade with only a couple of hard moves just above the second niche. There are some good hands-off rests available but watch out for the odd loose block.
FA. C.Curle 5.5.80

10 Out for the Count . . . ☆3 ☐ **E4 6a**
20m. A route that has such good moves that it deserves 3 stars in spite of the fact that the line is a bit close to *Too Much Pressure* at the top. Climb a crack past a bulge, traverse left on good holds then climb up some thin cracks to a no-hands rest. Step left and climb another crack to the top. *Photo on page 82.*
FA. Steve Monks 23.4.83

11 Under the Influence . Top 50 ☐ **E4 6a**
20m. This one also has good moves, managing to be pumpy and delicate at the same time! Follow the continuous crack line on the right-hand side of the wall after starting up *Out for the Count.*
FA. Nipper Harrison 25.4.82

12 Over the Hill . . . . . . ☆2 ☐ **E4 6a**
18m. This burly climb follows the steep crack in the narrow east facing wall. Of the climbs here, this one probably has more scalps on its belt than the others since not only is it steep and sustained, but it also has a mysteriously technical move at the top. Follow the crack above a small cave, past one rest to another below a steep section. There are plenty of holds, though lots of them are not very useful!
FA. Smiler Cuthbertson 1980

Afternoon | 20 min | Tidal

South West Face

Approach - Abseil from the tooth and walk round, abseil down *Abseil Groove*, or scramble down to the right (looking out) of the cliff and round to ledges below the face.
Conditions and Tides - Afternoon sun and a lowish tide are the ideal conditions to climb here.

South Face

A magnificent piece of rock which presents a pair of compact vertical faces. Great for E4/5 leaders!

Approach - Abseil from the tooth to ledges below the face, or traverse in from below the West Face.

Conditions and Tides - A sunny setting though it does catch the wind. The highest ledges are above the sea but beware of high tide and high sea combos.

13 Cripple Creek E2 5a

18m. The big corner between the narrow east face and the right-hand wall requires sustained laybacking and bridging leading to a loose finish. Start at the bottom of the corner, end at the top with a bit of a rest on a ledge on the left. Alternatively you could go and find a better route somewhere else.

FA. Charlie Heard 4.5.80

14 Downward Bound E4 6a

20m. The left-hand crack in the wall gives an unrelenting pitch, though it is quite low in the grade. Beware of the possibility of unzipping wires if your belayer is on the set-back ledge. The crack is followed except for a short excursion to some grooves and ledges on the left at 2/3 height.

FA. Ben Wintringham 9.8.80

15 Heat of the Moment . E5 6b

20m. The central crack on the wall is virtually continuous and has a tough lower half. Another climb which you can't really stray off route on. *Photo on page 85*.

FA. Nipper Harrison 22.5.82

16 Chasing Shade E5 6b

20m. A blank-looking start looks desperate but isn't too bad and can be protected by small wires. Once you have gained the crack, climb it with great difficulty to the top. Not done very often but a great route.

FA. Nipper Harrison 9.82

17 Vista E2 5c

18m. The right-hand arete of the wall gives an extremely unlikely looking route - honest it is only E2! Start below the arete at low tide. Climb up razor sharp rock to a ledge on the right. Step left onto the wall and move up using a crack out left. Continue up the left-hand side of the arete above in a fine position. A two star **S1/ F6a+** DWS with the right tide (a high one!)

FA. Nipper Harrison 9.82

St. David's
Flimston Bay
Mewsford
Castle/Rusty
Saddle Head
Bosherston Head
Huntsman's Leap
Stennis/Chapel
Trevallen
St. Govan's
Mowing/Stackpole
Mother Carey's

East Face

The East Face of the Castle has a great set of very steep routes. It is popular with Deep Water soloists and those going to do *Wishful Thinking*. A full survey of the routes is attainable from the old building opposite.

Approach - Most of the routes require precise abseil approach from above. Only at low tide can you navigate easily along the bottom of the crag. The topo should give the best clues to pick your point of descent, combined with a recce from the other side of the zawn.

Conditions and Tides - The crag is predominantly east-facing, so expect a lot of morning sun; things should dry out fairly early. You need a low tide to get involved in the trad routes here, as the lower stances are generally a little problematical at higher tides - a calm sea is also advisable. If your mission is DWS, take along a decent tide! Bear in mind that route lengths are usually given from a low-tide stance - a DWS traverse into a route at a higher level will shorten the route a little, and give it a more sensible S grade.

Approach the next two routes by abseiling down just left (looking out) of the Vista arete, to ledges just above high tide.

1 Bastille. . . . . HVS 5a

16m. The wall just right of the of the arete of *Vista*. From ledges at the base, climb the blocky face to the top. There's a few wobbly flakes in the upper bit.
FA. Ben Wintringham 15.6.80

2 Kramer vs Kramer 1 E1 5b

16m. The twin cracks right again give good climbing. Start by way of bridging, then follow the left-hand crack to the top.
FA. Gary Lewis 15.6.80

The rest of the routes require more accurate abseils down the lines, especially if you are intending to solo them.

3 Daze of the Weak. . . 1 E6 6b

17m. A good, hard addition, tackling the alluring pillar. From non-tidal ledges at the base of the pillar, climb the pillar (moving both left and right, to find the better holds) until a sloping, resting ledge is gained at two-thirds. Finish directly up the face.
FA. Frank Thompson 11.6.00

4 Anniversary Waltz . . 2 E3 5c

17m. Excellent climbing, ascending the south-facing wall of the bay. Climb diagonally rightwards up cracks to start, pass an overhang, then waltz up the superb finishing cracks.
FA. Ben Wintringham 28.6.80

5 Barbecuing Traditions 2 E5 6b

16m. Another line that gets soloed more often than led; the crux is around 6m above a good high tide. Climb through the low band of overhangs, moving slightly leftwards, to a hard move onto the face above. Further trickiness gains the right edge of the face and an easier finish. (**S1/2, F7b**)
FA. Gary Gibson 23.3.90

9 Trapdoor **E2 5b**
20m. A good line up the massive corner. You'll have a choice of stances, with lower or higher ledges available. Climb up to the overhang, trend left, then ascend the big corner above.
FA. Pat Littlejohn 19.4.81

6 Critical Masses **E4 6a**
16m. Another good line, and one that's also seen a number of solos. Break out rightwards from *Barbecuing*, to gain the steep arete. Move right to a big crack, then continue up and right to gain a thinner crack. Gradually move back leftwards, to finish more easily. (**S1/2, F6c**)
FA. Gary Gibson 26.3.90

7 Vengeance **E4 6a**
17m. The face to the right is wonderful, and a great DWS; expect a crux at about 11m. From the slender pillar at the high water mark, climb up to gain the face proper, and continue up to a blunt spike. Trend right into a groove, then make hard moves to gain better holds; follow these up and left to the top. (**S1/2, F6c**)
FA. Pat Littlejohn 7.6.84

8 Dead Choughed . **E6 6b**
18m. A hard modern classic, tackling the unrelenting wall right of *Vengeance*, it has been on-sight soloed! Pull over the lower roof, and continue up the crack above, until a leftwards move gains a big jug under the headwall. Climb the tricky headwall in a great position. (**S2/3, F7b+**)
FA. Steve Monks 25.6.00

10 Black Man Ray **E4 6a**
19m. This line offers some amazing climbing in the upper section. From the base of the big chimney, climb its left edge for 7m, to gain a thin crack in the steeper arete above. Push out onto the hanging left face, and tackle the bulges above with gusto, trending leftwards to a spike; finish directly.
FA. Gary Gibson 25.3.90

11 Wishful Thinking . . . **E1 5b**
19m. A classic trip at a more amenable grade; the upper roofs provide delicious, juggy entertainment. Climb the right wall of the arete, move back to the arete, and up to a good ledge on the left. Power rightwards through the roofs above, to a wide crack up on the left; follow this to finish through the well-positioned top roof.
FA. Gary Gibson 25.3.90

12 Tragedy and Mystery **E4 6a**
19m. A demanding wall climb to the right of *Wishful Thinking*. Sustained and bold in places. Climb the lower wall moving left to the break (thread). Climb a flake on the right then move up to the top overhang. Pull rightwards through this.
FA. Gary Gibson 25.3.90

Rusty Walls

	No star	1	2	3
Mod to S	-	-	-	-
HS to HVS	-	-	-	-
E1 to E3	1	2	2	1
E4 and up	-	2	2	1

A rugged west-facing slab suspended above a booming zawn, with one of Pembroke's classic ticks in the shape of *Lucky Strike* (E1). There are other worthwhile offerings here too, and although the rock looks a bit red and crusty, appearances can be deceptive. Access is by abseil and the place is best avoided in wild weather due to its open aspect.

Approach
From St Govan's car park, walk west on the coast path for about 1km (15 minutes). Shortly after you pass Huntsman's Leap, there is an MOD building on the long thin headland of Saddle Head. A road leads from this along the coast to another MOD building and off into the Range. Join the road and follow it until just before the second building. Then head down left to the square-cut corner of the bay, beneath the building. The climbs are reached by various abseils from the blocks at the clifftop.

Tides
The routes on the left (looking in) of the wall start from a ledge above the high tide level. The routes in the centre start from the boulder beneath the wall which is uncovered for 2 or 3 hours at low tide. The routes on the right can all be started from non-tidal ledges below them.

Conditions
It can get a bit rough when there is a swell running but often this is just what is required to make *Lucky Strike* even more memorable, although you won't be able to start it from the boulder. The rock is mostly solid and the friction on the upper slab is superb. Lower down it gets a bit grey and shiny which can affect *Circus Circus* and the routes to its right. The main wall faces west and only gets the afternoon sun.

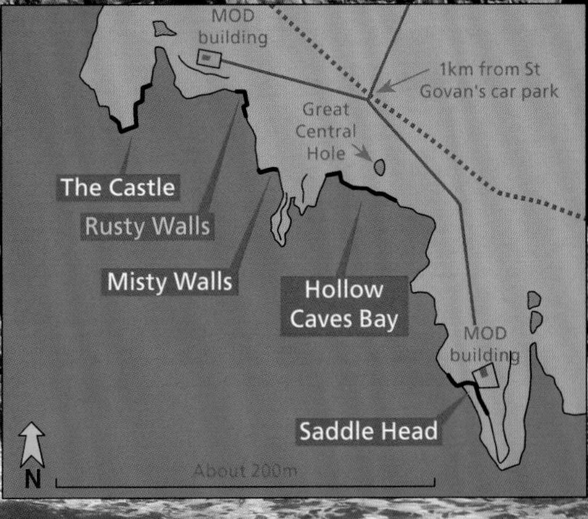

A team with a mid-pitch starting point on *Lucky Strike* (E1) - *page 93* - Rusty Walls, while more climbers await their turn on this ever-popular classic. Photo: Jack Geldard

The first routes take spectacular lines above the vast sea cave in the left wall (looking in) of the big corner. They start from a non-tidal ledge below the corner, which is reached by abseil.

1 Undertone. E5 6a
34m. A route which takes an 'edge of everything' line up the right-hand side of the large sea cave. Intimidating but well protected where it matters. From the ledge, climb up to another ledge then head leftwards up the wall towards some blocky overhangs. Pull left around the overhangs and make some steep moves up into a hanging groove above. Follow this to the top, past a dodgy block.
Photo on page 229.
FA. Nipper Harrison 9.6.82.

2 Poles Apart. E4 6a
30m. A slightly less exposed variation to *Undertone*. From where that route moves left, climb straight up a steep groove and pull out leftwards from its top. Continue up cracks to the top.
FA. Jon de Montjoye 27.3.82

3 Solidarity E1 5b
25m. A good and popular crack climb in an impressive position. Starting from the ledge at the foot of the corner, climb up the higher ledge beneath the wall. Gain and climb the obvious hand crack just left of the corner, to the top.
FA. Ben Wintringham 18.5.81

4 Good Luck, Mr Gronski . . E2 5b
28m. A decent route on rock that is better than it looks. Climb direct through the small recess right of the corner to a steep finale.
FA. Dave Scott-Maxwell, Paul Dearden 31.3.96

5 Strike Lucky E1 5b
30m. This route is most frequently used as a high tide start for *Lucky Strike* however it is a good pitch in its own right. From the ledge, traverse rightwards along good holds to the beginning of the rising flake line of *Lucky Strike*. Climb straight up the wall and crack above to the top.
FA. Ben Wintringham 17.4.81

Sarah Jane Dobner on *Lucky Strike* (E1) - *opposite* - Rusty Walls. Photo: Ian Parnell

For the next routes start from either the non-tidal ledge at the foot of the corner or, better, the large boulder beneath the centre of the wall which is covered at high tide. They are reached by abseiling down the corner.

6 Lucky Strike . . . Top 50 **E1 5b**
35m. The main line of the slab is yet another Littlejohn classic, one of the great climbs of Pembroke. The route has adequate protection (small wires) and is slightly serious for the second. Start from the huge boulder beneath the wall or, when the tide is in, as for *Strike Lucky*. Step awkwardly off the boulder and climb up into a groove to the left of a roof (possible refuge belay). Move up to gain the rising (chalk-covered) line on the wall. Follow this until 4m short of the corner, then climb straight up to the top.
Photo this page and page 90.
Happy Go Lucky Finish, E3 6a - 6m left of the normal.
FA. Pat Littlejohn 11.5.80. FA. (HGLF) Nick Dixon 4.84

7 Circus Circus 3 **E5 6a**
32m. This big route tackles the bulging wall beneath the slab with some superb, hard climbing. Start at low tide, on the large boulder under the wall. Climb up to a ledge below a roof. Traverse right along a break for 5m to a small ledge. Move up to reach a flat hold and then pull up and right with difficulty to gain a jug. Move right again to more good holds then reach back left to a thread. Climb past this onto the slab and have a breather. Finish up the wall between the two finishes of *Lucky Strike*.
FA. Gary Gibson 28.3.90

8 The Muppet Show . . 2 **E6 6b**
32m. The wall to the left of the long groove is climbed with great difficulty - super steep but with good gear. Climb pockets to a ledge. Move right to some cracks then back left to jugs on *Circus, Circus*. Climb a rampline back right to a pocket. Climb a thin crack above to reach the slab.
FA. Tim Emmett 4.98

The last three routes on the wall are situated around the large open corners on the right-hand side (looking in). They start from ledges beneath the corners which are reached by abseil.

9 Greased Lightning 1 **E4 6a**
28m. A well named route up the large corner which bounds the right-hand side of the slab. Start from a non-tidal ledge beneath the corner and slither your way up it.
FA. Ben Wintringham 17.4.81

10 Rust. . . . . 1 **(E3 5c)**
28m. The route up the large arete between the two corners on the right-hand side of the wall. Start from the ledge beneath *Greased Lightning* and climb up rightwards to the arete. Pull up to a ledge to the right of a bulge. Follow a short crack then step back left onto the arete. Climb this with a slight rightwards detour. There were three peg runners on the route though these may not be solid anymore.
FA. Paul Donnithorne 17.8.91

11 Flying Picket **E1 5b**
30m. From the non-tidal ledge at the base of the next corner right of *Rust*, climb over the bulge above and enter the corner. Follow this but move right at the top to avoid a loose bit.
FA. Ben Wintringham 18.4.81

Misty Walls

	No star	1 star	2 stars	3 stars
Mod to S	-	1	-	-
HS to HVS	-	-	-	-
E1 to E3	-	-	3	2
E4 and up	-	3	2	-

Which came first, the route names, or the crag name? Whatever way it happened it has to be said that the place is no more misty than any other Pembroke crag. It is rather compact and shiny though and also a huge sun-trap - get caught here in the wrong conditions and you'll find yourself slipping around on frictionless rock, above some tenuous microwire placements. Come when it is good though and you will find some great routes that tend to be more emotionally draining than butch and beefy.
The big tick for most is *Bon Voyage* (which does have a beefy crux) but equally good is its more direct variation *Play Misty for Me*. Once those are done there are plenty more lines in the E2 to E5 range.

Conditions

As previously mentioned, this south-facing crag can be an amazing sun-trap - keep away when hot since the slippery grey rock doesn't give much friction on sweaty fingers. Although it is sheltered from the wind, it does seem to attract some massive waves - I've seen them virtually hit the cave on *Bon Voyage*! Luckily it is possible to get a clear view of the tides and waves from the narrow headland. The rock is solid and the finishes are sharp.

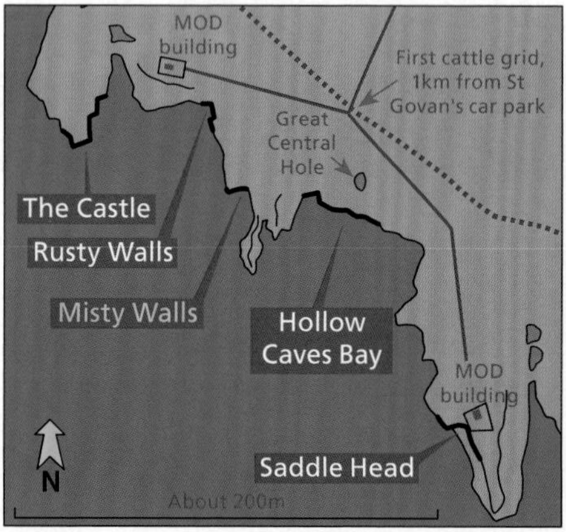

Approach and Tides

From St Govan's car park, walk west on the coast path past the Leap and the MOD building on Saddle Head. At the first cattle grid head diagonally leftwards to the cliff edge and locate a narrow headland which stretches out to sea. Misty Walls is tucked into the west (right looking out) side of this headland. The best approach for all the routes is to abseil down the right-hand side of the wall (the line of *Shadow Boxer*) from blocky ledges at the clifftop. This takes you to a narrow ledge which is separated from a large block below the face by a deep slot (top tip: don't abseil onto the block!) This ledge is not affected by the tide and gives easy access to routes from *Shot Across the Bows* rightwards. The other routes are reached by scrambling leftwards from the narrow ledge. This is possible from mid-to-low tide.

1 Misty Arete . . . . 1 star **Sev 4a**
35m. This well-positioned route follows the big arete, sadly the second pitch is both a bit loose and escapable. Start from ledges at the foot of the arete that bounds the left side of the face.
1) 15m. Climb a groove on the right to a sloping ledge out left.
2) 20m. Follow the left-hand side of the arete to the top.
FA. Mike Harber 9.7.78

2 Bon Voyage. . . . . . . Top 50 **E2 5b**
35m. A popular climb which happily repelled teams for years when graded E1. The traverse right from the cave usually proves to be a bit taxing, especially when damp. In such conditions the direct finish (as for *Play Misty for Me*) isn't any harder. Start on a good ledge below an open slanting groove on the left-hand side of the wall. Climb the groove and then trend rightwards along a crack to another, steeper groove. This leads to the cave. Hard layback moves up and right leave you beneath a easier groove. Climb this and the easy upper wall to the top.
FA. Charlie Heard 25.7.81

3 Play Misty for Me. . . . . 3 stars **E3 5c**
35m. The most popular of the harder routes on this wall takes an elegant line up the blunt arete right of *Bon Voyage*. Start 5m right of *Bon Voyage* and climb the rib with some tiddly fiddly wires for protection. Join the second groove on *Bon Voyage* to the cave and pull out straight above onto the headwall (easier than it looks). Wander up the wall above to the top.
FA. Gary Gibson 16.6.85

4 Fog Horn Blower . . . . . 2 stars **E5 6a**
35m. The wall below the cave has a beautiful open groove in it. Rack up all the microwires you can lay your hands on and climb the groove which is gained from the right. At its top move boldly left across the wall on good holds then make a hard move up to a groove which leads to the cave. Finish as for *Play Misty...*.
FA. Gary Gibson 16.6.85

5 Mistress of the Sea . . . . 2 stars **E4 6a**
28m. Yet another fine climb on perfect rock. Start below some cracks just left of the big corner in the centre of the wall (*Master Blaster*). Climb the cracks onto a slab which leads delicately to a groove. Step left and climb another groove to the diagonal break. Finish as for *Bon Voyage* or head off rightwards.
FA. Gary Gibson 15.6.85

St. David's
Flimston Bay
Mewsford
Castle/Rusty
Saddle Head
Bosherston Head
Huntsman's Leap
Stennis/Chapel
Trevallen
St. Govan's
Mowing/Stackpole
Mother Carey's

6 Master Blaster 2 E2 5b

28m. This sustained and popular route gives the easiest way up the wall. Start beneath the central groove-line. Climb the groove which gets trickier as you get higher. Step right at the top and climb the continuation grooves above to the top.

FA. Charlie Heard 26.7.81

7 Shot Across the Bows ... 2 E3 6a

26m. A good route with a steep finish. Start below the groove five metres right of *Master Blaster*. Climb the groove past a bulge to where a thin crack breaks out left. Climb the crack and difficult bulge above to a sloping ledge. Finish straight up.

FA. Gary Gibson 15.6.85

8 First Impulse 1 E4 6a

26m. The direct line above the groove of the last two routes has a steep crack above it. Gain the crack from the groove and climb it to the top. Sustained.

FA. Gary Gibson 10.4.85

Lots of sun | 18 min | Tidal

Abseil in

9 Shadow Boxer 1 E5 6a

24m. Bold. Start under a crack at the right-hand end of the ledge, left of the slot. Gain the crack from the right and climb it. Place a high runner then step left to a ledge. Move up onto a slab and continue to gear at the roof. Step right and join *Oratorio* to finish.

FA. Gary Gibson 15.6.85

10 Oratorio 2 E3 5c

24m. An entertaining pitch; take some microwires. Start below a groove, as far right as you can get before the slot. Move up into the groove and climb it to a good hold where the angle eases. Continue above to a square cut ledge then step 2m left to a crack. Follow this to the top. *Photo on page 11.*

FA. Gary Gibson 10.4.85

11 The Mad Death 1 E5 5c

22m. Unprotected climbing up the ramp and slab above the right-hand side of the sea trench. Rarely repeated due to its extreme seriousness - except on a top-rope!

FA. Gary Gibson 15.6.85

	No star	1	2	3
Mod to S	-	-	-	-
HS to HVS	-	-	-	1
E1 to E3	1	6	2	1
E4 and up	-	1	3	7

Hollow Caves Bay is one of those mad places that you'll just have to delve into at some point, mainly because it looks so damn exciting from the top! The classics are manifest, and include such forays as *Galactic Glory* (HVS), *Super Galactic Hammy* (E2), *Gravy Train* (E3), *Jabberwock* (E5) and *San Simian* (E8). The routes are generally steep and sustained, the gear is mostly good, and the geology is an absolute delight, although a little familarisation and care is required on your first visit, especially with regard to tides and the various traverses down at sea level. The Box Zawn (western) end of the bay provides a wealth of sustained three-star climbing in the higher grades, with the eastern end, accessed by abseil through the amazing Great Central Hole, giving stunning routes on a series of outstanding pillars.

Approach

From St Govan's car park, walk west on the coast path. Continue past the Leap and the MOD building on Saddle Head. Join the tarmac road briefly then head leftwards towards the cliff edge. There are some large holes here one of which is great Central Hole used for accessing some of the routes (see page 98). Further right (looking out) is the characteristic square-cut recess of Box Zawn at the base of a gentle rocky slope. To familiarise yourself, and check the tides, it is a good idea to walk to the narrow headland which stretches out from below Misty Walls. From here you can look back eastwards towards the bay.

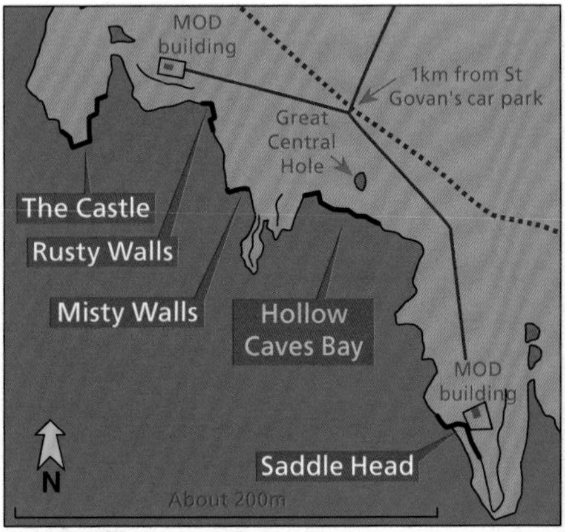

Tides

The routes in Box Zawn can mostly be done from mid-to-low tide although it is possible to get some of the routes at high tide from a small ledge below *Monster in a Box*. The routes in the *Gravy Train* area further into the bay need mid-to-low tide.

Conditions

The routes in Hollow Caves Bay are often not in condition due to seepage and condensation; only climb here on sunny days with low humidity, and ideally a light south/south-easterly breeze. If the rock is damp the Box Zawn routes become heinous.

The first routes are situated on the large back wall of the zawn. Beneath the right-hand side of this wall is a tidal ledge which can be reached by abseiling from blocks above the right-hand corner. The first route starts to the left of this ledge.

1 Jabberwock. . . . . . . 3 stars **E5 6a**
40m. A great route which is probably the most popular route on the wall, although that isn't saying much. Start at mid-to-low tide towards the left-hand side of the wall. Climb a crack through the roof and continue to a recess - a thread and a rest. Traverse left to a bottomless groove and climb this for 6m until it is possible to traverse left again around a hanging arete to the upper section of the left-hand corner of the zawn. Finish up this. The top is loose so a pre-placed rope down the last 5m is not a bad idea.
FA. Ben Wintringham 4.7.81

2 Airdrawn Dagger . . . 3 stars **E8 6c**
35m. Piles trouble on trouble when *Knock Yourself Out!* heads for safety! From below the thin crack on *Knock Yourself Out!* trend left up the steep wall to a position under the highest roof. Pull rightwards through this and finish up the wall trending right.
FA. Neil Gresham 7.04

3 Knock Yourself Out! . 3 stars **E6 6a**
35m. This impressive and unlikely route follows a very steep line roughly up the centre of the back wall. Start on the platform below a roof with a notch in it. Climb a crack for 5m and swing left onto the wall. Follow a leftwards rising line to a small ledge below and left of a thin crack. Gain and climb the crack (old peg - not crucial) to the large pedestal ledge. Finish straight up the steep headwall above, moving slightly left at the top.
FA. Martin Crocker 1.10.88

4 Grezelda, Grezelda . 3 stars **E6 6a**
35m. An extremely sustained stamina climb of the highest quality. Start as for *Knock Yourself Out!* but once past the roof trend right with difficulty to the hanging crackline. Follow this past a medium-cam placement and continue to the roof. Climb this leftwards past lots of in-situ gear to a groove. Move up and left to some jugs then back right to finish. Originally climbed with two pegs in the top groove; these are probably no good anymore but the grade is still E6 without them.
FA. Martin Crocker 11.9.88

5 The Obsession Box. . . . . 3 stars **(E6 6b)**
32m. The long crack is extremely pumpy and has a few really hard moves! The route is rarely dry and the peg on the upper wall is old - hence it probably hasn't had any ascents in recent years. From the right-hand end of the ledge, climb a short corner to the roof. Step left under it and make a hard pull back right. Climb a short groove to the crack which is followed to the high roof. Pull around this and then stretch left for a good side-pull. Move left again to join and finish up *Grezelda, Grezelda*.
FA. Martin Crocker 11.9.88

The side-wall has a series of steep cracks and walls topped off with some slightly unstable finishes.

6 Monster in a Box . . . . . . 3 stars **E7 6c**
25m. The big pillar in the back of the zawn. Start from a small non-tidal ledge and climb up to a shallow ramp. Follow this towards the corner of *Triad* (gear) then pull back left into a hanging groove. More hanging grooves lead up and leftwards with increasing urgency, to the top.
FA. John Arran 2001

7 Triad **E2 5b**
28m. The left-hand crack to a loose finish. Included to let you know what goes up there and not so that you might climb it.
FA. Ben Wintringham 20.6.81

8 Trefoil . . . . 1 star **E2 5c**
28m. The central crack is better but still not sparkling.
FA. Ben Wintringham 20.4.81

9 Love My Teddy Bear . . . . 1 star **E4 6a**
28m. The centre of the wall between the main two cracks gives good climbing and is more solid than its near neighbours. From the pedestal climb two cracks to the base of a groove. This can be reached more easily from the crack on the left. Follow the groove and make hard moves up right to a jug and a rest. Continue to a roof and climb straight over onto a slab. Finish direct.
FA. Martin Crocker 2.10.88

10 Trihedral. . . . . 1 star **E1 5b**
28m. The right-hand crack in the wall gives a worthwhile pitch on good rock with a steep finish. It is also the easiest way out.
FA. Ben Wintringham 20.4.81

11 The Black Box . . . . 1 star **E3 5c**
30m. An interesting little route which roughly follows the arete. Start as for *Trihedral* but move right onto a ledge. Climb the wall above, just left of the arete until the angle eases. Continue direct to a roof, pass this on its right and continue up the right-hand side of the arete to the top.
FA. Crispin Waddy 7.88

St. David's
Flimston Bay
Mewsford
Castle/Rusty
Saddle Head
Bosherston Head
Huntsman's Leap
Stennis/Chapel
Trevallen
St. Govan's
Mowing/Stackpole
Mother Carey's

Gravy Train

Hollow Caves Bay extends eastwards from Box Zawn presenting a series of amazing pillars and caves. The routes here are atmospheric and very rewarding.

Approach - The area is best approached via the Great Central Hole (see map on page 96). Walk down the scree into the hole towards the lower window (seen in photo). Either abseil off a spike and wires for 30m, or descend the lower black groove to a huge thread and abseil from here for 15m.

Tides - At low tide you can navigate around the caves by traversing and boulder-hopping just above the sea.

12 Ringolino . . . . 1 ☐ **E3 5c**

30m. A long diagonal pitch out of the back of the cave. From the back, move up and then make a traverse up and rightwards across the wall to a hanging orange slab. Continue traversing to the right-hand arete and climb up this to the top.

FA. Crispin Waddy 7.88

13 Great Dane . . . . 2 ☐ **E4 6a**

25m. A fairly direct line up the left-hand wall of the cave cutting through *Ringolino*. Start below a thread and climb up leftwards to a rest on a shelf-like bulge. Move up and right past a thread, onto a slab. Climb a flake crack on the left to an overhang and layback around it to an easier finish.

FA. Paul Donnithorne 5.7.92

14 S.L.R. . . . . 1 ☐ **E2 5c**

25m. A good route up the front face of the pillar. Start just right of the through-slot and pull up to gain the slab above. Climb boldly into a groove and continue up, finally breaking left to finish up the arete on the left.

FA. Steve Lewis 11.4.82

15 Storm Bird . . . . 1 ☐ **E1 5b**

25m. Steep moves gain a wide crack. Climb this then move left to a small ledge. Continue up to gain a thin crack, follow this to its finish then move right into a groove. The groove leads to an easier wall above.

FA. G.Lewis 26.7.81

16 Gravy Train 3 E3 5c
30m. An outstanding line up the back arete of the pillar, featuring some stunning rock architecture. Climb up the arete into the short corner, pull out right then move leftwards across a slab to the arete. Gain the upper groove and follow it in an amazing position to the top.
FA. Paul Donnithorne 31.5.98

17 Super Galactic Hammy . . 2 E2 5b
30m. A cracking line tackling the west face of the pillar, with slabby moves interspersed by steep pulls. Climb up on good holds then venture up the sloping diagonal shelf on the right until holds lead onto the slab above. Move up and left to a groove and climb this until a swing left leads to below an overlap. Pull through and climb the crack in the clean slab above.
FA. Steve Lewis 5.4.81

18 Galactic Glory . . . . 3 HVS 5a
30m. A connection of routes which offers some breath-taking terrain, however it is the easiest way out so make sure you are confident at the grade before committing. Follow *Super Galactic* through the initial diagonal shelf, then break out rightwards up to a rest on the arete. Move up and right to climb the steep juggy wall (shared with *Faded Glory*).

19 Faded Glory 2 E3 6a
30m. Another excellent route on this amazing pillar. Climb the crack to gain the corner and continue up this to a rest on the arete on the left. Move up and right to climb the steep juggy wall to the top.
FA. Ben Wintringham 26.5.80

20 Tranquillizer 2 E5 6a
30m. A stamina-sapping route up the cracked groove in the incredibly steep orange south face of the pillar. Start up *Faded Glory* then make committing moves up right onto the overhanging wall. Surge up this using a variety of cracks. Finish up easy ground.
FA. Stefan Doerr 16.7.00

21 The Fine Art of Surfacing
. . . . 2 E6 6a
26m. A superb route. The first ascent was done as a deep water solo but the route is well protected. From the ample but tidal ledges, follow the series of cracks and pockets up the impending wall. A pumpy upper section gains better holds followed by a step left to easier ground. *Photo on page 231.*
FA. Neil Gresham (solo) 7.04

22 San Simian . . 3 E8 6c
25m. This steep modern classic tackles the steep orange wall at its very steepest. It's steep. Considered hard **F8a** with good-but-spaced gear which is very pumpy to place. Climb the lower face then take on the grotesquely steep upper wall on pockets and side-pulls. Did we mention it was steep? Has been soloed (**S3**).
FA. Charlie Woodburn 7.04

Sun and shade | 18 min | Tidal | Abseil in

St. David's | Flimston Bay | Mewsford | Castle/Rusty | Saddle Head | Bosherston Head | Huntsman's Leap | Stennis/Chapel | Trevallen | St. Govan's | Mowing/Stackpole | Mother Carey's

Saddle Head

Pete Robins climbing *Blue Sky* (VS) - *page 102* - on Saddle Head. It doesn't really overhang that much! Photo: Jack Geldard

	No star	1 star	2 star	3 star
Mod to S	1	7	-	-
HS to HVS	-	5	4	1
E1 to E3	1	2	-	-
E4 and up	-	-	-	-

Saddle Head is one of the most popular locations in Pembroke because it contains the largest concentration of Diff to VS routes and many of them are classic sea cliff outings. Most of the routes follow short corners and walls above an accessible non-tidal platform and four of the routes listed here take wonderful long lines up the tall tidal buttress to the left of the platform.

Approach and Tides

From St Govan's car park, walk west along the coast path, past Huntsman's Leap. Continue to some natural arches on the left then head left towards an MOD building on a narrow headland. Scramble along the exposed crest of the headland to a saddle and drop down the west side beneath the cliff.
Only the first four routes are severely affected by the tide. At low tide you can abseil or scramble down onto the large platform beneath the arete of *Blue Sky*. WARNING: this is often wave-washed and is only completely revealed during low spring tides. At all other tides a tricky abseil/traverse may get you dry-shod onto the buttress. If you are unsure it is probably a good idea to walk around to have a look first.

Conditions

The rock is solid and compact grey limestone with great friction. The lower section of the *Blue Sky* wall is more water-worn at the bottom which can be slippery, but is still climbable. The cliff faces south east and receives plenty of afternoon sun and it is also more sheltered than you might expect for a headland.

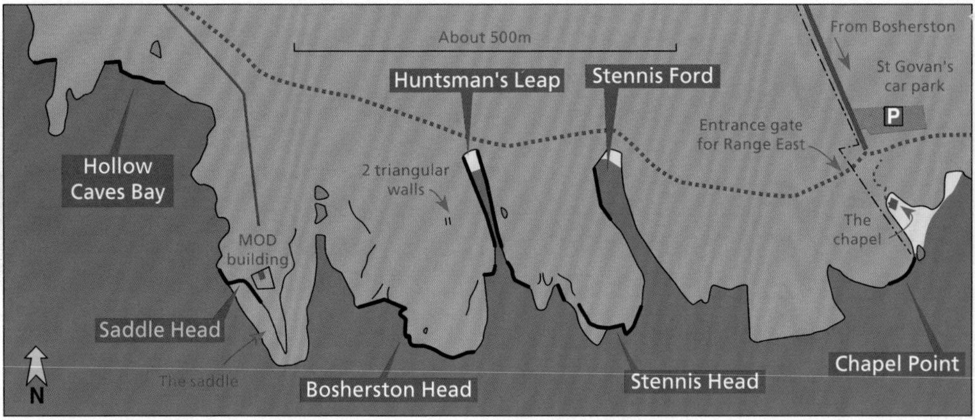

1 Eaves Dripper . . . . 2-star ☐ **HVS 4c**
56m. A fine climb to the left of the ever-popular *Blue Sky* making the most of the steep rock to the left of its upper section.
1) 4c, 26m. Start as for *Blue Sky* but continue leftwards up the long groove to a ledge and small cave to belay.
2) 4c, 30m. Climb two grooves in the wall above to the top roof. Pull left around this and continue to the top in a fine position.
FA. John Harwood, M.Rhodes 1.3.80

2 Blue Sky . . . . Top 50 ☐ **VS 4b**
56m. A popular Pembrokeshire classic which is one the best VS routes around. It climbs the huge arete of the main face of Saddle Head, above a tide-washed platform. Access is tricky and the overall atmosphere is added to by the awkward approach. Start as described above. *Photo on page 100.*
1) 4a, 28m. Climb a weakness on the left-hand side of the arete to reach a groove. Follow this onto the arete and then step right and climb the rugged cracked wall to a ledge and cave stance.
2) 4b, 28m. Climb up a crack above the stance and continue in a great position up the arete to enter the wide finishing groove.
FA. Pat Littlejohn, John Harwood 8.4.78

3 Blue Lagoon . . . . 1-star ☐ **E1 5b**
58m. A right-hand alternative to *Blue Sky* with a steep finish.
1) 4a, 28m. As for *Blue Sky* to the cave stance.
2) 5b, 30m. Step right from the stance and climb onto a small jutting nose. Follow cracks above to beneath a bulge then pull out rightwards up a steep diagonal crack for a spectacular finish.
FA. Gary Lewis 5.5.85

4 Landvetter . . . . 2-star ☐ **VS 4b**
56m. Another worthwhile but neglected route which follows the big groove above the right-hand side of the platform. Start at the base of the corner at low tide only.
1) 4b, 25m. Climb the big corner, with a deviation onto the right wall at the start, but mainly on the left wall above this. Belay on a ledge above a chockstone.
2) 4b, 32m. Climb the short subsidiary groove on the right, then traverse a long way left into the main groove and finish leftwards as for *Blue Sky*.
FA. Steve Lewis, John Harwood 3.9.78

Blue Sky

The main soaring buttress is home to one vaunted classic and several other offerings that are only a little less worthwhile. The difficulty of getting at the routes means they see a lot less attention than they otherwise might.

MOD Building

A closely packed set of short easy routes, on good rock and in a lovely setting. The easy accessible nature of the place means it can get crowded here - don't be surprised if you turn up and it is mobbed!
DO NOT belay to the clifftop fence.

5 Haze . . . . ☆1 ☐ **VS 4b**
26m. Start at the base of the slab at the left-hand end of the wall. Climb down to cross the groove then up and left to a ledge, then follow the narrow groove and cracked headwall to the top.
FA. Alec Sharpe 6.5.78

6 Sea Mist . . . . ☆2 ☐ **HS 4a**
26m. A great route which takes you into a wonderful position above the sea. Mild but it has quite an airy feel about it. From the ledge on *Haze*, step right and make easy but bold moves to the arete. Finish up the headwall above. *Photo on cover.*
FA. Alec Sharpe 6.5.78

7 Sunset Boulevard . . . . . . ☆1 ☐ **HVS 5a**
24m. From the low cave climb the left-hand side of the slab by a series of mantelshelves then finish easily up the headwall above.
FA. Dave Jones 16.4.81

8 Breaking Wind . . . . ☐ **E1 5b**
24m. A bit of an eliminate. From the cave pull directly onto base of the smoother section of the slab using a pocket and a flake. Continue more easily - pleasant!

To the right are five closely-packed corner grooves, all give pleasant climbing and all are popular.

9 Pink 'un . . . . ☆2 ☐ **VS 5a**
24m. The corner bounding the right-hand side of the slab gives an technically interesting little climb which takes as many runners as you can throw at it. Finish direct.
FA. Alec Sharpe 6.5.78

10 Infra Red . . . . ☆1 ☐ **Sev**
22m. Just right of *Pink Un* is another similar corner with some red rock at its base. Follow this as it jinks to the right.
FA. John Harwood 26.2.78

11 Wetstone . . . . ☆1 ☐ **Sev 4b**
22m. The next corner with a move left high up. Nice well-protected climbing suitable for sharpening up your technique perhaps.
FA. Gwyn Evans 26.2.78

The rest of the routes top out by the MOD building. The best approach is to take a belay at the edge and scramble off leftwards. DO NOT BELAY TO THE BUILDING OR THE FENCE.

12 Urchin . . . . ☆1 ☐ **Sev 4a**
22m. The fourth of the corner climbs has a short rib to reach it.
FA. John Harwood 25.2.78

13 Buff . . . . ☐ **VDiff**
22m. The last of the clutch of corners is a narrow affair and it joins *Urchin* higher up.
FA. J.Williams 22.7.78

14 Flake-Quake . . . . ☆1 ☐ **Sev 4a**
22m. At last not a corner! Climb the wider wall right of all the corners past two ledges and a flake - nice rock.
FA. John Harwood 25.2.78

15 Fel Gwyr . . . . ☆1 ☐ **Diff**
22m. Climb the right-bounding rib of the slab. Mild but still well worthwhile, again on great rock.
FA. C.Evans 25.2.78

To the right are two low caves.

16 Forgotten Corner . . . . ☆1 ☐ **HVD**
22m. The corner with a cave below and right of it is quite tough for the grade but the gear is good.
FA. D.Parsons 29.7.78

17 Small Beginnings . . . . ☆1 ☐ **VDiff**
22m. Climb the crack and short groove in the wall above the left-hand cave, reached from its right-hand side.
FA. John Harwood 25.2.78

18 Nameless Wall . . . . ☆1 ☐ **HS 4b**
22m. Climb the wall above the right-hand edge of the cave. Quite mild at the grade, but another with pleasant climbing.
FA. Pat Littlejohn 8.4.78

19 Follow the Chalk . . . . ☆1 ☐ **HS 4b**
22m. The long corner (the left-hand of a pair) gives nice climbing to a steep finish. One foot may stray into *No Hands* ... briefly!
FRA. Colin Binks, Chris Craggs 5.6.09. "The line was easy to spot owing to all the chalk on the holds"!

20 No Hands . . . . ☆1 ☐ **VS 4b**
22m. The larger cave has a pillar of rock in it and above this a long corner runs up the left-hand end of the roof high above. It can be reached direct (pull!) or from left or right and gives fine sustained climbing.
FA. Pat Littlejohn 8.4.78

21 Get on Lord . . . . ☆1 ☐ **E2 5b**
22m. Climb the steep wall above the right hand side of the cave. The bulge is crossed at an inverted niche then finish rightwards.
FA. Bill McKee 28.3.84

Lots of sun
15 min
6
7
8
9
10
5
A
11
12
13
14
15
16
17
18
19
20
21
Descent scramble to the wave-washed platform
Landvetter

Bosherston Head

Alan James finishing the brilliant traverse on *Sunny Corner* (HVS) - *page 114* - at Bosherston Head. Photo: Mike Robertson

Bosherston Head

	No star	1	2	3
Mod to S	-	-	-	-
HS to HVS	-	4	4	1
E1 to E3	-	5	8	3
E4 and up	-	3	7	5

Bosherston Head is the broad promontory between Huntsman's Leap and Saddle Head with huge solid faces on all sides. Despite this vast expanse of rock it has never been that popular mainly due to the intimidating nature of the climbing - you can't get a good view of it and the stuff you can see tends to be in the higher grades, plus the fact that we omitted the celebrated South Face from the last Rockfax guide.

The most popular spot on the headland is the Keelhaul Wall; a fine compact wall of excellent rock with a quartet of class routes - *Ghost Ship* (E3), *Intensive Scare* (E2), *Baker's Door* (E1) and *Keelhaul* (E2). Next door is the dramatic leaning wall made infamous by the controversial route *The Big Issue* (E9) and adjacent to this is the stylish *Ivory Tower* (E2). Moving further round, the South Face is glorious, smacking of wild abseils, grand-scale adventure and seat-of-the-pants daring. This is partly because it's impossible to gain a decent view of your chosen route before engaging, and partly because this terrific hunk of rock is home to one of Pembroke's finest adventures - *Preposterous Tales*, going at the thoroughly unlikely (caving) grade of HVS, or the E2 we give it here! However, if you are really in search of emotional and soul-searching leads of E4 and above, on wonderful rock, giving you an experience which you will be talking about for years, then you need look no further than the *Star Wars* area.

Ignoring warnings about winter storms, Larry the Limpet sets off on a daring solo ascent of Preposterous Tales.

Approach

The three areas require different approaches. To get to the headland, walk west along the coast path from St Govan's car park. After passing the Leap, head towards two curious triangular walls over on the left. For *Keelhaul*, *The Big Issue*, *Ivory Tower* and the South Face, keep slightly to their right, until you arrive at the other side of the headland. For *Star Wars*, walk along above the West Wall of the Leap. Virtually all the routes require abseil approach. See the information with each buttress for more details.

Conditions and Tides

The Keelhaul Wall faces south and gets all of the afternoon sun available. It is tucked in a bit of a bay which gives it some shelter from both the morning sun and strong winds. The rock is the shiny grey limestone which is peculiar to Pembroke. This has the friction of glass when damp, which is of particular importance on the hard routes, however it is solid and compact which means that at least your runners will be good. The *Ivory Tower* is composed of similar rock but gets the sun a bit later in the day. The south face is exposed to any wind and bad weather there is, but it can also be baking hot in calm conditions. The *Star Wars* area varies from perfect white limestone on its left to very steep blocky stuff on its right. It is also sheltered but is more exposed to the sun. Slap on the factor 50 if you intend to take a long time over *Star Wars*.

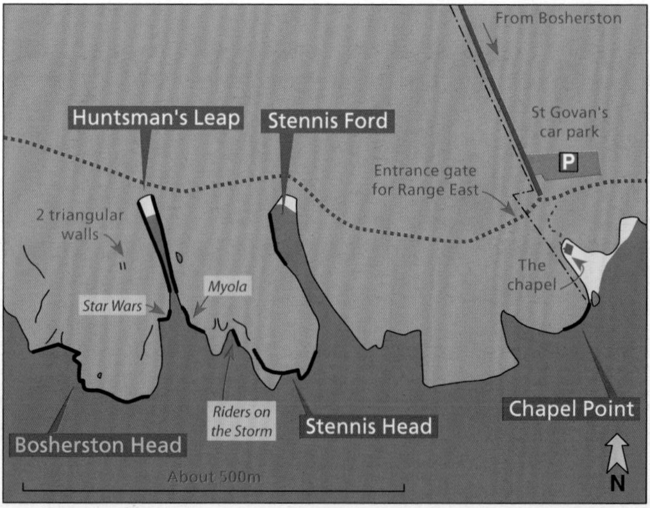

St. David's
Flimston Bay
Mewsford
Castle/Rusty
Saddle Head
Bosherston Head
Huntsman's Leap
Stennis/Chapel
Trevallen
St. Govan's
Mowing/Stackpole
Mother Carey's

Tom Graham enjoying classic of classics *Star Wars* (E4) - *page 119* - Bosherston Head. Photo: Scott Sadler

St. David's
Flimston Bay
Mewsford
Castle/Rusty
Saddle Head
Bosherston Head
Huntsman's Leap
Stennis/Chapel
Trevallen
St. Govan's
Moving/Stackpole
Mother Carey's

Keelhaul

A beautiful slabby wall of immaculate rock. The routes here are intense and fingery, usually with small wire protection. The upper section is the crozzly sharp rock that snags on everything.
Approach and Tides - The abseil leads to ledges below *Keelhaul* which are above the high tide line, but awash in rough seas. At high tide you can reach routes the routes from *Baker's Door* rightwards, and *Intensive Scare* with a bit of a traverse. All the routes can be reached from mid tide onwards. It is possible, at low-to-mid tide, to scramble down a wide grassy gully to the north of a knoll at the clifftop. Ledges lead back right under the face.

1 DEEsire . . . . 1 **HVS 5a**
40m. Start on the pedestal of *Fifty Lashes*. Climb the pillar on the left then follow cracks left of the final groove of *Fifty Lashes*.
FA. Alun Richardson 10.1.99

2 Fifty Lashes, Mister Christian 2 **E4 6b**
A well protected climb on slippery pink rock, slightly spoilt by the desperate crux which is significantly harder than much of the other climbing. Start at mid-to-low tide below a groove on the left-hand side of a recess, above a pool.
1) 6b, 25m. Climb the groove to the bulge and struggle around this onto the slab above. Move right to a crack in the bulge above and follow this to a ledge on the left arete.
2) 4c, 15m. Climb the groove in the arete above.
FA. Gary Gibson 30.4.83

3 Ghost Ship . . . . Top 50 **E3 5c**
40m. A magnificent route up groovy rock. The protection is good, after the start, but the climbing is steep and sustained until you get to the headwall. Start on a ledge right of the recess and traverse left to reach the left-hand of two grooves above the pool. Contort up the groove to reach a wide crack, follow this then traverse right and up across the steep wall. Step around the juggy arete, in a superb position, into another groove. Climb this and the bulge above with difficulty. Finish more easily up the razor sharp headwall.
FA. Pat Littlejohn 11.5.78

4 Mutiny on the Bounty 2 **E6 6a**
40m. Shiny rock, sustained bridging and minimal protection don't aid the popularity of this route, however it does give a great challenge for those up to it. Start below the right-hand groove above the pool and climb it with extreme difficulty until you can reach a crack above. Either finish as for *Ghost Ship*, or pull around onto the wall and follow it directly to the top.
FA. Gary Gibson 5.7.85

5 Man Overboard 2 **E5 6a**
28m. As with all of the routes here, the grey and slippery rock can be unnerving especially when you are pushing the boat out! Start below a curved left-facing groove. Climb the groove then step right (wire up and right) and back left above it. Continue moving left up the wall, over a bulge. Move up then step back right to the base of a long brown streak. Climb this and move right to belay in the approach gully.
FA. Gary Gibson 31.5.83

❻ All Hands on Deck 1 E5 6b

25m. An eliminate between two of the curving grooves. Climb the wall to the bulge (hidden wires) and make a long move around this. Join and finish up *Intensive Scare*.

FA. Gary Gibson 5.7.85

❼ Intensive Scare 2 E2 5c

25m. The first in a trio of fine wall climbs fortunately has a misleading name. Start beneath the large yellow-streaked curving groove. Climb up the barnacle-covered lower wall to gain the groove. Follow this to a roof then pull up above to a good hold. Finish up the short wall and blocky corner to belay in the open gully below the clifftop.

FA. Jon de Montjoye 4.4.81

❽ Baker's Door 2 E1 5b

25m. Start below the left-hand of two slim left-facing grooves in the wall below the high overhang. Climb up to the groove then step right to a short crack. Move up and left across the wall and then climb direct, just left of the overhang, to the ledge belay.

FA. Ian Carr 26.4.81

❾ Keelhaul........... 3 E2 5c

25m. The last of the trio takes a line up the wall directly below the overhang. Climb up to the right-hand of the two left-facing grooves, move up slightly rightwards then trend back left to a split in the overhang. Heave over this and finish up the crack.

FA. Jon de Montjoye 28.12.80

❿ I See No Ships........ 1 E4 6b

25m. Good climbing but often wet due to a seepage drip from above. Climb the easy (but bold) wall to a ledge. Make hard moves left to a groove in the edge of the overhang. Pull through and finish up the crack.

FA. Gary Gibson 20.4.84

⓫ Springboard 2 E1 5b

25m. A good tough route up the huge corner at the right-hand side of the wall with a high crux. Not surprisingly most of the climbing is on the less-steep left wall of the corner. It is often wet.

FA. Pat Littlejohn 8.4.78

From mid morning | 10 min | Tidal | Abseil in

⓬ Wage War. E3 5c
45m. Climb *Springboard* (previous page) to a break running across the wall, follow this to the cave and a widely positioned stance. From here follow the break rightwards (big holds - big exposure) to escape.
FA. Frank Ramsey 28.4.90

⓭ Punks in the Tea Room . . E5 6b
40m. Lacks line but not excitement! Start up *Springboard* and step right at 15m, power up the crack to the cave stance. Move right along the traverse of *Wage War* but where this heads uphill, swing down and pump along the lower traverse to easy ground.
FA. (Living in the Past - a well named aid climb) S.Hitchens P.Collis 12.12.88
FFA. John Gandy, Pete Oxley 8.92

⓮ Ocean Drive E6 6b
36m. Forge up the tilted wall above the cave to give a (very) well-positioned continuation to *Punks in the Tea Room*.
FA. Andy Long 4.8.96

⓯ The Big Issue . . E9 6c
36m. The big wall is taken up its centre by this (in)famous and arduous outing. Climb the soaring central line to the high break then continue up even steeper ground above.
FA. John Dunne 5.96. Previously bolted by Pete Oxley.

⓰ The Big Softy. . . E7 6c
28m. The other line on the wall follows right-trending holds and cracks to reach a niche. Finish more easily from here.
FA. Adrian Berry 6.6.00

The Big Issue
This obscenely-angled orange wall is home to one of Pembroke's more impressive routes. The routes often seep a bit and, for most, dry conditions are essential.
Approach - Abseil down the Keelhaul wall at any tide and scramble right to the non-tidal ledge below the face.

Ivory Tower

This splendid tower of rock is home to the popular *Ivory Tower*. Its companion *Agent Orange* is a little unbalanced. Included here also is *Gone with the Wimp*; an exposed trip for ambitious VS leaders!
Approach - Abseil from good belays to a non-tidal ledge below the route *Agent Orange*.

17 Ivory Tower . . . . 2 ☐ **E2 6a**
35m. Another route which is well established on the Pembroke hit list. Perhaps it has been slightly over sold, but it does give good climbing with some tricky moves. The dark left-hand side of the arete is often very greasy. From the high ledges, climb up and leftwards to the arete. Step around onto the dark wall and follow cracks up this until you are level with a small roof on the arete. Pull up and around onto the front face with difficulty. Swarm easily up the wall above on cheeze-grater rock.
FA. Pat Littlejohn 10.5.80

18 Agent Orange . . . . . 1 ☐ **E3 6a**
33m. The front face of the tower contains this difficult and steep route which is high in the grade but the protection is good. Start from the ledge of *Ivory Tower*. Climb straight up above the belay to a bulge. Pull over this frantically to much easier ground above.
FA. Nipper Harrison 8.84

19 Gone with the Wimp . . . . 2 ☐ **VS 4b**
A great adventure in a steep and intimidating setting and a fine first pitch. A confident leader and second is needed for this route.
1) 4b, 20m. Traverse horizontally right following an easy low line. Then climb diagonally right up and move right again onto a ledge.
2) 20m. Easy rock leads to the top.
FA. Dave Oxenham, M.Hill 5.5.84

Afternoon | 10 min | Abseil in

St. David's
Flimston Bay
Mewsford
Castle/Rusty
Saddle Head
Bosherston Head
Huntsman's Leap
Stennis/Chapel
Trevallen
St. Govan's
Mowing/Stackpole
Mother Carey's

St. David's
Flimston Bay
Mewsford
Castle/Rusty
Saddle Head
Bosherston Head
Huntsman's Leap
Stennis/Chapel
Trevallen
St. Govan's
Moving/Stackpole
Mother Carey's

Preposterous Tales

This superb and atmospheric section of cliff has plenty to offer at a reasonable grade although the exposed location and committing blind approaches tend to make the routes feel quite serious.

Approach - A walk southwards from the Keelhaul Wall along the cliff edge will take you past the *Preposterous Tales* exit hole, and then along to the headland proper. Locate the line of *Quoin*, which is effectively the south-west arete of the buttress. From here abseil in from wires and blocks. Please take note of any climbers already on the cliff and avoid extra ab ropes if they aren't necessary.

Conditions and Tides - South-facing, so expect plenty of sun. The routes in the middle of the face can be done at any tide, although calm seas are advisable. You need a lower tide for *Neurosis.*

For the first route, abseil down the right (looking out) side of the headland to a ledge at the base of a huge curving corner (also see photo on page 113).

1 Sunny Corner . . . . 3 **HVS 5a**

40m. A brilliant find which takes you to places other HVS routes don't reach. The location is intimidating though and you need a confident second. From the ledge at the base of the corner, climb a steep crack above on the left wall - usually a bit slippery, sometimes very wet. Pull over the bulge and squirm out onto the hanging slab. Tip toe delicately right across this until you can climb round the roof on its right-hand side. Wander easily to the top from here.
Photos this page and page 106.
FA. Paul Donnithorne 12.4.97

The next four routes mostly start from a ledge on the seaward face.

2 Quoin . . . . 1 **HS 4a**

34m. This exposed route is based on the south-west arete of the face. Expect a little crunchy rock and the odd loose flake in the upper section. Climb the easier lower section, then move a little leftwards, to finish up the left side of the upper arete.
FA. Scott Titt 14.4.79

3 Poltergeist . . . . . . 2 **HVS 5a**

34m. Excellent. Ascend the lower wall, breaking away from *Quoin* to climb into a deep groove. Follow this on steepening rock and great holds, to the top.
FA. Steve Lewis 2.9.78

4 Telekinesis . . . . . . 1 **HVS 5a**

34m. Similar to *Polergeist*, but a little less obvious. Move right out of the sister route to follow a steep groove system. Continue up this, with a few possible deviations, all the way to a steady finish.
FA. Alec Sharpe 18.6.78

5 Neurosis 1 **E2 5c**

36m. Less-often climbed. You need a low-ish tide and hanging stance tactics to get started on this one. Climb up on steep rock to gain a scoop, then continue through a bulge to reach the groove above. Follow this to the top.
FA. Nipper Harrison 25.7.83

Bean Sopwith on the wonderful line of *Sunny Corner* (HVS) - *this page* - Bosherston Head. Photo: Ian Parnell

6 Preposterous Tales . . . . Top 50 E2 5b(ish)

This route is a wild, crazy trip into the bowels of the earth. It starts as for *Quoin*, and traverses into the low sea cave to the right, thereafter firing up through a massive blowhole system, to arrive at the top blowhole exit (see photo right). Big, big adventure! Please note that the route is much harder when it's soaking wet. In perfect conditions it may only be HVS, in normal conditions it is around E2, and in wild conditions it is even harder and inadvisable. Check the blowhole exit before you commit, as this gives you an idea of how wet the route is likely to be - it does occasionally dry out, especially with a strong, dry southerly blowing. Head torches very much required (as is an easy-going sense of humour). But then again, there's also that first ascent date!

1) 5b, 15m. Traverse rightwards into the cave, aiming for its apex. Ape into the cave to reach a good belay 4m inside, on a boulder choke.

2) 5a, 10m. Bridge inwards to where the cave widens. Committing but surprisingly easy moves across the left wall lead to a corner beneath daylight. Belay here.

3) 5a, 25m. Follow the corner above to one of the strangest finishes at Pembroke.

FA. Dave Scott-Maxwell, Paul Dearden 1.4.95

St. David's
Flimston Bay
Mewsford
Castle/Rusty
Saddle Head
Bosherston Head
Huntsman's Leap
Stennis/Chapel
Trevallen
St. Govan's
Mowing/Stackpole
Mother Carey's

There is one final route which also starts from the Quoin belay - see previous page for the start and access.

❼ **High Life**.............☆☆ ☐ **E1 5b**

An excellent rising traverse which is a great way to experience this face, giving good exposure at a reasonably friendly grade.
1) 5a, 42m. From the ledge of *Quoin*, climb diagonally rightwards to a small ledge. Traverse right to a spike, then move up a little before continuing right to stance in the groove of *Wavelength*.
2) 5b, 20m. Traverse the break rightwards to reach a flake up which you finish.
FA. Paul Donnithorne, Emma Alsford 12.6.94

The next two routes require an abseil to a tiny ledge at the high water mark, just east of the Preposterous Tales cave. Both routes were originally climbed in two pitches, but can be done in one.

❽ **Frigid Digits** ....☆ ☐ **E2 5b**

35m. Climb the wall just left of the belay, then climb a sustained section to reach a sloping ledge on the right (possible belay). Continue up and leftwards on steep ground, to gain first a brown niche, then a groove above. Follow this to the top.
FA. C.Gibson 11.5.80

❾ **Dayglow Saracen**........☆ ☐ **E2 5c**

35m. Break out right from the belay, to gain a groove. Follow this to a rest on a sloping ledge (possible belay), then step right to a crackline. Follow this to the top.
FA. C.Gibson 10.5.80

Wavelength

The central section of the south face is a wonderfully remote feeling bit of rock. The face is a touch steeper here which nudges the grades up a little.
Approach - The abseils need a little thought since you can't see where you are going until you have committed. There are various belays from wires and threads in the crag-top blocks.
Conditions and Tides - The face is south-facing, so expect plenty of sun. It is exposed to wind and heavy seas so choose calm conditions. A mid-to-low tide is required for the lower belay points along the cliff, most specifically the alcoved ledge of *Exogen* and *Wavelength*. The other routes can be started a bit higher, especially if you belay on your abseil rope.

The next two routes need a fresh abseil, to gain a belay at the base of the curving niche. Aim for low-mid tide, and calm seas.

❿ **Exogen**.............☆ ⛏ ☐ **E3 6a**

36m. Step left off the ledge, and climb a steep crack to a short-lived groove; a hard move through a bulge gains a rest on a sloping ledge (possible belay, shared with *Dayglow*). Continue up the wall above, to reach the white groove; follow this briefly, until it's possible to pull rightwards, then climb directly to the top.
FA. Paul Donnithorne 14.6.92

⓫ **Wavelength**.........☆☆ ⛏ ☐ **E3 5c**

36m. A terrific line. Pull into the chimney-crack, and follow it until it abruptly ends; move up, then follow the leftwards-groove to gain the steep vertical groove above. Follow this on its natural course all the way to the finish.
FA. Nipper Harrison 7.8.83

See previous page for routes on this side

St. David's / Flimston Bay / Mewsford / Castle/Rusty / Saddle Head / Bosherston Head / Huntsman's Leap / Stennis/Chapel / Trevallen / St. Govan's / Mowing/Stackpole / Mother Careys

The next two routes start from good ledges at the base of the rib of Warm Waves.

12 Dope without a Rope ...... ☆1 ☐ HVS 5a

23m. This line makes the best use of the hanging, bottomless grooveline found high up on the crag. The route can be split into 2 pitches if you encounter rope drag. Start up the upper section of *Warm Waves*, then traverse leftwards towards the groove; then climb the right wall of the groove to the top.
F.A. Emma Alsford 11.6.94

13 Chakademus and Pliers .... ☆1 ☐ E1 5b

20m. A nicely out-there upper pitch. Start at the big ledges. Break left out of *Warm Waves*, to climb the excellent steep juggy wall above.
FA. D.Jones 28.5.94

14 Warm Waves............ ☆1 ☐ VS 4c

36m. This one's more amenable; good climbing, and good positions. Can be split into two pitches. From a belay close to sea-level (there's quite a few choices) climb the rib on the edge of the tall cave to arrive at the collection of big ledges. Continue up the rightwards-trending ramp above, then climb a short corner to the top.
FA. Alec Sharpe 9.5.78

15 Trade Wind .... ☆1 ☐ E4 6a

18m. This steep testpiece is mighty appealing. Recommended is starting from the big half-height ledges, as the original bottom pitch is much easier than the 'proper' top one. Climb up into the brown-streaked, pocketed overhanging crack, and follow it with difficulty to easier ground above.
F.A. Nipper Harrison 28.7.85

The last two routes here are reached by abseiling to a cleft just above the high water mark. You'll have to jiggle around a bit to find a good abseil point in the blocks above.

16 Ocean Passage .... ☆2 ☐ VS 4c

36m. A grand and engaging little adventure, with a comfortable half-height belay option. Climb out of the lower cleft, and continue past two bulges; continue up the wall above, to reach a rest (possible stance) below a corner in the right side of the upper arete. Climb the superb, balancy corner to a steep exit.
FA. Scott Titt 28.5.78

17 Lundy Road............ ☆1 ☐ E2 5b

36m. Another good route; steep, but well-littered with jugs. Move right from the lower stance, and climb the steep wall above, to a good ledge. Move up to get established on the exposed rib on the right, then tackle the steep crack above to complete the task.
FA. Nipper Harrison 6.8.83

Lots of sun | 10 min | Tidal | Abseil in

Star Wars

This fine wall at the entrance to the Leap is home to the majestic *Star Wars* and a collection of classic harder routes as well.

Approach - Walk along above the West Wall of the Leap to where it opens out at the seaward end. The wall is directly beneath you and can be viewed from further along the headland. The non-tidal ledge at the base of the corner can be reached by abseil direct from a stake at any tide.

1 Star Wars . . . . Top 50 **E4 5c**

38m. A magnificent and elegant climb. There is a lot more gear than the grade suggests and although there are hardly any easy moves, there are no desperate ones either. Start from the ledge at the foot of the corner. The original start followed the corner for 3m then traversed right to the arete but it is better to climb up the blunt arete from the right-hand end of the belay ledge. Continue to the mid-height break and the base of a long straight crack. Move right to a narrow groove then trend up and rightwards on improving holds to another break. Move right again and finish up a groove with an increasing sense of elation - beautiful!

Photo on page 109.

FA. Ben Wintringham 29.6.80

2 The Empire Strikes Back . 2 **(E6 6c)**

35m. A great hard route but with some old fixed gear that may not now be trustworthy. Climb *Star Wars* to the base of the long straight crack. Move left, with your feet in the break, then up (old peg) to a slanting roof (small cam). Pull leftwards head then up the wall with difficulty to a break. Finish easily above.

FA. Gary Gibson 2.5.87

3 Luke Skywalker 3 **E5 6b**

35m. The straight crack in the centre of the wall proves to be sustained and difficult but very well protected. Follow *Star Wars* to the crack then climb it to the top.

FA. Nipper Harrison 7.84

4 Eat, Drink and Beat Gary. 3 **(E6 6b)**

40m. A huge route up the wall right of the big roof. The climbing is superb but there is some crucial fixed gear which may be in a bad state. Start at the flake of *Big in America*, step left to a ledge then climb up and over a bulge (good nut slot). Move up and right to some good holds. Then move back left and climb up to the mid-height break. Pull up again then make a hard move rightwards into the base of a groove. Climb the groove to the top break and step right into the finishing groove of *Big in America*.

FA. Gary Gibson 18.3.90

5 Big in America. . 3 **(E6 6b)**

40m. A big climb, with a big grade, up big grooves, on a big wall! There is some fixed gear which may be in a bad state. Start at a prominent flake 30m right of the corner ledges. Climb the flake to the possible belay. Gain a groove and make some bold moves up rightwards then climb over bulges into the base of a long slim groove which runs the full length of the wall above. Make some hard moves up the groove to the mid-height break and a rest. Move onto the worrying block above and reach good holds above and use these to move back left into the groove. Follow this with a hard move to reach the upper break. Finish easily.

FA. Gary Gibson 12.4.87

6 Insignificance 2 **E4 6a**

An atmospheric route but with some suspect rock. Start at very low tide below a groove 6m right of the *Big in America* flake; or abseil to a flat spike on the upper left-hand side of this groove.

1) 6a, 25m. Climb the lower groove then step left to the flat spike. Trend back rightwards into a long groove - bold but easy. Climb the open groove for 4m then pull left onto the arete. Climb this straight over a small overlap to reach a ledge, grovel onto this then climb a short groove to a belay.

2) 6a, 15m. Climb juggy cracks in the left wall of the groove above to the second thread then pull rightwards in an exposed position onto the wall right of a rib. Move up to a thread and finish more easily above.

FA. Gary Gibson 17.3.90

Approach to base of wall - The cliff base is only uncovered during lower spring tides which doesn't always leave enough time for an ascent so time your approach to routes 4, 5 and 6 well. There is a small ledge above the tide line to escape an incoming tide. It can be reached from above with a bit of a swing.

Huntsman's Leap

Susan Hatchell making the stretch move on *Beast from the Undergrowth* (E2) - *page 131* - on the East Wall of Huntsman's Leap. Photo: Gareth Hallam

	No star	1 star	2 star	3 star
Mod to S	-	-	-	-
HS to HVS	-	-	-	-
E1 to E3	-	2	7	-
E4 and up	-	4	20	13

Opinions on Huntsman's Leap vary from the "best crag in the World" to "a grotty hole in the ground", but they rarely venture into the "quite good" category - you will either love it or you will hate it. For those to whom it does appeal, the experience of climbing in this dramatic location is unforgettable and once you have started tackling the routes, you will continually be looking for the next one to tackle as you creep up the grade ladder.

Most people will make their first acquaintance with the slabbier routes on the East Wall where the rock isn't quite as good, but the best lines are well-cleaned and popular. Routes like *Shape Up* (E1 and the easiest exit), *Beast from the Undergrowth* (E2), *Strap-Up* (E3) and *Quiet Waters* (E2) are all top-notch challenges. Further seaward is the well-named Monster Face with its spooky routes at the narrowest section of the Leap - *Mythical Monster* (E3) and *The Honey Monster* (E2) being the classics here.

The true connoisseur though will spend most of their time on the West Wall since this is where the best of the Leap's treasures lie. The entry level is quite tough though - *Bloody Sunday*, an E4 for ambitious E3 leaders. After that the tick list opens up with virtually every route being a classic - check the table to the right to monitor your progress and maybe you can become one of the elite group of professors!

Approach

Huntsman's Leap is situated 500m west along the coast path from St Govan's car park. It should not be mistaken for the wider Stennis Ford which you reach first. There is usually a collection of people and sacks at the top. The abseil point is on the corner nearest the path but this is slowly disintegrating so take care not to knock loose stuff onto people below.

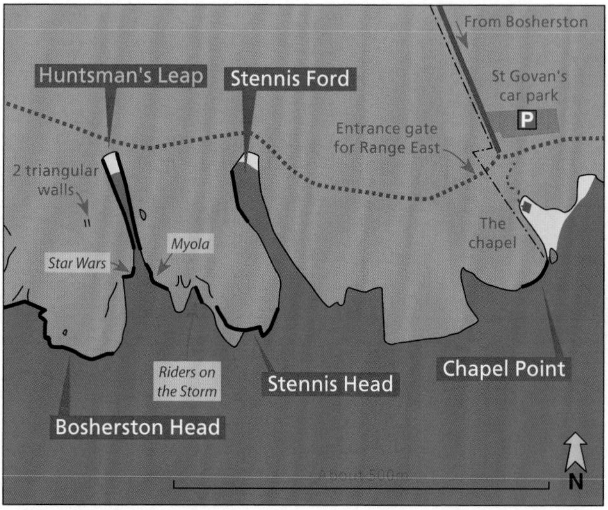

Tides

The sea seldom gets rough in the sheltered base of the Leap, although the debris in the back wall suggests that it sometimes does. In normal conditions high tide is about level with The Minotaur Block and the base of *Shape-Up* although the block itself remains accessible. Towards the sea from here the climbs are increasingly affected by the tide. At the narrowing beneath the Monster Face, a small pool forms during spring tides and the base is exposed for about 3 hours at low tide. During neap tides the pool doesn't form but some of the routes can still usually be reached, however the time window is only about 2 hours.

Conditions and Tides

The Leap is a strange place with strange rock and strange climbing conditions. The West Wall only receives a waffer thin slice of morning sun and can suffer from seepage although this is peculiar in that it doesn't always depend on how much rain there has been. The East Wall gets slightly more sun on the tops of the routes in the afternoon.

The base of the Leap is almost always cold. In baking hot summer days this can be very useful, however, just occasionally it isn't quite so hot. Top tip: if you are belaying, always take at least one more warm garment down than you think you will need.

Once the tide has gone, the lower walls sometimes dry in minutes and sometimes not at all; this depends on how fresh the atmosphere is and whether the wind is blowing through the Leap. As a general rule, sunny fresh weather gives the best conditions. When the Leap is sandy, the routes stay wet for longer and a rope bag is essential to keep your ropes dry. The seaward routes tend to be more slimy, however it is often worth a closer inspection because the rock often looks wet when it is in fact dry.

Leanne Callaghan on the second pitch of *Witch Hunt* (E4) - *page 124* - Huntsman's Leap. Photo: Ian Parnell

Route	Qualification
☐ Terminal Twilight	*Professor of Leapology*
☐ Souls	*Member of the Order of Huntsman*
☐ Pulsebeat	*Master of the East Wall*
☐ Darkness at Noon	*Doctor of Leap Obsession*
☐ The Minotaur	*Undergraduate in West Wall Studies*
☐ Bloody Sunday	*Aspirant Westwaller*
☐ The Beast from the Undergrowth	*A-Level in East Wall Studies*
☐ Shape-Up	*Apprentice Leaper*

1 Woeful **E5 6b**
A classic E5 and one on which you don't have to worry about any dodgy bits of fixed gear. Start next to the pool under the boulder choke, which is only revealed during spring tides.
1) 6b, 25m. Traverse leftwards to reach a crack and climb it and some layback flakes to a groove and rest on the left. Move up and left into a scoop and leave this leftwards to good holds. Follow these to a layback flake. Then, inside leg measurements permitting, bridge between the two walls under and around the chockstone.
2) 5b, 20m. Traverse left and finish as for *The Honey Monster*.
FA. George Smith 16.4.95

2 Darkness at Noon . . . . . . Top 50 **E5 6a**
An amazing climb which takes a wild line up the seaward end of the wall. The conditions of this route seem to vary from slippery and unclimbable to surprisingly dry. Take a lot of small wires.
1) 6a, 25m. Climb the ramp then step down and traverse left with difficulty. Move up the ramp above into a runnel and squirm up this to a tricky exit. Belay on a big thread in the groove above.
2) 5c, 10m. Undercut wildly rightwards around the roof, then step back left and look down at your second. Finish straight up to a big natural thread on the right.
FA. Pat Littlejohn, Tony Penning 15.4.84

3 Night-Seeker . . . . . . **(E6 6b)**
35m. The towering groove above the ramp gives a BIG pitch which needs re-climbing now the drilled old pegs have gone. Start up the ramp and climb the groove to a bridging rest below a step in the big roof. Zig-zag first left to some good footholds, then back right to reach better holds. Finish more easily up scoops above.
FA. Martin Crocker 26.7.87

4 Hunter-Killer **E6 6b**
35m. This magnificent route follows the pocketed crack line above the right-hand side of the ramp. The climbing is physical but well protected where it matters. Start by the grey ramp, climb up then make hard moves across left to some overlaps. Pull over these and layback with difficulty to a large hole (*the Mantrap*) which provides a welcome rest. More hard climbing gains the pocket line, which is followed to a small ledge below a bulge. Pull left around this and continue up and left to the top.
FA. Martin Crocker 10.5.87. DW soloed onsight by James McHaffie.

5 Nothing to Fear . **E8 6b**
35m. A huge climb which tackles the left-hand of two groove/runnels. Climb the lower wall (good small wires) to the roof (small cam). Cross the roofs at a step to a red pancake. Climb the runnel above and then pull round the bulge with difficulty into the upper runnel. This is followed by bold but easier moves to a bulge which is passed on its left. Finish up and left. The pegs used on the first ascent have now rotted away, hence the bump in grade.
FA. Martin Crocker 5.7.87. Repeated onsight by Ian Vickers!

6 Terminal Twilight . . . Top 50 **E7 6b**
35m. An ascent of the snaking runnel is a magnificent achievement. A strenuous struggle from the word go; the gear is good but hard-earned. Reach the runnel from the right and follow it past a slight rest to desperate moves over a smooth bulge. Keep it going up the headwall which eventually leads to good finishing holds.
FA. Pat Littlejohn 28.4.84. The hardest route climbed in the UK without chalk? Probably only one repeat in 25 years!

7 The Black Lagoon **(E7 6b)**
35m. The left-hand direct start to the finishing groove of *Witch Hunt*. Start under the runnel which is gained via a flake and some hard climbing. After a brief rest more hard moves gain holds at the base of the continuation runnel on the right. Follow this with some long reaches to join *Witch Hunt*. Most of the fixed gear has rotted and the route is probably unrepeated in its current state.
FA. Gary Gibson 5.7.87

8 Light at the End of the Runnel
. . . . **E6 6b**
35m. Yet another stupendous climb which reaches the upper section of *Witch Hunt* via two prominent hollows. Climb up to the first hollow (gear), and then the second (rest). A move left gains *The Black Lagoon* at its reachy runnel.
FA. Martin Crocker 4.5.87. Original done with a peg at E5.

9 Little Hunt **E6 6b**
35m. The direct version of *Witch Hunt* in one pitch. Start as for *Light at the End of the Runnel*, but break out right from holds on the lip of the second hollow to boldly reach the *Witch Hunt* belay from below (possible stance). Blast on up above with a long reach to leave the scoop above the belay. Continue up the headwall.
FA. Gary Gibson 24.5.87

10 Witch Hunt **E4 6b**
The original line up this bit of wall which is slightly spoilt by the crux move being much harder than the rest. *Photo on page 123.*
1) 6b, 25m. Climb the triangular niche and the crack above it. From here either move left and up to the pegs, or climb the flake on the right - both 5b. Make a desperate series of moves up and left into a scoop. Step left again to another scoop to belay.
2) 5c, 20m. Step up and clip a thread than move back down and traverse left in an impressive position to reach another runnel. Follow this direct to the top.
FA. Pat Littlejohn 3.4.84

11 Chupacabra E8 6c

35m. A very bold climb. From the rest in the scoop after the crux of *Witch Hunt*, pull out right and climb the bold wall above to a good threaded nut. Follow a flake, then move left and make hard moves to good holds and then the top. *Photo on page 33*.

FA. Ben Bransby 16.5.98

12 Boat to Naxos E7 6b

35m. An extremely bold undertaking. From the peg in the flake on *Witch Hunt*, step right and climb a scoop. Pull up onto the wall above and follow a faint flake to its end. Step right and climb direct to a grassy finish. *Photo on page 20*.

FA. Andy Donson 4.6.95. Originally done on bolts by Gary Gibson.

Witch Hunt

The seaward end of the West Wall is awesomely steep and impressive and contains one of the most stunning set of hard traditional routes to be found anywhere. Some of the routes rely on a lot of fixed gear, much of which is becoming old. This gear must be regarded as very dubious and an abseil inspection is advised.

13 Souls .... Top 50 E6 6b

35m. A solid E6. The crucial fixed gear is now in very poor condition and is difficult to back up. Start as for *Witch Hunt* but move right to a ledge. Step up to a small round scoop and then commit to the flake above. Climb this then move leftwards and up to two good threads. Here comes the blind crux - don't be tempted off left onto the good holds. Finish up the groove above.

FA. Gary Gibson 2.7.85

St. David's
Flimston Bay
Mewsford
Castle/Rusty
Saddle Head
Bosherston Head
Huntsman's Leap
Stennis/Chapel
Trevallen
St. Govan's
Mowing/Stackpole
Mother Carey's

St. David's
Flimston Bay
Mewsford
Castle/Rusty
Saddle Head
Bosherston Head
Huntsman's Leap
Stennis/Chapel
Trevallen
St. Govan's
Mowing/Stackpole
Mother Carey's

Minotaur

The landward end of the pink west (right looking out) wall contains some of the most accessible and popular hard routes in Pembroke. The main characteristics are the crack of *The Minotaur*, the (usually) well-chalked line of *Head Hunter* above the centre of the large block, and the popular line of *Bloody Sunday*. The finishes of all of these routes require care with loose rock and some tricky vegetable cornices.

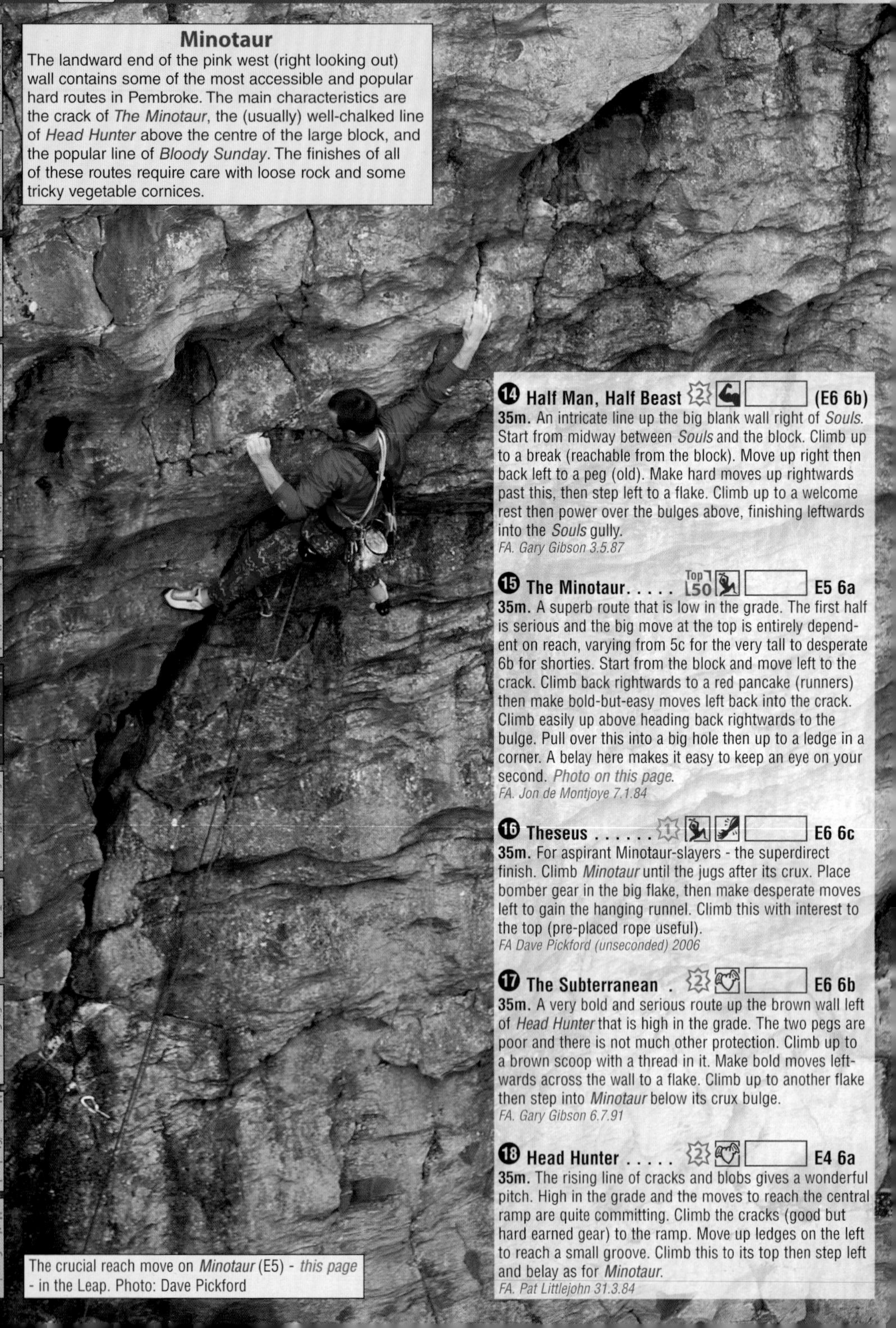

The crucial reach move on *Minotaur* (E5) - *this page* - in the Leap. Photo: Dave Pickford

14 Half Man, Half Beast 2 **(E6 6b)**

35m. An intricate line up the big blank wall right of *Souls*. Start from midway between *Souls* and the block. Climb up to a break (reachable from the block). Move up right then back left to a peg (old). Make hard moves up rightwards past this, then step left to a flake. Climb up to a welcome rest then power over the bulges above, finishing leftwards into the *Souls* gully.

FA. Gary Gibson 3.5.87

15 The Minotaur. . . . . Top 50 **E5 6a**

35m. A superb route that is low in the grade. The first half is serious and the big move at the top is entirely dependent on reach, varying from 5c for the very tall to desperate 6b for shorties. Start from the block and move left to the crack. Climb back rightwards to a red pancake (runners) then make bold-but-easy moves left back into the crack. Climb easily up above heading back rightwards to the bulge. Pull over this into a big hole then up to a ledge in a corner. A belay here makes it easy to keep an eye on your second. *Photo on this page.*

FA. Jon de Montjoye 7.1.84

16 Theseus 1 **E6 6c**

35m. For aspirant Minotaur-slayers - the superdirect finish. Climb *Minotaur* until the jugs after its crux. Place bomber gear in the big flake, then make desperate moves left to gain the hanging runnel. Climb this with interest to the top (pre-placed rope useful).

FA Dave Pickford (unseconded) 2006

17 The Subterranean . 2 **E6 6b**

35m. A very bold and serious route up the brown wall left of *Head Hunter* that is high in the grade. The two pegs are poor and there is not much other protection. Climb up to a brown scoop with a thread in it. Make bold moves leftwards across the wall to a flake. Climb up to another flake then step into *Minotaur* below its crux bulge.

FA. Gary Gibson 6.7.91

18 Head Hunter 2 **E4 6a**

35m. The rising line of cracks and blobs gives a wonderful pitch. High in the grade and the moves to reach the central ramp are quite committing. Climb the cracks (good but hard earned gear) to the ramp. Move up ledges on the left to reach a small groove. Climb this to its top then step left and belay as for *Minotaur*.

FA. Pat Littlejohn 31.3.84

19 Snake Charmer E5 6c

The cluster of tat with a bale-out krab on it marks the crux, although reaching it is no picnic.

1) 6c, 15m. Climb to the tat and make a desperate move up and right (6c for shorties) to reach a good hold. Belay on the ramp.

2) 6a, 20m. Climb the wall above the centre of the ledge past a thread. Move back left to join and finish up *Head Hunter* at its flake. The original ivy and grass finish is a desperate struggle. It can be climbed in one pitch.

FA. Gary Gibson 26.3.85

20 The White Hotel ... E6 6c

The elegant open groove is seldom climbed.

1) 6b, 15m. Climb the groove. Where it ends make hard moves up to eventually reach the sloping ledge.

2) 6a, 20m. Climb direct up the corner above the ledge to a big thread. Continue past a flake and some awesome ivy above.

FA. Pat Littlejohn 6.5.84.
This route marked a change in style for Pat - he started using chalk, hence the name.

Not much sun | 8 min | Tidal | Abseil in

21 The Witching Hour ★1 E6 6b

35m. Extremely bold and difficult to onsight and probably the hardest E6 in the Leap (now that *Terminal Twilight* has been upgraded to E7). It follows the wall mid-way between *White Hotel* and *Bloody Sunday* to the break. You could dive off left at this point but after putting in that effort, it makes more sense to try...

FA. Gary Gibson 1.6.84

22 Wicked Witch of the West . . . . ★2 E6 6b

35m. A direct finish to *The Witching Hour*. Climb *The Witching Hour* to a good rest at the large undercut flake. Climb direct up the hanging flake to join *Bloody Sunday* for its second crux. Then move left and climb the shallow groove in the final pillar.

FA. Dave Pickford, Nic Sellers 8.08

23 Bloody Sunday . . Top 50 E4 6a

35m. This magnificent Pembrokeshire classic should have a place on everyone's tick list. Arguments over its grade will continue for ever so consider it hard E3 or easy E4. Start 10m left of the end of the wall. Climb a series of cracks and bulges, with a hard move at 6m, to reach a rest below a big curving overlap. Pull out left and try and get your right hand in a slot which your left hand is in. Climb up and back right to reach the wide finishing flake/groove. *Photo this page.*

FA. Alec Sharpe 15.7.79

24 Just Another Day ★2 E4 6a

35m. The right-most climb on the wall is another classic which is probably best combined with *Scorch the Earth*. Start at the right-hand end of the wall beneath a wide crack high up. Climb up to the bulge and pull over directly to a peg (there is a sneaky little rightwards bypass around this move which is a bit easier). Move easily up to the base of the wide crack. A delightful traverse leftwards leads to a ledge below a bulge. Either finish direct (as for *Scorch the Earth*), or make a hard move up and left into *Bloody Sunday*.

FA. Gary Gibson 27.4.84

25 Scorch the Earth . ★2 E4 6a

35m. A well-positioned route which provides an excellent variation finish to either of the previous two routes. From the rest on *Bloody Sunday*, or the ledge half way across the *Just Another Day* traverse, make a hard move past a thread. Continue above this past a couple of large juggy flakes to a slightly loose finishing groove.

FA. Perry Hawkins 27.4.84

Steep moves on the upper wall of the classic *Bloody Sunday* (E4) - *this page* - in the Leap. Photo: Scott Sadler

St. David's | Flimston Bay | Mewsford | Castle/Rusty | Saddle Head | Bosherston Head | Huntsman's Leap | Stennis/Chapel | Trevallen | St. Govan's | Mowing/Stackpole | Mother Carey's

Not much sun
8 min
Tidal
Abseil in
S
25
22
White Hotel
High tide
21
23
24

1 Magazine People . . . 2 ☐ **E5 6b**
32m. The best route on this bit of wall has climbing much more in keeping with the fingery start which was the original way of doing *Quiet Waters*. Climb straight up past the threads to reach a curving line of holds (good nut slot). Follow this with difficulty to the bulge where another hard move gains *Quiet Waters*.
FA. Nick Dixon 10.4.85

2 Specimen Hunter . . . . . . 1 ☐ **E5 6b**
32m. A slightly easier method of climbing the wall which gives good technical climbing. From the third thread on *Magazine People*, make some fingery moves rightwards (good but hard-earned wires) to reach a ramp. Move back left over the bulge (as for *Magazine People*) then step right under a roof. A hard move over this gains the upper slab and the top.
FA. Gary Gibson 20.4.84

3 Quiet Waters Direct . . . . 2 ☐ **E3 5c**
32m. Originally this route started in the same place as *Magazine People*, but it is much better to start at the arete just left of *Shape-Up* (or the slab just left with a thread at **6a**). This gives a good enjoyable pitch at a more even grade. From the top of the arete make tricky moves up onto a ramp, then continue to reach a traverse line under the roof which is passed by puzzling moves on its left-hand side.
FA. Gary Gibson 29.5.83

4 Shape-Up . . . . 2 ☐ **E1 5b**
33m. The easiest climb in the Leap gives good climbing up the groove line right of the smooth brown wall. From the top of the lower groove, tricky moves back left gain the upper corner to the right of the large roof. Follow this, with care, to the top.
FA. Alec Sharpe 17.6.78

Quiet Waters

Most people's first climbs in the Leap are on the landward end of the east (left looking out) wall on the *Quiet Waters* area. The routes here tend to be a bit easier and less committing than on the Monster Face or the West Wall yet they still should not be underestimated. Before you abseil in you should at least be certain of being able to climb *Shape-Up* or *The Beast from the Undergrowth* since these are the easiest escape routes.

5 Fitzcarraldo. . . . . 2 ☐ **E5 6a**
35m. This popular E5 has a hard start and a bold finish. Start just left of *Shape-Up* below some pockets and cracks. Climb these and the easier flakes above to the overlap. Move left below the old peg and then up to the next overlap. Fill this full of gear, pause for a long time, and then climb direct to the top.
FA. Gary Gibson 8.4.83

6 Slap-Up/Fitz-In . . . . 1 ☐ **(E5 6b)**
35m. A combination of filler-in routes that may now be bolder due to the peg being old. The lower section follows the open scoop with loads of threads in it. (A decent **E3 6a** if you finish up *Wrap-Up*). From the top of the scoop, climb the slab above on its right edge (old peg) with some very hard moves.
FA. (Slap-Up) Alec Sharpe 3.9.78.FA. (Fitz-In) Dave Viggers 8.4.89

7 Wrap-Up. . . . . 1 ☐ **E3 6a**
35m. An enjoyable route up the crack left of the flake of *Beast from the Undergrowth*. From the top of the crack pull over the small roof leftwards. Continue up the wall above keeping just left of the overlaps. Step left at the top.
FA. Alec Sharpe 3.9.78

8 The Beast from the Undergrowth
. . . . 2 **E2 5b**

35m. This is probably the most popular route in the Leap, it starts at the big flake/groove left of the smooth black wall. Step right from the top of the flake and pull over a bulge. Follow a line of holds up rightwards to a roof. Step back left and make a l-o-n-g pull over this to reach good holds above. Shorties may want to use the two alternative sequences which don't need a reach. Follow the wall above with care, keeping slightly right.

Photo on page 120.

FA. Gary Gibson 19.3.84

9 The Pulsebeat . . 2 **E6 6b**

35m. The stunning lower black wall has some unlikely climbing which is protected by threads - check them before your ascent since there is little other gear. The friction is usually better than it looks but there isn't a single easy move before the crux which is a lot higher than you might think. Climb the wall up the line of the gear. Higher up step leftwards into a chossy groove.

FA. Gary Gibson 20.3.84

10 Compulsion. 2 **E6 6a**

35m. This very serious route follows the striking arete on its left-hand side to a junction with *Moving Away....* The gear is crap or non-existent: maybe the sand will save you.

FA. Gary Gibson 5.5.88

11 Moving Away from the Pulsebeat
. . . . 1 **E4 6a**

37m. The first half of this climb gives some good sustained climbing. Step out of the groove of *Strap-Up* at its first roof. Make an awkward move around the arete and then climb the sustained crack above. From here move right to the arete and take the most stable line up the tower above. Unfortunately the gear on the upper tower tends to be behind the dodgy blocks you are pulling on.

FA. Gary Gibson 30.5.84

The first two routes are on the slightly chossy section of rock to the left of the big cave.

12 Strap-Up. 2 **E3 5c**

37m. The route up the big corner which runs the full height of the wall is a strenuous undertaking. Climb the groove all the way stepping right around the first roof.

FA. Alec Sharpe 2.9.78

13 Vladimir on the Rocks . . 2 **E4 6a**

37m. This one follows the remains of the once-classic *Vladimir and the Beast.* Start right of *Strap-Up* up a crack, and trend leftwards to a thread. Continue to a peg near *Strap-Up*, then move back right and follow the gear up the steep wall to the top.

FA. Paul Donnithorne 15.5.93

Not much sun | 8 min | Tidal | Abseil in

St. David's | Flimston Bay | Mewsford | Castle/Rusty | Saddle Head | Bosherston Head | Huntsman's Leap | Stennis/Chapel | Trevallen | St. Govan's | Mowing/Stackpole | Mother Carey's

St. David's
Flimston Bay
Mewsford
Castle/Rusty
Saddle Head
Bosherston Head
Huntsman's Leap
Stennis/Chapel
Trevallen
St. Govan's
Mowing/Stackpole
Mother Carey's

The Monster Face

The Monster Face is the well-named seaward end of the East Wall. The climbing here tends to be intricate and mysterious with most of the routes following complex lines up the wall. The rock on the lower section often appears to be wet but the routes can usually still be climbed in these conditions.

⑭ Monsterosity 2 (E5 6b)

Good climbing but may now be more serious due to the missing peg.
1) 5c, 15m. Climb the grey flake and then move left to a hole. Step up rightwards to the poor belay in a hollow.
2) 6b, 35m. Finger traverse leftwards then move up to a flat ledge. Climb up (missing peg) and left past some threads and a crack to a ledge on the arete. Finish out left into the gully. Belay above the arete taking care not to dislodge any loose rock.
FA. Gary Gibson 23.2.86

⑮ The Monster Mash 1 E3 6a

A complex route up the wall above the grey flake.
1) 5c, 15m. Climb the flake then move up and rightwards into an open groove. Follow this until it is possible to step left into the wide crack and poor belay of *Monsterosity*.
2) 6a, 35m. Pull out above and step right. Climb straight up to a roof and pull over it leftwards. Easier climbing up left leads to the hole. Finish up and right onto grassy ledges.
FA. Gary Gibson 10.3.84

There are a couple of other routes here: **Monster-growth from the Underbeast (E5 6a)**, *tackles the hanging left arete but the rock is poor; and* **Monster Modello (E5 6a)**, *which takes a direct line where Monster Mash heads up and right. Both routes rely on a significant amount of fixed gear and probably haven't been climbed for years. The grades should be treated with caution.*

⑯ Mythical Monster 2 E2 5c

The most popular on the face. The climbing is never very hard but the situation is intimidating. It can be climbed in one pitch.
1) 5b, 25m. Climb the flake and step right in the open groove (as for *Monster Mash*). From the top of this pull out rightwards and climb the wall above to the small ledge belay.
2) 5c, 25m. Follow a diagonal line of cracks up and leftwards past a large thread. Easier ground leads to the grass ledges and the stake belays at the top.
FA. Gary Gibson, Andy Hudson 28.5.83

17 The Honey Monster .... 2 ☐ E2 5b

The easiest route up the face gives a popular and unusual excursion.
1) 5b, 25m. As for *Mythical Monster* to its step right from the open groove. Continue traversing rightwards beneath a bulge to reach a ledge.
2) 5b, 30m. Move right across a slab then climb up to a couple of holes keeping just left of some ledges. Pull out of these and climb the wall above, passing some more holes, to the top.
FA. Gary Gibson 23.4.84

18 Meet the Monster Tonight 2 ☐ E4 6a

The best route on the wall has a superb first pitch which is sometimes covered with unclimbable slime.
1) 6a, 15m. Start 5m right of the grey flake, below a runnel and an undercut hole. From a ledge climb up then move right into the runnel and climb this with a long reach for a hidden finger jug to leave the undercut. Continue to the belay of *The Honey Monster*.
2) 6a, 30m. Climb the wall on the right to a ledge. Step left into a crack and climb this with a hard move past a thread. Finish straight up.
FA. Gary Gibson 29.5.84

19 Release the Bats ... 2 ☐ E5 6a

Now things start getting really weird! Start just left of the pool at dead low tide, beneath the landward boulder choke.
1) 6a, 25m. Climb up to a ledge then follow a slim groove leftwards. Step down then pull up left into a rounded scoop. Pull out right on a hidden jug and continue to *The Honey Monster* traverse and belay on a ledge on the right.
2) 5c, 20m. Traverse 3m further than *The Honey Monster* and climb the scoop above to a crack. Finish up wobbly rock.
FA. Crispin Waddy 7.87

20 The Ducking Stool .. 3 ☐ E5 6a

An amazing route with a leg splitting first pitch. The rock can be drier than it looks, which is lucky. Start as for *Release the Bats*.
1) 6a, 25m. From a ledge at 3m traverse right and then climb a line of holds up and leftwards. (Possible belay at a large nut slot). Move left then back right to reach a ledge above the belay. Mantle onto this and climb the blank wall above on hidden holds. Where these run out, do the splits across the Leap, or move up a little higher and back and foot it up to belay on the boulder choke.
2) 5b, 20m. Step left over a bulge to join and finish up *The Honey Monster*, or finish direct from the boulder choke at around **5a**.
FA. Crispin Waddy 10.5.87

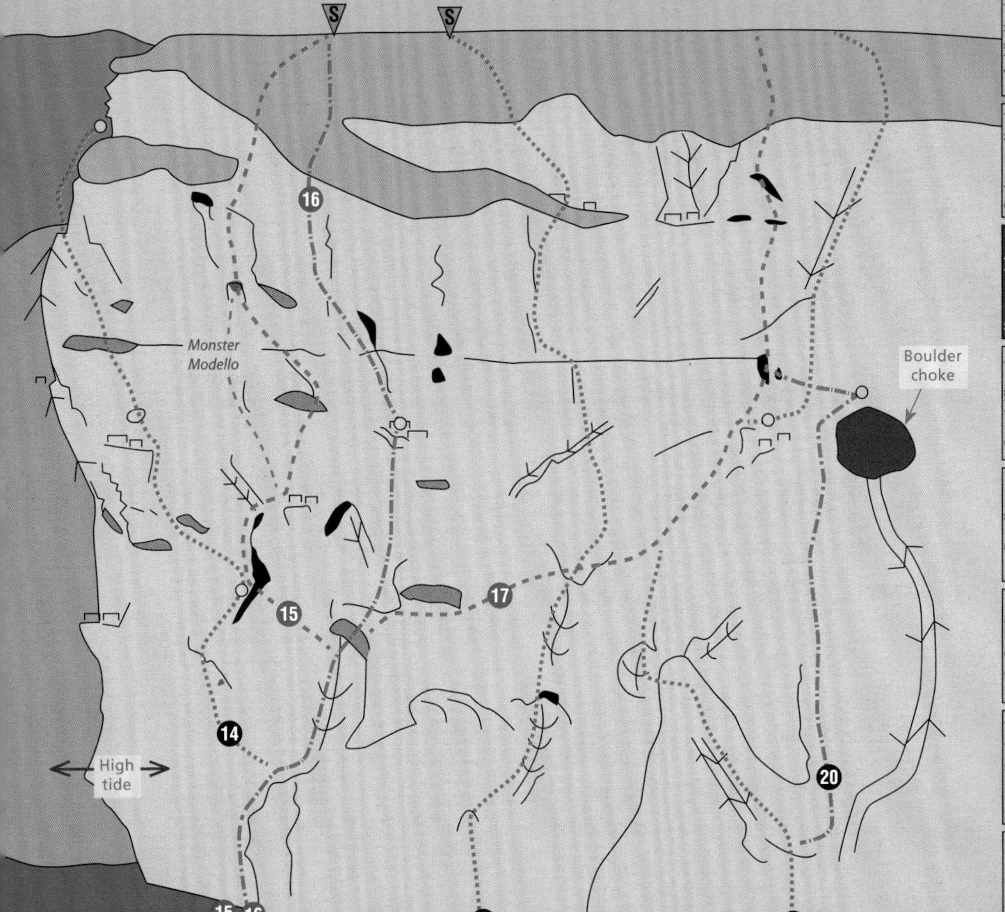

St. David's
Flimston Bay
Mewsford
Castle/Rusty
Saddle Head
Bosherston Head
Huntsman's Leap
Stennis/Chapel
Trevallen
St. Govan's
Mowing/Stackpole
Mother Carey's

Stennis Head
Stennis Ford
Chapel Point

Ali Kennedy pondering the crux of one of Pembroke's finest, *Pleasure Dome* (E3) - *page 144* - Stennis Head. Photo: Jamie Moss

St. David's
Flimston Bay
Mewsford
Castle/Rusty
Saddle Head
Bosherston Head
Huntsman's Leap
Stennis/Chapel
Trevallen
St. Govan's
Mowing/Stackpole
Mother Carey's

	No star	1	2	3
Mod to S	2	2	-	-
HS to HVS	2	7	4	2
E1 to E3	1	12	2	3
E4 and up	-	3	3	3

The glorious and easily-accessed venue of Stennis Head has long been the place for beginners and experienced climbers alike, with its steady scramble-in approach, tempting spread of grades and terrific fused limestone - the only thing wrong with Stennis Head is the fact that it's on the wrong side of the dreaded red flag!
The classics here include *Hercules* (HVS), *Manzoku* (E1) and the aspirational mega-route *Pleasure Dome* (E3) - quite possibly the best E3 in the land. Add to this the long, diagonal slash of *Myola* (HS), the hanging grooves of Stuntsman's Buttress, the *Dream of White Horses-esque* traverse of *Riders on the Storm* (HVS) and the outlying corner gem of *Bludgeon* (HVS), and you have a recipe that goes down well on just about every visit.

Approach

From the St Govan's car park, walk west along the coast path. After passing the inlet of Stennis Ford, turn left across the grass and walk towards the end of the headland. Head slightly rightwards to an eroded red gully. Descend down here to the pleasant non-tidal ledge beneath the cliff. Slightly different approaches are needed for *Bludgeon*, *Myola* and *Riders* areas.

Conditions and Tides

The main faces of the buttress face south and get all the sun that is going. *Myola* and *Riders* walls face more westerly getting the sun later in the day, and *Riders on the Storm* is a particularly good late afternoon route. As with most areas the sections of rock away from the sea tend to dry quickly, especially on the exposed arete of *Manzuko*. As you get closer to the sea the slippery morning slime can be a problem on the shiny rock. Only the *Myola* and Stuntsman's Buttress require a low tide.

Pembroke perfection; Rob Howell finishing *Riders on the Storm* (HVS) - *page 140* - Stennis Head. Photo: Tim Wilkinson

Myola and Stuntsman's Buttress

This region is another one of those lesser-known Pembroke crags, mainly due to the lack of an obvious viewing point. With a bit of effort, it should be possible to negotiate your way around without too many dramas. The plum here for lower grade climbers, is the magnificent *Myola* (HS) which is surely the Leap's answer to Mowing Word's *Diedre Sud* (but without the queues and/or the bird restrictions). You'll also find a sprinkling of sustained groove lines.

The routes just to the north (right looking out) of *Myola* are restricted due to nesting birds. None of the routes described on this page are effected by the restriction.

Approach - For *Myola*, abseil from wires and spikes in blocks, and take a line slightly left (looking out) of the bird restriction red pot found on the crag top. This will also get you to a ledge below *Myopia* and the routes around *Blind Magic* - low tide only.

For the Stuntsman's Buttress, abseil down the left side (looking out) of the face, from blocks, to ledges at the base that are uncovered from mid-tide onwards.

1 Life Jacket E6 6b

32m. Terrific, sustained climbing. It's possible (and easier) to tackle the hardest section of this route DWS-style (S1), or even trail a rope to use for the upper 5b bit. From the belay at the very base of *Myola*, nip off leftwards, to climb the centre of the steep prow direct. At the 18m mark, join *Blind Magic* to finish.

FA. Ben Bransby 27.4.96

2 Blind Magic. E1 5b

32m. Start as for *Myola*. Climb that route to a chockstone at about 8m, then head up and left to small ledges. Continue up the line of weakness to a good rest, then climb the top wall above.

FA. Paul Donnithorne 9.7.94

3 Bedrock E2 5c

32m. Climb *Myola* for about 14m, then swing leftwards, tackling the brown groove above. From the top of that groove, step left and finish up the steep wall above.

FA. Paul Donnithorne 24.7.94

4 Myola . . . . Top 50 **HS 4b**
32m. A classic line, taking the absorbing diagonal line that rises from the very depths of the zawn. It can be clearly viewed from above *Star Wars* if you want to check it out before committing to the abseil. There are no hard moves, it's just damn good all the way! Climb the long, diagonal groove that slashes the crag from top to bottom.
FA. D.Roberts 13.4.78

5 Myopia . . . . 1 **VS 4c**
32m. Another rewarding line, although this one's a little trickier to follow. Climb diagonally rightwards on flakes from the lower belay ledge, and trace a line up the face about 6m right of *Myola*. The route weaves about a bit and don't expect a straight line!
FA. Tim Daniells 25.5.81

The following routes are approached with an abseil from the top of Stuntsman's Buttress, to gain a selection of spacious ledges below. You'll normally be able to pick and choose where to lay your ropes down. One further note: even though the topo makes it look fairly obvious, it's not super-easy to orientate yourself (lots of roofs/grooves!) once you've set off; so recce your exact line carefully in advance.

6 Oversight . . . . 1 **Sev 4a**
28m. The easiest line here which is useful as a quick exit but also good for those getting used to climbing on sea cliffs. From the left side of the lower ledges, climb easily up the left side of the buttress. Move left of the left-most roof, and then climb diagonally leftwards across the upper slab, mostly on good foot ledges, to reach the top of the *Myopia* slab.
FA. L.Shore 14.4.84

7 Two Men and a Scrote . . . . . **HVS 5a**
24m. The first groove on the buttress. Climb confidently up to gain the lower groove, then make hard moves to enter the steep V-groove above. Follow this to the top.
FA. Paul Donnithorne 2.7.94

8 Big Sea Running 1 **E1 5b**
24m. Up a notch on the last one. Share the easy lower bit with *Two Men* (or from the right at the same grade) then break out rightwards to make tricky moves into the even steeper groove to the right. Follow this, not without interest, to the top.
FA. Damo Carroll 8.4.89

9 Traction Action 1 **E3 5c**
24m. A feisty and pumpy route, firing directly through the central, steepest part of the crag. Climb the amenable start, then pull through the roof above, to gain the crack above. Climb this strenuously up to a second set of roofs, and pull through those to finish more easily.
FA. Dave Viggers 2.4.89

10 Stuntsman 1 **E2 5b**
24m. This line (almost) skirts the overhangs on their right. Climb the short face at the bottom, to reach a good ledge; from here, follow the cracked wall above, moving left to by-pass the small roof to gain a niche. The finishing cracks pull you slightly leftwards.
FA. Damo Carroll 2.4.89

There's one more route here that needs attention since it is definitely nearing classic status. It takes the hanging arete/upper groove just to the south of the Stuntsman's Buttress, and is situated above an almost bottomless pool.

11 Out of my Mind 3 **E5 6a**
28m. Outrageous, exposed climbing. The original line dived in from the cave on the right; but the variation start from the left is also very good. Climb out across the left wall of the cave, using a rising crack, to reach a thread runner. Continue via a break, to reach the arete - and a rest on the left. Then climb the long, slender grooveline above, to a tricky exit.
Variation, E5 6a - Traverse in from the Stuntsman ledges, and traverse the lower break to reach the left side of the arete. Climb the left side of the arete to join the parent route.
FA. Gary Gibson 28.3.90. FA. (Variation) Crispin Waddy 1996

Afternoon | 10 min | Tidal | Abseil in

St. David's
Flimston Bay
Mewsford
Castle/Rusty
Saddle Head
Bosherston Head
Huntsman's Leap
Stennis/Chapel
Trevallen
St. Govan's
Mowing/Stackpole
Mother Carey's

1 Riders on the Storm . . . . Top 50 **HVS 5a**

28m. Brilliant! Great positions, some of the biggest (and sharpest) jugs known to man, but steep rock and not one for a timid second. From the belay ledge, step down and make a tricky pull up across onto the wall to gain the base of a flake. Continue traversing left, going up and down a bit, as far as a tricky move up past a big undercut. Trend up leftwards from here towards the finishing corner, finish up this, or belay on the ledge on the left if you need to watch your second.

FA. Bill Lounds 9.9.84

2 Middle C. . . . . 2 **HVS 5a**

26m. More great climbing. This line was originally a massive wander-fest, utilising the lower, tidal ledges - it's described here with the more straightforward *Riders* approach. Follow *Riders* to within 5m of the corner, then follow your nose up the steep wall above, trending left to finish.

FA. Bill Lounds 28.6.95

3 Big C 1 **E1 5a**

35m. From a point halfway across the *Riders* traverse (before the big undercut), sprint up the wall above until it slabs out a little (spaced gear), then tackle the crack in the headwall above.

FA. Reece Williams 9.9.84

4 Lucky Find . . . . 1 **HVS 5a**

34m. From the *Riders* traverse, dive up the wall just to the right of *Big C*, to reach slabbier territory. Follow the slabby groove rightwards under a roof, then follow the corner above to the top.

FA. Bill Lounds 1.9.84

Riders on the Storm

The *Riders on the Storm* face is one of those spots which has eluded climbers for years, simply because it is hidden. So now you have the knowledge, and thus no choice but to go and climb possibly the best single-pitch traverse route in Pembroke - *Riders on the Storm*. That route, with its many huge spiky jugs proves to be the cream, but there's more to get pumped on here, and all at about the same magic HVS grade.

Approach - From the ledges below *Limbo*, either abseil in to the route from good spikes, or scramble down at about VDiff, to reach the lower belay ledges, where there's sufficient room for ropes and bodies.

Conditions and Tides - It's only the roughest seas that will keep you away from the exciting traverse that feeds all the routes described here, although a big tide and a calm sea might persuade you to go DWS-style on *C++*! More important is the sheen of moisture that often seems to coat the rock in the mornings - the crag is west-facing, and will generally get drier the later you leave it. So bide your time, let the sun come around, and make it your afternoon/sunset venue.

5 C++ . . . . 1 **HVS 5a**

20m. The shortest line here is most often climbed these day as a DWS (**S2, 5+**) although there is gear! Pull across that first crimpy move on *Riders*, traverse a few metres further, then climb the first line of big jugs found above your head. This brings you to a short cracked orange slab - climb this on its right edge, heading rightwards to traverse-off.

FA. Bill Lounds 15.9.95

Stephen Yeoman on the magnificent *Cool for Cats* (E1) - *page 142* - at Stennis Head. Photo: Nick Smith

St. David's
Flimston Bay
Mewsford
Castle/Rusty
Saddle Head
Bosherston Head
Huntsman's Leap
Stennis/Chapel
Trevallen
St. Govan's
Mowing/Stackpole
Mother Carey's

1 North Corner . . . . **VDiff**
15m. The corner at the left-hand (north!!) end of the first wall.
FA. Colin Mortlock 8.69

2 Highland Fling . . . . 1 **HS 4b**
18m. Start just left of a small corner and roof.
FA. R.Smith 12.8.78

3 Quickstep . . . . 1 **VS 4b**
18m. Climb the small corner and roof to a ledge. Follow the rightwards leaning flake above.
FA. Mike Harber 12.8.78

4 Limbo . . . . 1 **VS 4c**
20m. A good route. Start beneath a corner and overhang in the centre of the wall. Climb around the roof on its right, then move back left above to reach a diagonal crack which leads to another roof. Traverse right beneath this to the finishing corner.
FA. Mike Harber 12.8.78

5 Dire Straits 1 **E2 5c**
18m. Climb up the wall just right of *Limbo* with a hard move to reach two juggy pockets on the right. Continue up left of these to the roof. Pull straight over this on big, but slightly loose, holds.
FA. Jon de Montjoye 30.5.81

6 World War III Blues . . . . **HVS 5b**
18m. The wide crackline on the right-hand side of the upper wall.
FA. Chris Pound 13.8.78

7 Plankwalk 1 **E5 6b**
18m. This outrageously strenuous route follows the groove in the prow to the right of the first short wall. It is gained from beneath the crack of *World War III Blues*. Moving right around the bulge may prove to be just one strength sapping move too many.
FA. Nipper Harrison 18.7.81

8 Hercules . . . . 2 **HVS 5a**
30m. A fine climb up the tall corner above a small cave, where the ledge below the cliff drops down. Climb the corner then move back left and make a grovelling pull onto a ledge (possible belay). Move up and right into the higher corner and climb this to the top.
FA. J.Williams 12.8.78

9 Flash 2 **E4 6a**
30m. A well-named route where a fast approach is vital. Step across the trench and move up into a groove. Sustained climbing above this leads to a break and three small roofs. Pull over these to another break and move leftwards, then make some hard moves into a crack back right. Finish more easily above.
FA. Nipper Harrison 1.9.84

10 Stennis Elbow 1 **E2 5c**
35m. An interesting route which has a very hard initial section which stops many attempts, and then eases considerably above. At the base of the wall is a cave. Climb up into this and step out rightwards along a break. Make a difficult move up the wall right of the cave, then move up and left across the wall to reach the easy upper section. This can be climbed almost anywhere.
FA. Jon de Montjoye 2.5.81

From mid morning
10 min

Manzuko

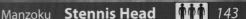

The left-hand side of Stennis Head offers one of the more friendly and accessible crags in Pembroke. It is non-tidal, you can easily walk to the base and comfortably gear-up under your chosen route. The presence of a few superb routes makes it one of the more popular sections of crag around.
Tides and Conditions - It is non-tidal and quick-drying and free from spray from all but the very roughest seas.

⑪ Manzoku . . . . Top 50 E1 5b

35m. 'Satisfaction' in Japanese - the wall left of the arete is superb, popular, polished and usually occupied. Move up to the break below and right of the cave. Traverse this rightwards until it is possible to pull up left into a groove. Move back slightly right to another groove then make a tricky move up left to gain good holds. Follow the wall above on some amazing juggy rock, keeping left of the finishing corner.
FA. Ken Wilkinson 27.8.78

⑫ Cool for Cats 3 E1 5b

35m. Another excellent route. Start as for *Manzoku* but make an extra move right on the traverse from the cave. Pull up onto good holds and continue direct above. Trend slightly leftwards into a groove which leads easily to the top. *Photo on page 141*.
FA. C.Connick 22.4.79

Pleasure Dome

The broad platform below the crag drops down and the walls rear up above impressively culminating in a huge sweep of rock above a permanently-filled inlet. This magnificent wall is crossed by one of the most iconic routes in the country - *Pleasure Dome* (E3) - which traces a beautiful line across a rising weakness, above this beckoning pool. The other routes here tend to be sidelines to the main event but all are worthwhile, although you need to be operating in the E-grades to get the most out of the place. Everything here is intimidating and committing.
Conditions and Tides - None of the routes are tidal although the sloshing pool can catch some big spray if there is a swell running. The lower section is prone to dampness early in the day especially on *Grey English Morning*.

13 Anyone for Stennis . . . . . ☆1 ☐ **E2 5b**
35m. The prominent crackline has a strenuous start with good but hard-earned gear. The crack is gained either directly or from the right. Follow it past a large open bay near the top.
FA. C.Connick 4.5.79

14 Loco Dementia . . . . ☆1 ☐ **E3 6a**
35m. An excellent and underrated route which has a very difficult section on its lower wall. Start down and right of the crack of *Anyone for Stennis*, below a ledge at 3m. Climb with difficulty to the ledge and then make a testing series of moves above to reach a groove which leads to an open bay at the top.
FA. Doug Hall 7.4.80

15 Stennis Pillar . . . . ☆1 ☐ **HVS 5a**
To the right is a trench which turns into a chimney above. This fun route takes the easiest line up the chimney and wall.
1) 25m 5a. Climb the right wall of the chimney past a ledge. Step left to a cave and move left again around a rib. Finish up the bay.
2) 10m 4a. Climb the right-hand side of the bay.
FA. Colin Mortlock 31.5.69

16 Gold Fever . . . . ☐ **E2 5c**
35m. The direct finish to *Stennis Pillar* is seldom climbed. From the small cave at the top of the chimney, climb directly up cracks above to the top.
FA. Ben Wintringham 8.6.80

17 Diagnosis . . . . ☆1 ☐ **E4 6a**
35m. The thin crack left of *Mean Streak*. Climb the rib to a ledge, then move left before stepping up a groove and shuffle left at the bulge for a rest. Follow the crack above to the top of *Mean Streak*.
FA. Nipper Harrison 18.7.81

18 Mean Streak . . . . . . ☆2 ☐ **E5 6a**
35m. The thin right-hand crack above the ledge gives painful, finger-shredding climbing. It is in a very impressive situation but prepare yourself for a real battle; the climbing is not to everyone's liking. Climb easily up the rib as for *Diagnosis*, to a ledge. Move up into the crack and climb it all the way to the top.
FA. Pat Littlejohn 6.4.80

19 Pleasure Dome . . . . Top 50 ☐ **E3 5c**
42m. One thing that makes a route truly great is when it goes somewhere that you don't think is possible at the grade. *Pleasure Dome* must be one of the most classic examples of such a route. It is quite a hard E3 but it is only E3. Climb the rib to the right of the trench to a ledge. Step up to gain the flakeline and follow it rightwards with just enough runners and nowhere near enough foot-holds. Where it blanks out, make a hard move to a non-rest at the top of a rightwards-facing ramp. Move up to some good gear, then climb back down, then move up again and back down, and up and down. Finally pull up again, slightly right of the obvious line and move left to a ledge below the easy finishing corner. Sort your runners out to reduce the rope drag. *Photo on page 134*.
FA. Pat Littlejohn 6.4.80

20 Stennis the Menace / The Great Elmyra
. . . . ☆3 ☐ **E6 6c**
38m. This modern combination of two half routes has become the classic hard tick of this wall. It gives sustained and technical climbing which bisects the *Pleasure Dome* traverse. Climb the bulging wall below to a flake and a bit of a rest. Move up the wall above to an undercut then up to *Pleasure Dome*. Gain a big hold below the thin crack in the headwall (old peg - not crucial). Pull up into the crack with great difficulty and follow it to the top.
StM Original Finish - Move right along *Pleasure Dome*, then pull through the bulge and climb direct to the finishing corner of *Pleasure Dome*. *Photo on page 1*.
FA. (StM) Ron Fawcett 7.82. FA. (TGE) Gary Gibson 25.5.86

21 Grey English Morning . . . ☆3 ☐ **E5 6b**
35m. An amazingly-positioned route which gives sustained climbing up the wall below *Pleasure Dome* after a devious start. The rib at the bottom is often wet and greasy. It has seen few ascents in recent years and may well be bolder now that the peg is old. Start below the short leaning wall and make a juggy traverse right into a corner. Move up and right to reach the (wet) rib. Climb this until it is possible to swing left onto the face (old peg - not crucial). Continue direct above to the base of the ramp on *Pleasure Dome*. Move rightwards up the wall to reach easier ground, and the top. The original start was from a hanging stance in the chimney but this is an uncomfortable stance and your belayer is above you when you start climbing the rib.
FA. Gary Gibson 27.9.87

22 Grey English Wimpout . . . . . ☆2 ☐ **E2 5b**
35m. A combination of other routes but a great way to enjoy this amazing wall at a more-accessible grade. Follow *Grey English Morning* to below its rib, then step across the void and climb the corner to the top. Alternatively, belay at the base of the corner and finish up *Walk on the Wild Side* for an even better **E3 5c**.

23 Walk on the Wild Side . . ☆2 ☐ **E3 5c**
25m. An underrated route which is a good way to get more experience of this wall for people who have already done *Pleasure Dome*. Either abseil down the corner to a ledge just below where the chimney closes, or do the previous route. Climb up into the corner and then step left onto the wall about 3m above where the chimney closes. Follow the easiest line of holds leftwards up the wall until it is possible to move back right to a ledge. Finish direct.
FA. Dave Jones 24.5.81

24 Superbrat . . . . ☆1 ☐ **E2 5c**
A right-to-left traverse of the wall which uses the traverse line below *Pleasure Dome*. Only the first two pitches are included here. Abseil to a ledge near the base of the chimney.
1) 5b, 30m. Step across the chimney and traverse into the corner. Climb up the corner and follow the flake line leftwards to the ledge on the rib at the beginning of the *Pleasure Dome* traverse.
2) 5c, 20m. Climb the red groove above to a bulge, then step left into the corner (this is part of *Diagnosis*). Climb straight up the groove above.
FA. Jon de Montjoye, Ian Parsons 6.12.81

St. David's
Flimston Bay
Mewsford
Castle/Rusty
Saddle Head
Bosherston Head
Huntsman's Leap
Stennis/Chapel
Trevallen
St. Govan's
Mowing/Stackpole
Mother Carey's

Lots of sun
10 min
24
20
22
17
18
19
16
23
24
13
14
15
22
20
21
High tide

Stennis Arete

The east side of the headland contains a number of good routes and an interesting method of gaining the slabby wall right of the enormous chimney below *Pleasure Dome*. The mostly give great adventures and can be done at any tide, in fact they are better at high tide!

Approach - Walk along above the west wall of Stennis Ford and find a grassy ramp which leads to a disappearing rock platform beneath the cliff - gear-up here. Most of the routes start by traversing along the bottom of the face, above the high tide line.

❶ Stennis Chimney . . . . ①☆ Sev

A good trip which gains a ledge below the arete right of the big chimney by a long traverse. Considering the grade, a rope is advisable for this first pitch.

1) 40m. Descend from the end of the disappearing rock platform to and pick the easiest line leftwards, above the high tide line, to a ledge on the arete.

2) 30m. Climb left from the belay then move up onto the wall. Either move left into the corner and climb it or, better, climb the wall to the right of the corner.

FA. Colin Mortlock 31.5.69

❷ Stennis Arete . . . . ②☆ HS 4b

A superbly-positioned route up the prominent arete.

1) 40m. As for pitch one of *Stennis Chimney* (originally the first pitch followed an artificial traverse line above this).

2) 4b, 30m. Climb grooves above the belay up leftwards to the base of *Maelstrom Chimney*. Step right and climb a crack in the arete to the top.

FA. Colin Mortlock 31.5.69

❸ Maelstrom Chimney . . . . ①☆ Sev 4a

Start at the end of the disappearing platform, level with the mid-height break.

1) 4a, 40m. Follow the break leftwards to a ledge on the arete.

2) 15m. Climb up left into a wide blocky chimney.

FA. Colin Mortlock 22.4.69

The next routes take lines up the wall to the right of the arete. The starts are reached by following the easy traverse of Stennis Chimney which can be soloed, for routes of these grades. The most prominent feature is the big corner of Bludgeon. 10m left of this is the crack of Merchant of Stennis.

❹ Fetish. . . . . ①☆ E5 6b

30m. A good technical pitch with a hard finish. Start below and left of the crack of *Merchant*. Climb a corner to a small roof, step right and pull up a wall to a thin crack. Climb this to the top.

FA. Nipper Harrison 8.5.82

❺ Merchant of Stennis . . . . ②☆ E3 5c

30m. A hard classic. Start below and 10m left of the big corner of *Bludgeon*. Climb up to a niche below the crack. Pull up to the mid-height break and then launch yourself into the upper crack (usually past some stuck wires). Climb it to the top.

FA. Brian Wyvill 4.5.81

❻ Bludgeon . . . . ②☆ HVS 5a

30m. An excellent climb up the big corner. This is the first feature encountered when traversing leftwards below the wall. Start below a slim groove below and slightly right of the corner. Climb the groove then step left into the corner and follow it to the top.

FA. Scott Titt 15.4.79

To mid afternoon | 10 min

St. David's | Flimston Bay | Mewsford | Castle/Rusty | Saddle Head | Bosherston Head | Huntsman's Leap | Stennis/Chapel | Trevallen | St. Govan's | Mowing/Stackpole | Mother Carey's

	No star	1	2	3
Mod to S	-	-	-	-
HS to HVS	-	-	-	-
E1 to E3	-	-	-	1
E4 and up	-	3	-	4

This impressive zawn is just a 5 minute walk west along the coast path from St Govan's car park. It is one of the most stared at pieces of rock in the area with ascents regularly attracting a gallery of onlookers. Whether those watching can tell the difference between the regular ascents of the beautiful if slightly unbalanced line of *Mysteries*, from tenuous top-end repeats of *From a Distance*, *Ghost Train* or *Point Blank*, is debatable. If you are the subject of the gazing hoards, then enjoy it, climb smoothly and don't curse too loudly if you fall off!

Approach and Tides

The most usual method is to make a long and spectacular abseil from the stake above *Ghost Train*. It is also possible to scramble down a short path to a ledge on the back wall of the Ford. From here you can set up a wire and sling belay to abseil from.
Most of the base of the Ford is covered at high tide. This includes the bottom of *Mysteries* which is inaccessible for about 2 hours. All of the routes can be reached from mid-tide onwards.

Conditions

Stennis Ford is a place for morning sun, afternoon shade and shelter from the wind. The base of the wall can be a bit slippery just after the tide has gone, or in humid weather. The last few moves on most of the routes involves some gnarly grass crimping so take care.

Italian climber Erik Svab *From a Distance* (E7) - *page 150* - in Stennis Ford. Photo: Mick Ryan

St. David's | Flimston Bay | Mewsford | Castle/Rusty | Saddle Head | Bosherston Head | Huntsman's Leap | Stennis/Chapel | Trevallen | St. Govan's | Mowing/Stackpole | Mother Carey's

1 Questions and Answers **E4 6a**

45m. Good climbing but high in the grade, and take lots of small wires. Start left of the smooth wall from blocks below a large ledge with a square cut corner on its right-hand side. Climb easily up until you are just below the ledge. Traverse right to another corner and climb it to ledges on the left above the corner. Move up above to gain an open continuation groove and follow this to a ledge at the break. Finish easily above.
FA. Pete Whillance 7.5.79

2 The Warsaw Pact . . **E5 6a**

40m. A weaving line up the arete to the left of the smooth wall. Start from boulders below a short crack. Climb the crack and groove above to join *Questions and Answers*. Where that route steps left, move right into another groove in the arete. Follow this and move out right to a flake. Boldly climb the arete above to the ledge at the break. Finish direct.
FA. Gary Gibson 26.4.86

3 From a Distance **E7 6b**

42m. Originally climbed with some bits of drilled gear, the right-hand side of the smooth wall now gives an awesome route which has become surprisingly popular (**F7c**). Start at a thin crack below and right of the smooth wall (as for *Hysteria*). Climb the crack for 5m then move left to a ledge. Attack the desperate crack above to gain some reasonable but hard-earned protection. Move left to a thread and a rest - crucial runner in slot to back-up thread. Climb up above then make a difficult undercut traverse rightwards and move back left to two threads. Move up into some scoops (old pegs - not crucial) above then climb the wall to a wide crack which leads to *Mysteries*. Finish direct up the headwall which is still taxing. *Photo on page 148.*
FA. Steve Monks 16.6.91

4 Point Blank **E8 6c**

45m. The dramatic wall left of *From a Distance*. Very sustained climbing (F8a) with long run-outs, however a huge drop zone means you'll only clock up air-time should you fall from the final hard section at 38m! Follow *From a Distance* until after its second crux (peg and thread). Step left and follow the line of holds leading out into the heart of the wall. Some long moves on crimps and slopers lead up and left to a respite (good peg). Blast up the wall above until a 'point-blank' shot for a shallow pocket marks the end of the difficulties. Finish direct above the break of *Mysteries*. *Photo this page.*
FA. Dave Pickford (unseconded) 4.5.09

Dave Pickford on the first ascent of his route *Point Blank* (E8) - *this page* - in Stennis Ford. Photo: James Marshall

5 Hysteria . . . . . 1 star E5 6a
One star for the top pitch. The first pitch has some frightening and hard moves on shattered rock. Combining pitch 1 of *Mysteries* with pitch 2 of *Hysteria* gives a good **E4 5c,6a**. Start at a crack below a rightwards facing groove.
1) 6a, 20m. Climb the crack and then undercut steeply rightwards and pull around the bulge. Teeter up the groove above, then step right onto the *Mysteries* ramp to belay.
2) 6a, 20m. Climb *Mysteries* for 5m then undercut right under a bulge. Pull over where the angle eases and climb the left-hand crack to the top.
FA. Gary Gibson 31.8.82

6 Suspense . . . . 3 stars E4 5c
Sustained and well protected where it matters and easily as good as *Mysteries*. Start at a small scoop left of *Mysteries*.
1) 20m. Climb the scoop then step left onto the wall and move up to a hole. Pull strenuously around the bulge and continue to *Mysteries*.
2) 25m. Climb up and right above the stance. Either traverse directly rightwards to a flake or step down and swing right on a good hold then move up to the flake. Move right again then climb up to a long ledge. Climb straight up the wall above moving left or right to finish.
FA. Pat Littlejohn 10.5.80

7 Mysteries . . . . 3 stars E3 5c
After a hard start the most famous route in the Ford gives steady HVS climbing up the impressive scoop-line. The lack of grade consistency slightly detracts from the route and it is a fairly low E3 but the start shouldn't be underestimated since it is a little bold. Start below the long scoop-line.
1) 5c, 20m. Climb the scoop with difficulty then follow the ramp up leftwards for 10m and belay where it is most comfortable.
2) 5a, 25m. Continue up the scoops, past a small bulge, to the horizontal break. Move left for 5m then climb past some holes in the wall to a corner on the left. Finish up this.
FA. Pat Littlejohn 13.11.77

8 Ghost Train . . . 3 stars E6 6b
This route looks okay until you abseil down it. It is only then that you realise how steep the wall is. Has been described as a **F7a+** with one long and serious run-out. Start at a crunchy flake to the right of *Mysteries*. Climb the initial wall past flakes (very low thread) to the large break and huge thread runners. Take a deep breath and attack the wall above, moving right to a thin flakeline. Climb this in a position of increasing seriousness to hopefully gain another thread. Follow the easier flake to a break then step right and climb direct to the top.
FA. Mike Owen 18.4.90

	No star	1	2	3
Mod to S	-	-	-	-
HS to HVS	-	-	-	-
E1 to E3	-	5	2	-
E4 and up	-	1	-	-

The Chapel - Pembroke's biggest tourist attraction? Photo: Ian Parnell

Chapel Point is the closest venue to the St Govan's car park, although it sees much less traffic than its neighbours. This is probably due to a combination of seasonal bird restrictions, tidal considerations and a slight lack of well-starred routes. That said, it's well worth a gander, as the two obvious ticks of *Ultravixens* (E1) and *Ultravox* (E2) are brilliant, and the rest of the wall harbours some pretty impressive territory, if not quite up to the same high standard. Alongside the crag you'll find the atmospheric Chapel Cove itself, which might well qualify as Pembroke's most popular tourist trap; random people falling about on slimy green boulders, that sort of thing. It's quite a spot for a bunch of peregrines to hang out.

Access

NO CLIMBING from 1st March to 1 August.

It is also important to remember that Chapel Point IS in the Range even though you can get to it without going through the gate. When the flag is flying, keep away. There is a permanent ban on climbing in the cove itself.

Approach and Tides

Follow signs to the Chapel from the car park.

Low tide approach - Walk down some polished steps, with little bits of sandpaper glued on them, to the remains of the old chapel. Continue through this and head rightwards to a spectacular narrow arch. Walk through this, or around it, to a gently rising platform on the other side. This leads to the non-tidal ledge at the base of the routes.

Mid tide approach - The approach walk is covered but you can abseil in from above to the platform below the face which is only covered at high tide.

Conditions

The cliff is slightly exposed and can be a bit windy. It receives all the available sunshine.

St. David's
Flimston Bay
Mewsford
Castle/Rusty
Saddle Head
Bosherston Head
Huntsman's Leap
Stennis/Chapel
Trevallen
St. Govan's
Mowing/Stackpole
Mother Carey's

No climbing
1 March to 1 August

Lots of sun | 2 min | Tidal

St. David's
Flimston Bay
Mewsford
Castle/Rusty
Saddle Head
Bosherston Head
Huntsman's Leap
Stennis/Chapel
Trevallen
St. Govan's
Mowing/Stackpole
Mother Carey's

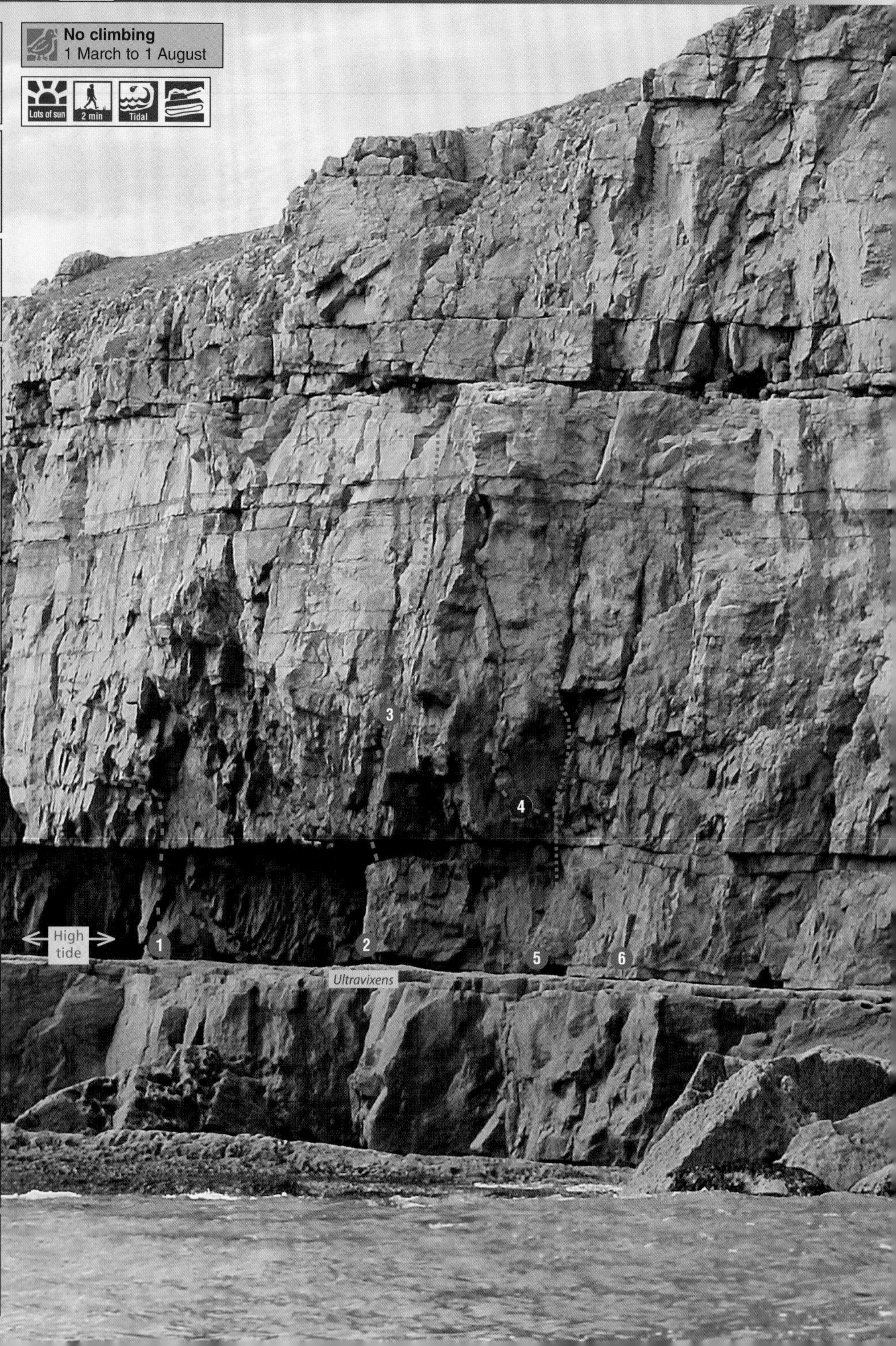

❶ Weekend Warrior . . . . . . ☆1 **E3 5c**
28m. A good, sustained pitch. Climb the low rib, then traverse leftwards just above the overhang, to gain the crack in the face above. Follow this all the way to a small ledge a few metres below the top, then trend a little left to finish.
FA. Pat Littlejohn 18.4.81

❷ Ultravox . . . . ☆2 **E2 5b**
26m. This is only slightly harder than *Ultravixens* and equally as good. Climb *Ultravixens* over the initial roof, into the groove. Then trend up and leftwards to a small ledge. Climb the wall above past a thin break to the wide upper break. Step left and finish up a left-facing corner.
FA. Jon de Montjoye 8.6.81

❸ Ultravixens . . . . ☆2 **E1 5b**
26m. A popular route which is another one on the Pembroke 'tick-n-go' list. Start beneath the narrow projecting block. Climb up this and pull over onto the wall above. Follow a grooveline up and rightwards then move up to a crack. Climb this, with some hard moves past a bulge, to the top break. Step left, pull over the small roof at a wide crack and climb the easy wall above to the top.
FA. Dick Swinden 27.4.80

The next two routes start below a long crack which is about 4m right of the right arete of Ultravixens.

❹ Missing Lynx . . . . ☆1 **E4 6a**
26m. A good climb, start as for *Blockheads*. Climb the crack for 3m and place some gear above. Move left into a blunt flakeline and climb this to the better main flake. Continue to a niche then pull around the arete using a fin of rock. Climb up to a ledge and finish direct up the easy wall above.
FA. Gary Gibson 6.3.88

❺ Blockheads . . . . ☆1 **E2 5c**
27m. The long crack gives an interesting route. Climb the crack to a small roof and pull over this with difficulty. Continue above past some pockets to a ledge. Move right up the wall into a groove above and finish steeply over the small roof.
FA. Steve Lewis 2.9.78

❻ Green Peace . . . . ☆1 **E1 5b**
28m. Start about 3m right of *Blockheads*. Climb up and rightwards, swinging back left to gain the corner above. Climb this to the big ledge, then continue up the well-positioned crack and ramp to the top.
FA. Nipper Harrison 17.4.81

The next routes are 15m to the right, past a rockfall area.

❼ Octobrina . . . . ☆1 **E2 5b**
Some good climbing, and at a consistent grade.
1) 5b, 16m. Climb the lower slab to a thin crack, use this to get to better holds, then move left to the belay ledge.
2) 5b, 18m. Step right, and make a reach for a horizontal break, then continue up for 4m, moving right to gain a decent standing ledge. Pace across the slab to gain the groove of *Promised Hand*, and finish as for that route.
FA. J.Eastham 26.5.81

❽ Promised Hand . . . . ☆1 **E2 5b**
30m. The original line of the two, with some great positions. It's possible to split it at two places in order to reduce rope drag. Take on the edge of the lower slab, to arrive at a small ledge (possible stance). Then traverse leftwards, to climb a slab. Pull through a steepening, to gain a groove (possible stance) follow this then tackle the steep top wall which is short and hard!
FA. J.Jones 27.4.80

No climbing
1 March to 1 August

Trevallen

David Noddings making the most of the incredible exposure on the top pitch of ***The Fascist and Me*** (E4) - *page 165* - at Trevallen. Photo: Alan James

	No star	1 star	2 star	3 star
Mod to S	-	-	-	-
HS to HVS	1	1	1	-
E1 to E3	2	4	5	1
E4 and up	3	10	8	8

For some people the hardest thing about Trevallen is getting back out again. There will be a few climbers out there who have abseiled down to do the classic *The Hole* (HVS) and then struggled to do the start move only to realise that there is no easier escape; persistence usually gets you up though, since above the start it lets up considerably. If you get through this initiation test un-scarred then a whole host of treasures awaits, in fact there is more quality hard climbing here than anywhere else apart from Huntsman's Leap. The climbing follows a distinct series of bands which slope downwards towards the St Govan's end. The lower band contains the meat of most of the routes - some with good gear, like *Sunlover* (E3) and *Yellow Pearls* (E5); and a few big run-outs like *Ships that Pass in the Night* (E5); but all have immaculate and steep rock. The middle band is much more compact giving some bold sections on many routes like *Dogs of Hoare* (E5) - usually more technical than pumpy though. The top of the crag has a series of huge juggy breaks which is nowhere better experienced than on *The Fascist and Me* (E4).

Conditions

The crag faces south and gets all of the afternoon sun. It is actually a bit more sheltered than you might think and the Sunlover Wall is a total sun-trap.

Sunlover end - It dries quickly and it doesn't retain much morning slime. Above the mid-height break, the rock quality deteriorates.

Trevallen Pillar end - As the sea gets nearer, the lower sections can get a bit more greasy. The middle band is composed of shiny grey limestone which is particularly slippery in misty or humid conditions.

Approach and Tides

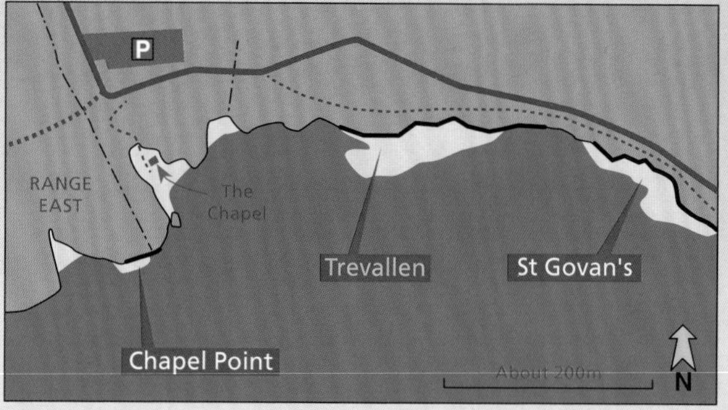

Trevallen is situated to the east of the St Govan's car park, along the headland towards St Govan's. From the car park, walk along the path towards the coastguard lookout. Head right off the path, across the grass, to the clifftop and follow this until a large dusty abseil gully with rope marks is reached. For most of the routes you can abseil down here to the platform at the cliff base. Take extreme care with this gully since it is becoming very loose. Only the routes to the east of the big corner of *Gypsy Lane* and *Romany* are affected by the tide and it is very easy to see what level it is at from the clifftop before you abseil in. The platform below *Trevallen Pillar* is exposed for about 3 or 4 hours at low tide, however, if you are belaying there, be aware that the sea can sneak up on you through the boulders at the base and there are no ledges on the wall which you can scramble up to.

Heugamont

This first area is at the extreme west end of the platform beneath Trevallen, just past the prominent arete of *Sunlover*. The routes here tend to be either steep and savage crack climbs, or bold wall climbs and they are all in the upper E-grades. These routes see few ascents.

There are 3 hard routes left of Heugamont - **Not Tonight Josephine (E5 6a)**, **Waterloo (E6 6b)** *and* **Napoleon Bone Apart (E6 6b)** *all of which rely on a lot of old fixed gear.*

1 Heugamont 2 **E5 6a**
28m. The long slim groove has an 'ankle breaker' start. Climb the right wall of the groove, to a semi-rest. Continue past some uninspiring gear to a pseudo-haven on the left arete. From here easy, but extremely worrying moves, lead to the break. Finish rightwards over the roof and up the loose wall above. Bold!
FA. Gary Gibson 29.5.84

2 Man from Uncle . 2 **E6 6b**
28m. A nasty pitch which keeps getting harder. Bold climbing up the wall leads to a poor peg (good wires). Make a long move to an unhelpful crack with more good wires. One more desperate move is needed to gain a good flake which leads to easier climbing and a ledge on the right. Finish with care up the wall.
FA. Gary Gibson 29.5.84

3 Versaille. 2 **E4 6a**
28m. In the centre of the wall is a long crack. This proves to be a sustained test of barn-door moves and awkward-to-place wires. It eases as you approach the ledge at the break. Finish as for *Man from Uncle*.
FA. Gary Gibson 27.3.85

4 Fat Finger Exercise . 1 **E5 6a**
28m. A beefy route up the wide crack, which is difficult to protect and you need more than just fat fingers to climb it. Start from the right-hand end of the pedestal, gain the crack and climb it. A hard move is needed to reach the wider upper crack. Where it closes climb the wall above to the break and finish up the flake on the left.
FA. Gary Gibson 1.6.84

5 Physical Jerks 1 **E5 6b**
30m. A desperate struggle up the wicked cracks just right of the pedestal. Climb the cracks then slap rightwards into a groove. Move back left to a blunt arete and climb this to the ledge. Finish up the wobbly wall above.
FA. Gary Gibson 10.4.85

6 The Bitch 1 **E5 6b**
30m. This well-named route follows the middle of three cracks left of the *Sunlover* arete. Climb the crack with some difficulty and move left to a ledge. Climb the right-hand side of the scoop above to a ledge. Step left and finish as for *Physical Jerks*.
FA. Pat Littlejohn 21.4.82

7 Joan. 1 **E4 6a**
30m. An easier-than-it-looks climb up the *Bitch-like* crack right of *The Bitch*. Slightly artificial since it is too close to its neighbours. Climb the crack then move up the slabby wall above to the big ledge, stepping left where it blanks out. Finish as for *Physical Jerks*.
FA. Steve Lewis 10.6.84

The top section above the big break can be a bit loose so take care and follow the most stable line. Alternatively pre-place a rope at the top and lower off.
Lots of sun
5 min
Abseil in
1
2
3
4
5
6
7

St. David's
Flimston Bay
Mewsford
Castle/Rusty
Saddle Head
Bosherston Head
Huntsman's Leap
Stennis/Chapel
Trevallen
St. Govan's
Mowing/Stackpole
Mother Carey's

8 Sunlover . . . . Top 50 **E3 5c**

30m. One of Pembroke's most famous routes follows the shiny arete. There is a bit of polish at the start, but not higher up where it matters. Make a steep pull up to the break, then swing left and move up to place some wires (possibly the crux). Climb the fingery wall above to reach better holds. Trend rightwards under some bulges then move up onto a large ledge. Climb the corner above and exit a little further right than is obvious.

FA. Nick Colton 5.4.80

9 Pearl Powder 1 **E6 6b**

30m. This direct variation on *Sunlover* has some excellent climbing. It is technically slightly easier than *Yellow Pearls* but has poorer gear which is also hard to place. Climb direct from the initial crack on *Sunlover* to reach the break. Follow the wall just right of *Sunlover* to the big ledge. Step left and climb the arete to the top.

FA. Gary Gibson 9.4.85

Sunlover

The Sunlover Wall is the big white wall, behind the huge block on the platform, to the left (looking in) of the abseil. It is probably the most popular spot at Trevallen with some superb climbs which mostly follow steep and strenuous cracklines, between horizontal breaks.

Karin Magog setting off on the traverse of *Youth on Fire* (E3) - *opposite* - on the Sunlover Wall. Photo: Alan James

⑩ Yellow Pearls . . . . . Top 50 E5 6b

30m. A stunning climb which follows the crackline above and right of the *Sunlover* start. Move right out of *Sunlover* then climb up to the fingery cracks which swallow wires. Hard moves lead to the break where a grovelling mantel gains the ledge on the right. Climb the easier, but still testing, wall on the left to a junction with *Sunlover* at the ledge. Finish as for this. Feels around **F7a+**.

FA. Ron Fawcett 7.82

⑪ Boss Hogg 2 E6 6b

30m. Yet another savage climb which follows the vague crackline above the centre of the undercut base - take loads of small wires. First get established on the wall (well hard) then struggle up the cracks above with small breathers at the breaks. Eventually you may arrive at the large break (big breather). Climb the easier wall above to the top. Around **F7b+**.

FA. Ron Fawcett 7.82

⑫ Barbarella. . . . . Top 50 E5 6a

30m. A strenuous and well-protected crack climb to the break, with a technical and slightly bold direct finish for dessert. Start below a groove and prominent crack, in the centre of the wall. Climb the groove to a flake on the left. Make a hard move into the crack above which gives sustained climbing to the big break. Pull over onto the upper wall, place some wires, and climb it to the top via some tricky and committing moves.

FA. Pat Littlejohn 30.4.80.FA. (Direct) Gary Gibson 16.3.86. It originally moved left along the big break to where Boss Hogg now finishes.This version is also worth E5.

⑬ Orange Robe Burning Top 50 E6 6b

30m. Some find this the best climb on the wall, especially if you are tall. Climb the rib right of *Barbarella* (thread out left) then follow a line of holds up right to a small groove. Climb the groove (microswires and a peg) and make a hard move left to a crack and the first bomber wire. Move left again then back right and up to the break. Arrange gear above, then make an outrageous l-o-n-g move to a good hold with a thread. Finish any way you can above.

FA. Gary Gibson 11.3.85

⑭ Fulmar Pants. . . . . HVS 5a

The corner at the right-hand side of the wall.

1) 5a, 20m. Climb the flaky corner to a ledge and belay.

2) 5a, 15m. The corner above the belay is followed to a roof. Hand traverse left and pull onto a ledge. An easy corner above leads to the top.

FA. J.Jones, Dick Turnbull 26.4.80

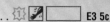

⑮ Youth on Fire. 1 E3 5c

30m. A worthy eliminate line which has some good positions. Step left out of *Fulmar Pants* across the steep wall. Climb past a thread then move back right to a ledge at the break. Ledges on the wall above lead to the finish of *Fulmar Pants*. *Photo opposite.*

I Saw, E6 6c - Traverse left out of *Fulmar Pants* at a lower level to a small hole, then climb direct before moving back right above the break.

FA. Gary Gibson 24.3.85. FA. (I Saw) Gary Gibson 17.3.87

Lots of sun | 5 min | Abseil in

St. David's
Flimston Bay
Mewsford
Castle/Rusty
Saddle Head
Bosherston Head
Huntsman's Leap
Stennis/Chapel
Trevallen
St. Govan's
Mowing/Stackpole
Mother Carey's

1 The Energy Funnel . . . . . 1 star — **E3 6a**

12m. Climb out of the cave down and right of the abseil, using some big undercuts, to reach a crack. Follow this to a wider crack and some threads to lower from.
FA. Paul Donnithorne 5.1.88

2 Hands of the Hunter . . . . 1 star — **E4 6a**

35m. A good wall climb. From a ledge right of the cave, climb the testing and bold wall above, first right then left to a small ledge. Move up to a break and continue past a wide crack rightwards to the upper break. Finish as for *Enter the Goat.*
FA. Rab Anderson 19.4.84

3 Goats that Go Gnash in the Night . — **E3 6a**

35m. Climb straight up the wall to the left of *Enter the Goat.* From the break, step left and climb the wall past some threads.
FA. Paul Donnithorne 3.1.88

4 Enter the Goat . . . . 1 star — **E2 5b**

35m. A popular route. Start below a right-trending line of holds in the middle of the wall. Move up to a ledge then climb the wall above to the break (old peg). Step right to a crack and follow this until it is possible to move left across the wall, on good holds, to a wide break. Finish straight up the wall above.
FA. Jon de Montjoye 17.7.82

5 The Hole . . . . 2 stars — **HVS 5b**

35m. Even if most of Trevallen is beyond you at present, this route is well worth seeking out. It climbs the remarkable tube high on the wall right of the abseil. Start below and left of the tube, at a rising line of holds. Climb these from the left (or climb directly to them from below at **E1 5c**). The wide crack and wacky tube above are then followed more easily to the top. *Photo opposite.*

6 Travellin' Man . . . . — **E4 6a**

35m. Climb the steep groove directly below the tube. Move up and right onto the wall and continue to a ledge. Step right and climb the wall above past a peg. Either move left into *The Hole*, or step right and climb direct to the top (harder but still only **E4**).
FA. Gary Gibson 16.1.88

7 Dead Ringer . . . . — **E2 5b**

38m. The vast corner at the right-hand end of the wall gives a big expedition. Start at a groove 5m right of the corner. Climb this then step into the corner proper. Climb past a bay then move onto the left wall which is followed to the roof. Move around this on its left-hand side and finish up the groove above. It can be started direct via a squirmy chimney.
FA. Jon de Montjoye 26.6.82

The Hole

The wall beneath the abseil at Trevallen hasn't got buckets of stars but there are some interesting contrasting pitches and two of Trevallen's more popular routes. It is non-tidal and a reasonably sheltered sun-trap.

St. David's
Flimston Bay
Mewsford
Castle/Rusty
Saddle Head
Bosherston Head
Huntsman's Leap
Stennis/Chapel
Trevallen
St. Govan's
Mowing/Stackpole
Mother Carey's

Ben Sutton climbing the lower wall of *The Hole* (HVS) - *opposite* - at Trevallen. Photo: Chris Sims

St. David's | Flimston Bay | Mewsford | Castle/Rusty | Saddle Head | Bosherston Head | Huntsman's Leap | Stennis/Chapel | Trevallen | St. Govan's | Mowing/Stackpole | Mother Carey's

1 Gypsy Lane . 1 **HVS 5a**
The route up the open corner at the east end of the large platform beneath the abseil has a good first pitch. After that it is a matter of "any way out will do!"
1) 5a, 20m. Climb the corner, moving right around the roof to a large hole. Belay on the ledge.
2) 4b, 15m. Climb the groove and corner on the left to the top. Take care with loose rock.
FA. Richard Crewe 1981

2 Romany 2 **E3 5c**
20m. A 2-star first pitch up the right wall of the corner is high in the grade. Climb the bold lower section to a small ledge. Move up to the break then right to some cracks which are followed to the large break. Either traverse left to belay and finish up *Gypsy Lane*; or better, traverse right to the large ledge and abseil from threads.
FA. Jon de Montjoye 15.11.82

3 Breaking the Habit 2 **E7 6c**
20m. The magnificent right arete gives a desperate challenge. Climb over steep bulges into the hanging groove then head straight up to the mid-height ledge.
The Meaning of Life, E4 5c - The upper groove can be reached by a rightwards traverse from *Romany*.
Abseil off from threads on the ledge.
FA. Pete Oxley 5.88. First climbed from the start of Romany with two bolts. The direct version described, without the bolts, had a peg and a spike but these have disappeared making it bolder.

Pete Davies and David Noddings cutting it fine with a wild incoming sea on the first pitch of *The Fascist and Me* (E4) - *this page* - at Trevallen. Photo: Alan James

The section of Trevallen which stretches east towards St Govan's is one of the most dramatic bits of rock along the coast line. The cliff is so steep here that there are only a few weaknesses, hence the existing routes are a bit sparse. The most popular route by far takes an unlikely line up the buttress right of the deepest cave.

4 The Fascist and Me Top 50 **E4 6a**

A stunning route up the big wall right of the cave. The top pitch is like climbing a line of bolt-on jugs up the bow of a ship! *Photo this page and page 156.*

1) 6a, 20m. Climb the awkward lower wall to a small roof. Move up and left onto a nicely-placed sloping ledge. Step left to a hole then climb up and back right via a hard move and continue easily to the ledge.

2) 5c, 20m. The loose groove on the right leads to a ledge below a flake crack. Arrange some gear in this, then swing left along a finger traverse line to a thread. Make a hard move up then move right onto the arete which is followed to the top.

FA. Gary Gibson 26.2.88

5 The Coriolis Affair . 2 **E2 5c**

A good route in some impressive territory but lacking slightly in line.

1) 5c, 20m. Make a steep footless pull up left then move up to a roof. Pull over to gain a break up then climb up towards the arete. Pull around onto the front face and climb up to the wide ledge above.

2) 5b, 25m. Walk left (re-belay) then climb direct up the brown wall and break-covered wall above to the top.

FA. Paul Donnithorne, T.Mean 26.1.88

St. David's
Flimston Bay
Mewsford
Castle/Rusty
Saddle Head
Bosherston Head
Huntsman's Leap
Stennis/Chapel
Trevallen
St. Govan's
Mowing/Stackpole
Mother Carey's

S
S
Lots of sun
8 min
Tidal
Abseil in
High tide
1
2
3
4
5

Trevallen Pillar

As you walk under Trevallen the crag gets bigger and bigger as the platform tapers away into the sea. The next prominent feature is also the location of one of Trevallen's best known routes - *Trevallen Pillar*.

❶ Trevallen Pillar . . . . Top 50 ☐ E4 6a

45m. A majestic climb which provides an excellent introduction to Pembroke E4s. It was traditionally climbed in two pitches with a belay at the break on the left. Now most people link them into one long pitch due to the difficulty of belaying the initial move of the old pitch 2. Step off the monster pebble and climb a short groove and crack to the break. Move right and pull up into a leftwards rising line of holds. Follow this to its end then make a tricky pull up above and continue to the small cave (possible belay). Arrange some gear above then swing right and climb the shiny grey slab - hard at first but it gets easier. Continue up the steep wall above to the top. *Photo on back cover flap.*

FA. Jon de Montjoye, Ian Parsons 20.6.81

❷ Ships that Pass in the Night . . . . 3 ☐ E5 6a

The right arete of the pillar gives an elegant experience in head climbing which just merits the grade.

1) 6a, 20m. Climb the right-hand side of the arete until it is possible to pull around onto its left. Tip-toe up this side past a small roof (old peg). Move up past a small wire to a square hold, then climb the dinky groove above with some excitement.

2) 5b, 25m. Climb the shallow groove behind the belay to the next ledge, then move left into *Trevallen Pillar*. Finish up this.

FA. Gary Gibson 30.4.83

❸ Abandon Ship . . . . . 2 ☐ (E5 6a)

The next route was always a very top-end E5. Now that the peg is probably not trustworthy anymore, it is almost certainly worth E6.

1) 6a, 20m. From just right of the arete, follow a thin line of holds rightwards to the base of a crack - this is the bold bit so take some microwires! Climb the crack, then move right to an old peg. The groove above leads to the ledge.

2) 5b, 25m. Finish as for *Ships that Pass*.

FA. Gary Gibson 15.6.85

❹ Sachsenring . . . . 2 ☐ E5 6b

Another brilliant and bold climb. Start below the twin grooveline.

1) 6b, 20m. Climb the lower groove and move right to a spike. Step back into the upper groove, lace the bottom with gear and start climbing it until you reach the ledge or your confidence fails!

2) 5b, 25m. Move left along the ledge and finish as for *Ships...*

FA. Jon de Montjoye 2.5.82

❺ Dogs of Hoare . . . . 3 ☐ E5 6a

Here we go again, another superb route with a bold bit! This time you are allowed a pitch to warm up on. Start below the groove midway between the arete and the big central corner.

1) 6a, 20m. Climb the groove to a crack. Move right to another crack and follow this to the ledge.

2) 6a, 25m. Climb a short way up the flake above the belay and stick some gear in. Move right to a tiny wire then right again to a chunky side hold. Make a committing move upwards to large holds - bold because you will hit the ledge if the wire pulls, which it probably will. Step back left and climb up the wide crack and superbly-exposed groove above.

FA. Jon de Montjoye 20.3.82

See next page for routes on this side

St. David's
Flimston Bay
Mewsford
Castle/Rusty
Saddle Head
Bosherston Head
Huntsman's Leap
Stennis/Chapel
Trevallen
St. Govan's
Moving/Stackpole
Mother Carey's

The Mercenary

To the right of Trevallen Pillar is a vast wall which gives a series of stunning climbs. The cliff is divided into three distinct bands. The lower band has the main steep wall pitches, the middle band tends to give short bold sections, and the top band is steep and juggy. Most of the routes are split into two pitches with belays on one of the breaks.

Tides and Approach - The routes are all best approached using the usual abseil. The base is covered from mid to high tide.

6 Just Another Dog E5 6b

45m. Start just left of the big groove of *Soldier of Fortune*. Climb the wall above via a thin flake then move back left to gain a diagonal crack (bold). Follow this and exit leftwards up the tricky wall to the big break, which has inconveniently turned into a roof since the last route. Move right and pull over the roof and continue to a ledge (possible belay). Finish up the crack left of the corner.

FA. Gary Gibson 6.3.88

7 Soldier of Fortune E1 5b

The big central groove provides a welcome relief from the sustained hard boldness around it.

1) 5b, 35m. Climb up into the groove and follow it to the break. Lean around the roof and reach a bucket. Heave around the lip and continue up the loose-looking (but solid) wall to a ledge.

2) 4c, 10m. Climb the crack/groove just right of the corner.

FA. Jon de Montjoye 21.3.82

8 Private Schultz E4 6a

A wandering eliminate which, even though it lacks line, does cover some impressive territory.

1) 6a, 25m. Start as for *Soldier of Fortune* but step right to reach the small subsidiary groove to the right. Follow this to the break then hand traverse right until you are below a hanging crack. Climb the hard wall and crack to the cave.

2) 5c, 25m. Finish as for *High Pressure*.

FA. Gary Gibson 11.3.85

9 Fortune Cookie E6 6b

The wall just right of *Soldier of Fortune* gives a big hard pitch which makes some of the others on this wall look like Sunday afternoon strolls. A big cam is crucial for the start.

1) 6b, 35m. Climb the wall moving slightly left to a small groove (thread). Move up and left and climb the right arete of the groove above to a good flake hold. Hard moves gain the break and yet more hard moves gain a standing position above the roof. Exit left to better holds and the belay ledge on the right.

2) 5c, 10m. Finish up the crack in the left wall of the recess.

FA. Gary Gibson 3.90. Originally it was climbed with drilled gear, this was removed and the route re-climbed.

10 High Pressure E4 6b

The next route continues the theme of testing technical wall climbs with thought-provoking gear. 10m left of the arete is a shallow groove which turns into a wide crack.

1) 6b, 20m. Climb the groove with increasing difficulty to eventually reach the crack with some relief. Follow this to a break, then traverse left until you are below another crack. Climb this crack to a cave and hanging belay.

2) 5c, 25m. Step 3m left then pull over into a thin crack which leads to a ledge on the left. Move back right and climb the bulging groove above to the top.

FA. Jon de Montjoye 18.4.82

11 The Honeymoon Killers E5 6a

Yet another bold pitch.

1) 6a, 20m. Start just right of the line of *High Pressure*. Climb the wall to a good jug at 6m. Move left to a crack and climb this past an undercut to the half-height ledge.

2) 5c, 25m. Either walk off rightwards to St Govan's, or climb the last pitch of *The Mercenary*.

FA. Gary Gibson 19.3.84

12 Reach for the Sky. . . E3 5c

The big right arete of the wall gives a fine route.

1) 5c, 20m. Start just left of the arete and climb up onto a small ledge on the right. Move back left onto the arete and climb it. The move that the route is named after is at the top.

2) 5c, 25m. Walk off right to St Govan's, or finish up *The Mercenary*.

FA. Nipper Harrison 15.8.82

13 Storm Trooper E2 5b

20m. The left wall of the corner has a crack snaking up it which gives a good pitch which is a bit of a hand-shredder. Start as *Reach for the Sky* and climb up to a ledge below the crack. Climb the crack to the ledge. Walk off to St Govan's.

FA. M.Butler 23.5.81

14 The Mercenary E3 5c

A great route with two testing pitches and a magnificent 'pat-on-the-back' finishing arete.

1) 5c, 20m. Climb the corner, which is hard at first but eases above, to a small roof. Swing right to a wide crack which leads to the ledge.

2) 5c, 25m. Climb the left-hand of two blank corners to another ledge (small microwires useful). Swing like an ape up the steep crack in the left-hand side of the arete to the top.

FA. Jon de Montjoye 5.12.81

15 Dinkum Wall E3 5c

This popular route has two contrasting, high quality pitches. The first pitch is an excellent **E1 5b** in its own right and from the top you can easily walk off to St Govan's.

1) 5b, 20m. Start 5m right of the corner and climb the wall to reach a vague crack. Follow this to a break and traverse right to another crack. A hard move at the top of this gains a short groove which leads to the ledge.

2) 5c, 25m. Climb the leftwards slanting groove behind the stance, to a ledge. Then follow the steep wall and groove above to the top.

FA. Ian Parsons, Jon de Montjoye 20.6.81

16 Brown Bess. E4 6a

20m. This minor eliminate up the wall left of *Dinkum Wall* has a short hard section. Start as for *Dinkum Wall* but move out left to reach a small groove. Swing left out of this to reach a wide crack which leads easily up to join *The Mercenary*. Walk off, or finish up *The Mercenary*.

FA. Gary Gibson 11.3.85

17 Perth Pink. E4 6a

20m. The steep crack in the wall right of *Dinkum Wall* pitch 2 is a lot harder than it looks. Start from the belay of *Dinkum Wall*, reached either from St Govan's, or from below. Climb the groove of *Dinkum Wall* then move right to gain the crack which leads, somewhat steeply, to the top.

FA. Doug Hall 15.3.86

Lots of sun
8 min
Tidal
Abseil in
S
S
17
St Govan's
8
13
16
7
High tide
6
9
10
11
12
14
15

St Govan's

Alan James making the traverse on the classic *Army Dreamers* (HVS) - *page 175* - at St Govan's. Photo: Mark Glaister

	No star	1 star	2 stars	3 stars
Mod to S	1	2	-	-
HS to HVS	8	6	3	1
E1 to E3	5	11	6	5
E4 and up	5	9	6	2

This army-free region needs little introduction for most seasoned visitors; just about every Pembroke devotee has spent time and energy devouring the crag's colossal spread of highly-charged classics. These mega-lines include *Tactician* (HVS), *The Arrow* (E1), *Deranged* (E2), *Space Cadet* (E3), *Tangerine Dream* (E4) and *Get Some In* (E5). Have no fear; your ticklist will prove to be almost unquenchable. The one minor glitch in the proceedings is the mammoth rockfalls that have taken place during the last decade - gone is *Conscientious Objector* and its close neighbours, along with much of the quality of the Zodiac Face. But what remains still provides a stupendous number of high-quality routes, including some of the very best ticks in the county. Enjoy, and return often.

Conditions

The starts of the routes often involve heaving up the steep juggy breaks which run along the base of the cliff. These breaks tend to be moisture magnets although they are usually still climbable because the holds are big. Higher up it is often drier. All the buttresses are well sheltered from the most common wind directions and, if the sun shines, it can be an unbearable sun-trap.

Tony Whitehouse on the neglected soaring crack of *The Kraken* (E1) - *page 179* - St. Govan's. Photo: Alan James

Approach and Tides

From St Govan's car park, follow the path towards the coastguard lookout at the end of the headland. The first cliff you pass is Trevallen. As the path veers rightwards you arrive at a grass-less area by a large detached block.
The most common approach from here is to abseil from stakes down the corner of *Gandhi*. As an alternative, scramble down the chimney behind the large block (a shiny Diff). Both left and right branches are about the same difficulty. Another alternative is to abseil down the Deranged Area onto the ramp below.
Another reason for the popularity of St Govan's is that it is mostly non-tidal. Everything up to *The Arrow* is above the tide level. High spring tides just reach the base of *The Arrow* but only cut it off, and access beneath it, for about an hour at most. The Deranged Area is always accessible by abseil and most of the routes are clear of high water.
As you travel further east (right looking in) the base drops away and the tide becomes more significant.

Front Line

The dominant arete of *Front Line* gives one of the first popular ticks of St Govan's. To the left (looking in) of this are a series of cracks and aretes with some less popular but still worthwhile routes.

1 The Candlestick Maker . . . . . 1★ **E1 5b**
20m. The arete is approach from the right.
FA. Nipper Harrison 4.5.86

2 Lemming Way . . . . 1★ **Sev**
20m. A decent easier route up the corner. A bit cramped.
FA. H.Parsons 22.9.79

3 Exit Corner . . . . **VDiff**
20m. Straightforward climbing up the open corner with ledges.
FA. Pete Whillance 30.12.76

4 Sandbagged . . . . 1★ **VS 4c**
20m. Gain and finish up the cracks right of *Exit Corner*.
FA. Charlie Heard 17.9.92

The lines of the original versions of the next two routes are unclear. The two listed below take the most logical lines up the wall and adopt the names of the original routes, but have different grades.

5 Just Before Dark **E1 5a**
20m. Climb up to the central groove. Follow this then the wall above on the left to the top. Thin gear on the lower section.
FA. Charlie Heard 17.9.92

6 Rock-a-Block . . . . **HVS 5a**
20m. Start up a short groove left of the arete then follow the flake up left. Steep cracks above lead to the top. Strenuous but good gear.
FA. Paul Donnithorne 22.1.87. Given E3 5c so probably a different line.

7 On Wenlock Edge . . . . . . 1★ **E4 5c**
25m. The left (looking in) arete of the descent gully gives a good steep route with an exciting finish. Climb the short groove of Rock-a-Block but move right to climb the arete, then move onto the right-hand side above to gain a thin crack. Contemplate putting some wires in this, then push on to the top while your strength lasts.
FA. Gary Gibson 27.3.85

8 Rub-a-Dub-Dub **E2 5c**
25m. Start *On Wenlock Edge*. Move right onto a ledge and step right to gain a crack. Climb this to the top.
FA. Gary Gibson 29.5.84

9 Stacked Against . . . . **VS 4b**
25m. Start up the arete then move right to a short groove which leads to a ledge. Continue up the arete above.
FA. Barry Clarke 7.8.81

10 Kinvig . . . . 1★ **E1 5b**
25m. Climb cracks up the face left of *Front Line*. Rough rock.
FA. Andy Pollitt 10.81

11 Front Line . . . . 2★ **HVS 5a**
25m. The magnificent hanging groove in the front arete of the block gives a popular pitch. Start by climbing up on the left then pulling across to gain a short groove above the roof. Move right into the main groove and climb it.
Variation, E1 5a - The steep groove left of the main groove.
FA. Dave Armstrong 31.12.76

St. David's | Flimston Bay | Mewsford | Castle/Rusty | Saddle Head | Bosherston Head | Huntsman's Leap | Stennis/Chapel | Trevallen | St. Govan's | Mowing/Stackpole | Mother Carey's

Army Dreamers

Army Dreamers is one of the great Pembroke classics up the steep cracks in the front face of the block. The other routes on this wall offer little quality competition to *Army Dreamers*, being either bold wall climbs or wide cracks, but *Bomb Bay* is worthwhile.

Right of the arete is a wall split by a series of cracks.

12 The Baker E2 5c
30m. The actual arete of the block gives an escapable pitch. Pull over a roof to gain a crack on the right-hand side. Climb this then continue up the arete above to the top.
FA. Andy Pollitt 21.9.81

13 Army Dreamers . . . . Top 50 HVS 5a
25m. An extremely popular route, especially on bank holidays. Start below a very wide crack in the east wall of the block. Climb up into the crack then make a slippery traverse left to a well-positioned thinner crack. Follow this to the top. *Photo on page 170.*
Direct Start, E4 6a - The crack can be reached direct by a bold sequence of moves on rounded holds. Much harder than it looks.
FA. Steve Lewis 3.80. FA. (Direct) Andy Pollitt 21.9.81

14 Shell Shock. . . . . VS 4c
20m. This route gives a graunchy experience up the monstrous wide crack in the east wall of the block.
FA. Dave Armstrong 2.1.78

15 Sharp Shooter E4 5c
20m. The wall in between the two big cracks has a bold little route. Climb the wall fairly directly, with the bold bit just above the first line of breaks.
FA. Tony Mitchell 25.9.85

16 Bomb Bay . . . . VS 4c
20m. This route follows the *big-but-not-as-big-as-the-other-one* crack, in the right-hand side of the wall.
FA. Pete Whillance 2.1.78

17 Bomb Scare E4 6a
20m. The wall between the two cracks is both bold and technical. It may be harder than E4 since the jammed wire used on the first ascent has long gone.
FA. Gary Gibson 18.5.86

18 Panzer II. . . . . HVS 5a
20m. The last of the crack climbs in this wall follows the thin crack just left of the descent gully.
FA. Sid Siddiqui 4.80

St. David's
Flimston Bay
Mewsford
Castle/Rusty
Saddle Head
Bosherston Head
Huntsman's Leap
Stennis/Chapel
Trevallen
St. Govan's
Mowing/Stackpole
Mother Carey's

The Butcher

One of the most popular walls in Pembroke is dominated by the big arete of *The Butcher*. All the routes here are worth doing although most pack a punch and should not be underestimated. This is not a good place to start your Pembroke career yet often it turns to be just that for many first time visitors.

Approach - There is an abseil down *Incest* but check first if people are climbing. The scramble descent is better - see page 173.

1 Up Against the Wall . . . . HVS 5a
25m. Climb the harder-than-it-looks lower wall to gain a niche and finish direct. Not as well protected as you might think.
FA. Sid Siddiqui 4.80

2 Chieftain . . . . 1 VS 5a
25n. Start just left of the arete and follow the crack to the top.
Variation, E1 5b - traverse right from high on the route to reach another crack.
FA. Jeff Lamb 31.12.76

3 The Butcher . . . . Top 50 E3 5c
25m. Easy E3 or hard E2, the discussions will go on for ever - this time we have gone with the harder grade, next time, who knows? Start below the arete and climb a crack in its right-hand side. Make a satisfying move leftwards to a jug on the arete, then move back right to finish. Some people accidentally continue direct from where the crack ends which makes it about 6a (and proper E3!). *Photo opposite and on the back cover.*
FA. Pat Littlejohn 26.4.80

4 Vice is Nice 1 E2 5b
25m. Steep climbing up the left-hand of the two cracks under the abseil. It can be dirty but is good when clean and dry.
FA. Steve Bancroft 5.4.80

5 But Incest is Best 1 E1 5b
25m. The right-hand crack is equally popular but tends to be a little dirtier if anything due to it being right in the abseil line.
FA. Steve Bancroft 7.4.80

6 Gandhi . . . . VS 4c
25m. The route up the left-hand side of the open corner tends to be too dirty to be much fun. High in the grade.
FA. S.Blackman 1982

7 Centurion . . . . 1 Sev 4a
25m. The right-hand side of the corner is not as dirty as *Gandhi*. It sees few ascents but is a useful grade for this crag. The pull around the bulge near the top needs determination.
FA. J.Taylor 2.1.78

8 The Loosener . . . . 1 HVS 5a
25m. To the right of the open corner is a blunt arete which is undercut on its right-hand side. This route follows the crack to the left of the arete. Not very well named, thankfully.
FA. Bernard Newman 7.4.80

9 Clean Hand Blues Band . 2 E1 5b
25m. A popular route which is often found hard by people who climb it too directly. Start just left of the detached flake on the ledge. Climb up to the bulge then pull round virtually on the arete to gain the finger-traverse which leads back right. Move up and back left to gain the delightful finishing slab.
FA. Steve Bancroft 5.4.80

10 Munchies . . . . HVS 5a
25m. Climb the groove above the large detached flake/block.
FA. Al Evans 4.80

Lots of sun | 8 min

Luke Roberts on the big hold on the arete of *The Butcher* (E2.5?) - *opposite* - at St Govan's. Photo: Nick Smith

1 Let Him Babble On. **E4 6a**
25m. A decent route which packs it in above the roof. Start at the right-hand end of the ledge. Climb up then move right onto a small slab and follow this on its left-hand side to the roof. Arrange some gear then pull onto the wall and climb it with some urgency.
Babbalonia, E4 6a - The right-hand line around the roof.
FA. Gary Gibson 24.3.85. FA. (Babbalonia) Gary Gibson 27.4.86

2 Desire **E1 5b**
28m. Start from the right-hand end of the ledge underneath the *Vice/Incest* wall. Climb easily up to the ledge beneath the corner (possible belay to reduce rope drag and improve communication). Climb the corner to the top.
FA. Sid Siddiqui 15.8.80

3 Piggy's Crack **E1 5b**
30m. This thuggy climb tackles the steep curving crack to the right of the corner of *Desire*. Although the difficult section isn't that long, it does pack a lot in. Start as for *Desire*, to the ledge beneath the corner. From the right-hand end of the ledge, launch up the crack.
FA. Al Evans 4.80

The next section is the home of some long testing pitches which tend to give steep and sustained climbing above the ledge which runs across at 1/3 height. The wall below this ledge has three approach lines up it which are easy but a bit thin on gear.

4 Charisma **E4 6a**
35m. A good route with one hard move. The peg can be backed up but the route is probably now worth E4. Climb the lower wall to the ledge. Move up to the base of a ramp and follow it to its end. Make a difficult move up the wall above, then move right into a groove and climb this to the top.
FA. Al Evans 15.8.80

5 John Wayne **E5 6a**
35m. A steep and taxing pumper. From the ramp on *Charisma*, follow a crack up and left to a small roof (old peg - other gear available). Pull over this into another crack and continue past a thread to the top.
FA. Gary Gibson 4.7.85

Mark Glaister tackling the sustained moves up the groove of *Test Case* (E3) - *this page* - at St Govan's. Photo: Alan James

6 Test Case . . . . Top 50 E3 5c

35m. An excellent and popular route which follows the main line of the wall. The climbing in the groove is superb and very pumpy. The upper wall is much easier but has some loose rock so make sure you get some good gear in. Start beneath the weakness in the lower wall. Climb up to the flake/crack and follow good holds up its left-hand side. From the top of the pedestal move up into the groove and follow it leftwards. At a small bulge pull back right onto the upper wall. Follow this to the top. *Photo this page.*

FA. Pat Littlejohn 21.7.78

7 Semaphore Signals . 1 E4 6a

35m. A seldom-climbed route up the wall right of the pedestal on *Test Case*. Climb the lower wall to the ledge. Step left then make steep moves back right to gain a flake. Continue above until it is possible to step right for a rest. Climb the wall above and move right around a roof. The crack above leads to the top.

FA. Nipper Harrison 23.5.81

8 Space Cadet 3 E3 5c

35m. A brilliant direct route up the wall. Climb the lower wall to the ledge. Move up and right towards a niche in the roof. Swing about on the huge holds and wave to your mates, then realise that the jugs disappear at the top of the niche and start to panic a bit. Climb up to another roof, pass it on its right then move back left into the awkward finishing corner.

FA. Nipper Harrison 17.4.81

9 The Call Up. 1 E4 6b

35m. A savage climb with a very uncomfortable crux. Follow *Space Cadet* to its first roof. Traverse right beneath this then pull over into a groove. Follow this to the next roof which is crossed with great difficulty. If you manage this, and your hands are still intact, then step out left to reach an easier finishing crack.

FA. Nipper Harrison 17.7.81

10 In Orbit. 1 E5 6b

38m. A beefy route which makes the most of the good rock around the rubble-filled chimney. Start 6m left of the prominent crack of the *Kraken*. Follow the easiest line up the bulging wall until it is possible to bridge across to the left wall of the chimney. Pull left and climb up to the niche of *The Call Up*. Pull up right-wards through the roof into a hanging niche and layback urgently up the wide crack on the right. Easier ground leads to the top.

FA. Andy Donson 11.6.94

11 Kraken 2 E1 5b

35m. The prominent crack in the side wall of the rubble-filled gully. Start at the bottom of the crack and climb to the top. Steep and awkward but quite satisfying. *Photo on page 172.*

There is an eliminate called **The Wake, E4 6a** which starts up the *Kraken* and tackles the wall on the right.

FA. Steve Monks 10.78

St. David's
Flimston Bay
Mewsford
Castle/Rusty
Saddle Head
Bosherston Head
Huntsman's Leap
Stennis/Chapel
Trevallen
St. Govan's
Mowing/Stackpole
ther Carey's

The Arrow

As the platform below St Govan's slides into the sea, a huge tower-like buttress stands in front of the rest of the cliffs. Between its two aretes are some excellent mid-grade routes which follow the prominent features.
Tides - Virtually non-tidal although the base of the wall can be caught by high springs and rough seas.

1 Flanker. . . . . VS 4c
30m. This pleasant route wanders up the left-hand side of the buttress. Climb the lower wall beneath the big open groove of *Ricochet* to a ledge. Trend up and leftwards to some cracks above a ledge. Climb the crack to another ledge and finish up the groove above. Take care with loose rock on this upper section.
FA. Dave Armstrong 2.1.78

Lots of sun | 8 min

2 Ricochet **E2 5c**
30m. A superb climb which leads you on with a lazy lower groove and then smacks you with a savage finishing crack. Start below the open groove and stroll up this to the left-hand of three cracks which sprout from its end. Arrange plenty of gear then attack the crack with everything you've got. Traverse right and finish easily above.
FA. Pete Whillance 2.1.78

3 Poisoned Arrow **E4 6a**
30m. A good technical pitch. Start as for *Ricochet* but move right to below a crack in the wall. Climb the crack and its continuation above, which leads rightwards to the top of *Cupids Bow*.
Photo on page 3.
FA. Steve Lewis 1982

4 Cupids Bow . . . . **HVS 5a**
30m. This thuggy route follows the huge flake crack in the centre of the buttress. It requires some large clanking gear to protect it. Start below the flake-crack, gain and climb it to the roof at the top and pass this on its left.
FA. Pete Whillance 12.12.76

5 Stupid Cupid **E5 6a**
30m. A fiddly eliminate. Move right from the base of the flake on *Cupid's Bow*. Make some hard moves up the centre of the wall to a ledge. Pull up and right and climb the wall above to the top break. Finish up the headwall.
FA. Gary Gibson 20.4.86

6 The Arrow . . . . Top 50 **E1 5b**
30m. One of the most sought-after routes in Pembroke. It tackles the cracks and flakes up the right-hand side of the buttress. The climbing is never too difficult but there are some hard moves, and there have been many accidents on the lower section. Start just to the right of the flake of *Cupid's Bow*. Climb up - make sure your gear is good - and gain a rightwards-trending line of cracks. Climb this to a tricky move right into a groove. Most people finish rightwards to a ledge and easy groove above, but it is better to pull straight through the roof, with no increase in grade.
Photo this page.
FA. Pete Whillance 19.2.77

7 Flight Path **E3 5c**
30m. Although this route does have one independent section, most of the good climbing is on other routes with better lines. Starting just right of *The Arrow*, climb up steep juggy rock to a small ledge. Step up and make a hard fingery traverse rightwards to the arete. Pull around the corner into a crack (on the route *Raw Recruits* - next page) which is followed for 4m. Step back left into an easy finishing groove on the left-hand side of the arete. The crack of *Raw Recruits* can be avoided at no change in grade.
FA. Pat Littlejohn 5.4.80

8 The Rising Tide **E4 6a**
30m. An excellent and underrated route which tackles the smooth white wall directly by some surprisingly amenable climbing. Start as for *Flight Path* and climb the wall with a hard move to gain a curving overlap at half-height (reasonable gear and two stainless pegs). Move left then continue up the easier but scarier upper wall trending left to finish up *The Arrow*. The original start was slightly to the right but is a bit artificial.
FA. Gary Gibson 23.10.82

Gareth Hallam climbing the brilliant route *The Arrow* (E1) - *this page*. Photo: Alan James

St. David's
Flimston Bay
Newsford
Castle/Rusty
Saddle Head
Bosherston Head
Huntsman's Leap
Stennis/Chapel
Trevallen
St. Govan's
Mowing/Stackpole
Mother Carey's

Tactition

This steep section of cliff hangs over a raised ramp which trails off rightwards under the face. The walls above mostly have hard undercut starts but surprisingly there are a few mid-grade routes which weave their way up the grooves and juggy breaks reaching some delightfully exposed positions.

Tides - Most of the routes are not affected by the tide but reaching them can be problematic when the tide is very high, or when the sea is running a swell. The base of *The Arrow* is sometimes cut off in these conditions, however it is almost always possible to reach the ramp with a well-timed run and an easy scramble up the wall under *Flight Path*. Alternatively abseil direct onto the ramp.

Lots of sun | 8 min

1 Raw Recruits. 1 E3 5c

30m. Strenuous climbing up the steep crack. Gain the crack from the right and climb it to a rest below a steeper section (junction with *Flight Path* - previous page). Hard moves above lead to easier ground. Finish up a short groove.

FA. Pete Whillance 6.5.79

2 Get Some In . . . . Top 50 E5 6a

30m. Sustained and well protected climbing and, like all good cruxes, it's at the top! Start at the same point as *Raw Recruits*. Climb to the right-hand side of a roof and break rightwards up the crack which is followed with increasing difficulty to a big flat hold. The next bit is best climbed as quickly as possible without thinking too much about your gear. Finish up a short groove above.

FA. Bob Berzins 22.8.81

3 You Got Me Into This! (E5 6b)
35m. The wall between *Get Some In* and the corner. One of the pegs has gone and the other is old - treat the grade with caution. Climb up to a flake crack and then move out leftwards to a small ledge. Hard moves lead past an old peg to a good jug. Continue to the roof then traverse left to *Get Some In*.
FA. Gary Gibson 3.5.86

The main corner, above the ramp, is covered in grooves and roofs. The lines look complex until you get on the routes. Then, with most of them, there is only one way to go.

4 Hangover '77. . . . . E1 5b
35m. The line is up the left-hand groove of the big open corner above the ramp. Gain the groove from below and follow it to the roof. Pull steeply around this and finish more easily above.
FA. Jeff Lamb 1.1.77. A New Year's Day hangover.

5 War Crime E2 5b
35m. The right-hand groove of the big open corner gives an excellent route with a exciting and exposed finish. Pull over an undercut nose below and right of the groove then move left and climb up to the second of two pedestal ledges. Move up then swing right into a line of broken cracks which lead to an awkward position below a roof. Move right to a rest below another roof, then pull back left and climb the groove to the top.
FA. Derek Furze 7.4.85

6 Get Out of That! E4 5c
35m. The wall just to the right of the corner is a lot steeper than it looks. Start as for *War Crime* but step off the first pedestal onto the wall. Climb this to a huge hanging flake. Continue past another flake to the upper groove which leads to the top.
FA. Gary Gibson 24.5.86

7 No Man's Land E4 5c
35m. This route isn't technically very hard, or badly protected, it is just extremely steep. From the first ledge on *War Crime*, climb a steep graunchy crack into a large triangular niche. Swing left out of the niche onto a steep wall. Climb this on very good holds until you are forced around the arete on the right. The slab above leads more easily to a block strewn ledge. Finish up the groove above in a good position.
FA. Nipper Harrison 14.8.82

8 War Games. E1 5b
35m. An underrated route which is probably as good as *Tactician*. Start as for the last three routes but move right and climb a crack to gain a left-trending scoop. Follow this into the triangular niche and then move up to a ledge. Make a deceptive move up the groove above to reach a ledge, then climb the wildly-positioned corner to the top.
FA. Pete Botteril 4.4.79

9 Tactitian . . . . HVS 5a
35m. This excellent and popular route follows the big corner above the centre of the ledge but it does have a bit of a stopper move at half-height. Climb a short corner and then move right into the main corner. Follow this to the top.
FA. Jeff Lamb 31.12.76

10 Blucher. E5 6a
35m. The arete left of the big groove of *Tactician* usually has a tempting thread dangling from its upper section. Start as for *Tactician* but break left along a crack to a junction with *War Games*. Move right around the arete and then climb a hard crack to a ledge. Finish up the arete above in a magnificent position.
FA. Gary Gibson 3.5.86

St. David's | Flimston Bay | Mewsford | Castle/Rusty | Saddle Head | Bosherston Head | Huntsman's Leap | Stennis/Chapel | Trevallen | St. Govan's | Moving/Stackpole | Mother Carey's

11 Depraved E2 5c

35m. A direct line up the wall between *Tactician* and *Deranged* - not quite as good as its neighbours but still very worthwhile. Start just right of *Tactician* and climb up a crack rightwards to meet *Deranged*. Follow this for 4m then step left and climb a groove to a ledge. Finish straight up the wall above.

FA. Jon de Montjoye 3.86

12 Deranged E2 5b

35m. A superb route which follows an intricate line up the wall. Start in the centre of an undercut roof, below a left-trending grooveline. Pull onto the wall, climb the groove then, at its top, step right into another groove and follow this to a roof. Move right around this then make a hard move back left above it to a flake/pillar which leads to the top.

FA. Alec Sharpe 24.6.78

13 A Shot in the Dark . . E5 6b

35m. A hard eliminate to the right of *Deranged* on which a long reach is essential. Move right from the base of the groove on *Deranged* and gain a crack by a hard move. Continue to a rest then make another hard move up a slim groove above to rejoin *Deranged*. Step right and finish up a steep wall.

FA. Gary Gibson 24.5.86

14 Draught Dodger E5 6b

35m. The route up the wall right of *Deranged* has a steep start with a wicked move. Start 4m right of *Deranged*. Pull up the wall on huge holds until they run out then make a hard move to a ledge. Move up then swing right onto a slabby groove which leads more easily to a break below the overhanging headwall. Finger traverse right to the arete, then move back left to a large hold above. Finish direct.

FA. Bob Berzins 22.8.81

15 Shot by Both Sides. . E5 6b

35m. Just right of *Draught Dodger* is an attractive short groove with some bits of fixed gear in it. Climb straight up the steep wall, keeping just left of a roof, into the groove. Follow this with great difficulty to a rest at the top. Continue up the right-hand edge of the wall above with some hard moves up steep cracks to gain a ledge on the arete. Finish more easily above.

FA. Gary Gibson 4.5.86

16 D-Day. E2 5c

35m. A nasty thuggy start leads to a pleasant groove higher up. Start below the steep flake and climb it to a groove (very aerobic). Follow the groove then move left around a roof and pull up onto a ledge (possible belay). Climb the fine groove above to an easy finish.

FA. Jeff Lamb 2.1.77

The next area used to be home to the classic routes **Conscientious Objector, E3, Mission Impossible, E5** *and* **Fire Power, E3**. *The wall collapsed in the winter of 1995/96. The remaining rock is still loose and shouldn't be reclimbed.*

Deranged

The wall right of *Tactician* offers more steep routes. The intimidating steep starts are usually the least of your worries since the thoughtfully-placed juggy breaks allow easy access onto the upper walls but, once there, you are on your own.

17 New Lookout Arete E3 5c
35m. A version of an old route which skirts the edge of the rockfall. Climb a steep crack to an easing in angle. After a move on *Range Rider*, move back left to the arete which is followed to the top.
FA. Paul Donnithorne 11.6.00. FA. (original) Dave Armstrong 1977

18 Range Rider E3 5c
35m. Another good climb. Start on the right of the arete at the right-hand end of the ramp. Climb the wall then pull around leftwards onto a ledge. Follow a series of open grooves above to reach an easy finishing crack.
FA. Dave Armstrong 16.4.79

The next routes are on the more broken wall around the corner from the ramp.

19 Photocall E2 5b
35m. Start just left of a roof and climb the wall above to reach a wide crack. Follow this into a niche and continue to a ledge (possible belay). Step left and thrash your way up the crack above.
FA. Steve Bancroft 5.4.80

20 The Alamo E4 6b
35m. Start as for *Photocall* but break out right and climb a thin crack with great difficulty. Continue to a ledge then climb the easier arete on the right.
FA. Gary Gibson 3.5.86

Range Rider
There are one or two good lines on the rounded buttress just right of the rockfall, and then the isolated majestic crack of *Tangerine Dream* further right again.
Tides - The boulders at the base of this wall are just cut off at high tide and in rough seas.

21 Zero Hour . . . . HVS 5b
35m. A boulder problem start is used to gain the rampline above the roof. Follow this more easily, finishing up a wide corner.
FA. Dave Armstrong 31.12.76

22 Nightmare. . . . . HVS 5a
35m. A badly-named route starting at a wide groove right of the roof. Climb the groove easily to ledges (possible belay). Finish up the pleasant slim groove above.
FA. J.Williams 30.6.79

After 50m of poorer rock, a wonderful orange wall rises from the boulders. The base is more tidal here.

23 Tangerine Dream . . . Top 50 E4 6a
38m. The first half of this route gives some of the best steep crack climbing around. Higher up the crack is much wider and easier to climb. Climb the twin thin cracks in the lower wall, with increasing difficulty and some haste - don't place too much gear - until a last difficult pull up and left gains a rest. Climb the wide crack above moving left at the top.
FA. Pete Whillance 4.5.79

St. David's
Flimston Bay
Mewsford
Castle/Rusty
Saddle Head
Bosherston Head
Huntsman's Leap
Stennis/Chapel
Trevallen
St. Govan's
Mowing/Stackpole
Mother Carey's

	No star	1	2	3
Mod to S	-	-	-	-
HS to HVS	1	3	-	-
E1 to E3	2	5	5	1
E4 and up	1	7	4	1

St. David's
Flimston Bay
Mewsford
Castle/Rusty
Saddle Head
Bosherston Head
Huntsman's Leap
Stennis/Chapel
Trevallen
St. Govan's
Mowing/Stackpole
Mother Carey's

Steve Crowe on the final section of *Juicy Lucy* (E4) - *page 191* - at St Govan's East. Photo: Alan James

Tucked away at the end of the most popular crag in Pembroke is a great crag with routes which see a fraction of the traffic. This is another one of those typical Pembroke crags that has a classic route - *First Blood* (E2) - which attracts people for their first visit but which tends to get forgotten a bit after that. Unlike some of the one-hit-wonder crags, St Govan's East actually has a lot more to offer. Routes like *Calisto* (E1), *Hidden Secrets* (E2), *Round the Horn* (E2), *Forbidden Fruits* (E3), *Howling Gale* (E3) and the magnificent *Brave New World* (E4) make a return visit well worth thinking about, especially if you are exasperated by crowds elsewhere.

Approach and Tides

From St Govan's car park, walk along the headland, past Trevallen and on towards the coastguard building. About 200m after the popular area at St Govan's, head across the grass to a solid abseil stake at the clifftop (about 50m left of the coastguard station). The routes on the right-hand (looking in) side of the crag start from a non-tidal platform. Working left from *First Blood* the routes become more tidal with a low tide required to get right under the arete of *Round the Horn* to reach the left-most routes.

Conditions

For some reason St Govan's East has got a reputation for only getting the sunshine in the morning. It is certainly true that it does get more morning sun than most areas in Pembroke, but I have also done the route *Forbidden Fruits* in sunshine at 4pm. All the stuff on the right-hand side is solid (except for the finishes of course) and the starts are usually dry. The more tidal routes do suffer a bit from greasy rock on their initial sections.

St. David's | Flimston Bay | Mewsford | Castle/Rusty | Saddle Head | Bosherston Head | Huntsman's Leap | Stennis/Chapel | Trevallen | St. Govan's | Mowing/Stackpole | Mother Carey's

Brave New World

The undercut walls on the left (looking in) of the crag are significantly less popular than the attractions to the right, but have just as much to offer in quality. The tidal nature and the savage starts tend to keep people away but *Brave New World* is an essential tick and there is quite a bit of other stuff to keep you busy while you are down this end.

Approach and Tides - The section below *Round the Horn* is only revealed for 3 to 4 hours at low tide (less in neaps). You need to walk across here to get to the other routes from the main abseil. Direct abseil is possible if you want to get in early to do *Brave New World*.

1 Sideshow . . . . **VS 4c**
25m. Start below the narrow slab on the end wall left of the corner. Climb the slab by the diagonal cracks leading rightwards.
FA. Jon de Montjoye 23.5.82

2 Blood and Flesh **E2 5c**
25m. Start below a thin crack which splits the roof of a cave. Climb to the crack then hard moves lead up to another crack. Follow this until you can step left onto a slab. This leads easily to the top.
FA. Damo Carroll 12.6.88

To mid afternoon | 10 min | Tidal | Abseil in

3 Flesh and Blood **E2 5c**
30m. Climb a crack just left of the cave to the break then follow the crack up right to a bulge. Move first right then back left to a ledge. Climb the corner on the right to the top.
FA. Lyndsey Foulkes 24.5.82

4 Hidden Secrets **E2 5c**
30m. Start below the left-hand side wall of the cave. Climb the wall and pull around onto the face - tricky. Move up then traverse right delicately into the corner and heave up onto some hanging flakes, then swing left to a ledge. Step back right into a corner and follow this to the top.
FA. Emma Alsford 4.7.92

5 Brave New World Top 50 **E4 6a**
32m. A stunning line, amazing rock and intensely thuggy climbing make this one of the most unforgettable routes around. Start beneath the crack in the corner and pull up into it (requires a shoulder-aid for shorties). Heave up to the roof, power around this then thrash up the crack above. Bridge up the finishing groove before you wilt.
FA. Pat Littlejohn 30.4.82

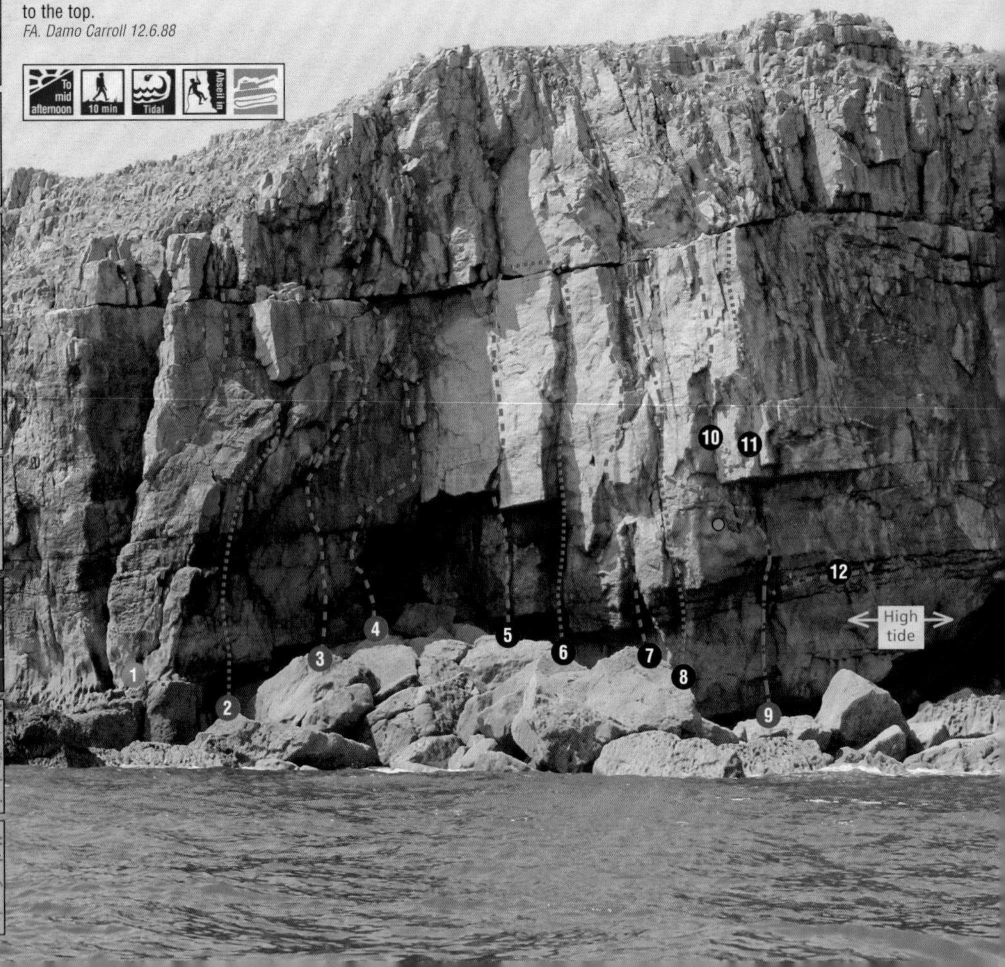

6 Ghostly Galleon . . . . 2 stars E4 6a
32m. The hanging groove right of the hanging arete. Like all of the starts around here, it is sometimes damp. Start on a boulder below the groove. Climb over the bulge to below the roof. Pull around this with great difficulty, then climb the groove above. Step left onto the ledge and finish up *Brave New World*.
FA. Nipper Harrison 4.7.82

7 Sea Fever . . . . 2 stars (E5 6a)
32m. Climb into the left-hand of two grooves, then move left to another groove. At the top of this reach around into a vanishing face-crack. Climb this for 4m then reach right to the arete. Continue up the arete, first on its left-hand side (old peg) to the break. Climb boldly leftwards across the blank wall to the top.
FA. Pat Littlejohn 22.5.86

8 The Savage . . . . 1 star E4 6b
32m. In the upper right-hand section of this wall is a long groove. This well-named route gains the groove from below. Pull up a steep crack and reach a wider crack above. Move up into the groove and follow it to the top (a lot easier then the first 10m!)
FA. Pat Littlejohn 14.5.82

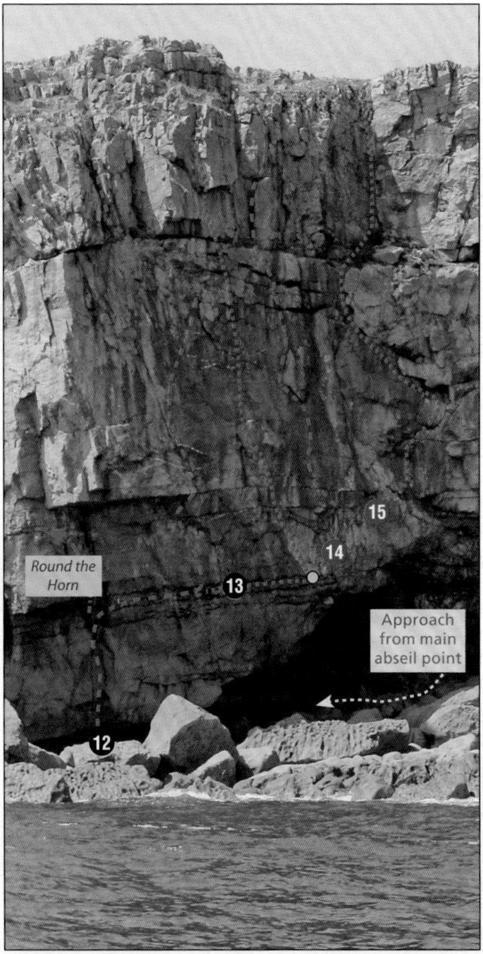

9 Round the Horn . . . . 2 stars E2 5c
35m. A enjoyable way of reaching the long groove of *The Savage* without all that mucking about with strenuous cracks. Start up an undercut corner beneath the right arete of the wall. Pull into the groove and climb it steeply to a small roof. Contort around this (wacky bridging helps) to a rest above (possible belay if tide threatens). Traverse delicately leftwards to reach the groove and climb it to the top past a section of unstable rock to the more-familiar unstable finish.
FA. Nipper Harrison 3.7.82

10 White Rhino . . . . 1 star E5 6a
32m. The direct finish to *Round the Horn*. From the traverse of *Round the Horn*, climb the groove above to its top. Continue up the wall above to the break. Head left across the wall to finish.
FA. Pat Littlejohn 20.5.86

11 Hotspur . . . . 1 star (E5 6a)
32m. Fix a runner in the groove on *White Rhino* and traverse to a small groove in the arete (old peg). Climb this, then the arete above, on its left-hand side, to the break. Finish easily up the groove above.
FA. Pat Littlejohn 23.5.86

12 Imagination . . . . 2 stars E4 6a
40m. A long pitch up the wall above the large roof. Beware of rope drag if you do it in one run-out - extend your runners. Alternatively, split it at a hanging belay in the breaks. Start up the steep groove below the roof and climb to a traverse line by a thread on the right. Move right for 6m until below a crack on the right edge of the roof. Climb up through the roof and up the wall above to a small ledge on the left. Now head rightwards across the unprotected wall to a wide crack. Move up then back leftwards to reach an easy finishing corner.
FA. Jon de Montjoye 18.7.82

13 Vision On . . . . 1 star E5 6b
The blank grey wall right of the crack of *Imagination*.
1) 5c, 15m. Follow *Imagination* but continue along the traverse line to a hanging stance above the cave.
2) 6b, 25m. Climb directly over the bulge above the stance and move left onto the slab. Climb straight up the slab to the high break and then continue up the front face of the pillar to the top.
FA. Gary Gibson 3.7.85

14 Just an Illusion . . . . 1 star E3 5c
Another wandering line which makes the most of the rock above the highest point of the black cave.
1) 5c, 15m. Climb *Vision On* to the belay.
2) 5c, 25m. Continue traversing right over the roof, then move up into a niche on the right. Pull left through the bulge above, onto the blank grey slab, and climb straight up to a hanging flake. Continue above to a grassy ledge and climb onto the top of a large pinnacle on the right. Finish straight up.
FA. Gary Gibson, S.Whalley 9.4.85

15 In Your Dreams E3 6a
This route takes the traversing a bit too far.
1) 5c, 15m. As for *Vision On*.
2) 6a, 30m. Keep traversing rightwards across the cave then move up to a break. Keep climbing upwards to a roof and then follow a leftwards trending line to a large ledge. Finish up the corner on the right.
FA. Lyndsey Foulkes, D.Meek 6.86

St. David's
Flimston Bay
Mewsford
Castle/Rusty
Saddle Head
Bosherston Head
Huntsman's Leap
Stennis/Chapel
Trevallen
St. Govan's
Mowing/Stackpole
Mother Carey's

First Blood

A popular wall and justifiably so. It gets morning sun and is relatively non-tidal and also has a tidy little set of routes including the Top 50 tick of *First Blood*. While you are down here, *Calisto*, *Forbidden Fruits* and *Howling Gale* are all worth a look too.

Approach and Tides - Abseil direct to a non-tidal ledge. The base of *First Blood* is cut off for a short time at high tide but you can usually still traverse in.

16 Black Rambo...... 1 E5 6a

35m. Start 8m left of the arete of *First Blood*, at the left-hand end of a narrow overhang, below a vague line of grooves. Power determinedly over the initial bulges into a groove. Climb this then move up left across a slab. Climb back right to gain a hanging crack and follow it, on dodgy rock, to a ledge. Step left around an arete and climb the wall above, via a good flake, to the top.

FA. Pat Littlejohn 20.5.86

17 Body Language . 2 E4 6a

30m. A fine companion to *First Blood* but quite a bit harder with a beefy start thrown in. Start beneath a small projecting rock tongue below the horizontal break band. Climb up to the tongue then psyche up and pull leftwards, eventually arriving on a small ledge above the bulge. Climb up some cracks above, over a bulge, into an open groove. Follow this to a ledge then finish up the corner above.

FA. Pat Littlejohn 30.4.82

18 First Blood .... Top 50 E2 5c

25m. A magnificent route which should be on everyone's Pembroke tick list. Start below the arete at the left-hand end of a platform which runs along the cliff base from beneath the abseil. Climb up, on huge holds, to the bottom of a thin crack. Follow the crack, with a bit of assistance from some holds on the right. Continue past a flowstone section (beware of nesting birds) to a groove. Move left onto a ledge then climb the pinnacle, and wall behind it, to the top.

FA. Pat Littlejohn 30.4.82

19 Calisto 2 **E1 5b**

25m. This pleasant route roughly follows the arete right of *First Blood*. Climb an open groove on the right-hand side of the arete to a large loose-looking flake. Move up to a ledge on the arete and then climb the arete on its right-hand side, past good but widely spaced gear. From the break move left behind a large pinnacle, step up onto this and climb the corner on the left.

FA. Pete Finklaire 18.4.81

20 Mother India 1 **E4 6b**

25m. The thin crack in the wall right of the arete has a desperate move in its middle section. Watch out for the loose finish.

FA. Keith Sharples 31.10.84

21 Ganymede . . . . 1 **HS 4b**

25m. A friendly grade. Start just right of the arete of *Calisto* below a long corner. Climb the corner with an awkward move onto a ledge near the top.

FA. Richard Crewe 18.4.81

22 The Vicar's Goat **E2 5b**

20m. Climb over the jumbled blocks to reach a leftwards leaning groove. Follow this to a loose finish.

FA. Damo Carroll 7.84

23 Silent Running **E4 6b**

20m. In the centre of the buttress is a line of thin cracks. Climb up these with lots of hard moves and good runners.

FA. Steve Monks 1983

The wall to the right is taken by **Quiet Please, E5 6b** *which used a drilled peg for protection. This has now gone.*

24 Mud Pie in Your Eye . . . . **HVS 4c**

20m. If you avoid touching any mud, by bridging up the edges of the chimney, then this is actually quite a good little route.

FA. Gary Gibson 9.6.88

25 Adam's Rib 1 **E4 5c**

20m. A bold route up the left arete of the buttress. Start below the left arete of the square buttress right of the mud-filled chimney. Climb up to a small roof and pass this on its left. Move back right above it and follow the right-hand side of the arete above. This is easy at first but it steepens up at the top.

FA. Bill Lounds 7.6.86

26 Forbidden Fruits 2 **E3 5c**

20m. A great route up the centre of the square buttress to the left (looking in) of the abseil line. Start in the centre of the buttress, below a left-leaning ramp. Climb the ramp to a good flake on the arete - lace this with gear, then make a tricky traverse back right to a hard move past an old peg. Finish strenuously right or left.

FA. Jon de Montjoye 17.7.82

27 Juicy Lucy 1 **E4 5c**

20m. A direct version of *Forbidden Fruits*. From the base of the ramp, climb straight up the wall above to a flake. Move right and up a thin crack to join the last moves of *Forbidden Fruits*.

Photo on page 186.

FA. Pat Littlejohn 1.4.86

20m right, past the abseil, is a large flying arete.

28 Rear Wind . . . . 1 **HVS 5a**

24m. The left side of the arete is great, and well-protected, too. Jump on board from the left, and trace a line all the way up the left side to the top.

FA. Tony Sawbridge 8.85

29 Whispering Wind 1 **E1 5a**

24m. Another good line. Engage the arete from under the initial overhang, and follow the cracks in the right side of the arete, passing a good ledge, to finish up a groove on the right (taking care with the rock).

FA. Lyndsey Foulkes 25.5.82

30 Howling Gale 2 **E3 6a**

24m. The superb face to the right is taken pretty much in its centre. Although it has some old fixed gear, this can all be backed up although it may be worth E4 when the peg eventually goes. Climb the wall to a break and a thread, then climb up and slightly right (two old pegs) to reach easier ground. Continue leftwards, to the loose finish of *Whispering Wind*.

FA. Alun Richardson 5.86

Mowing Word and Stackpole

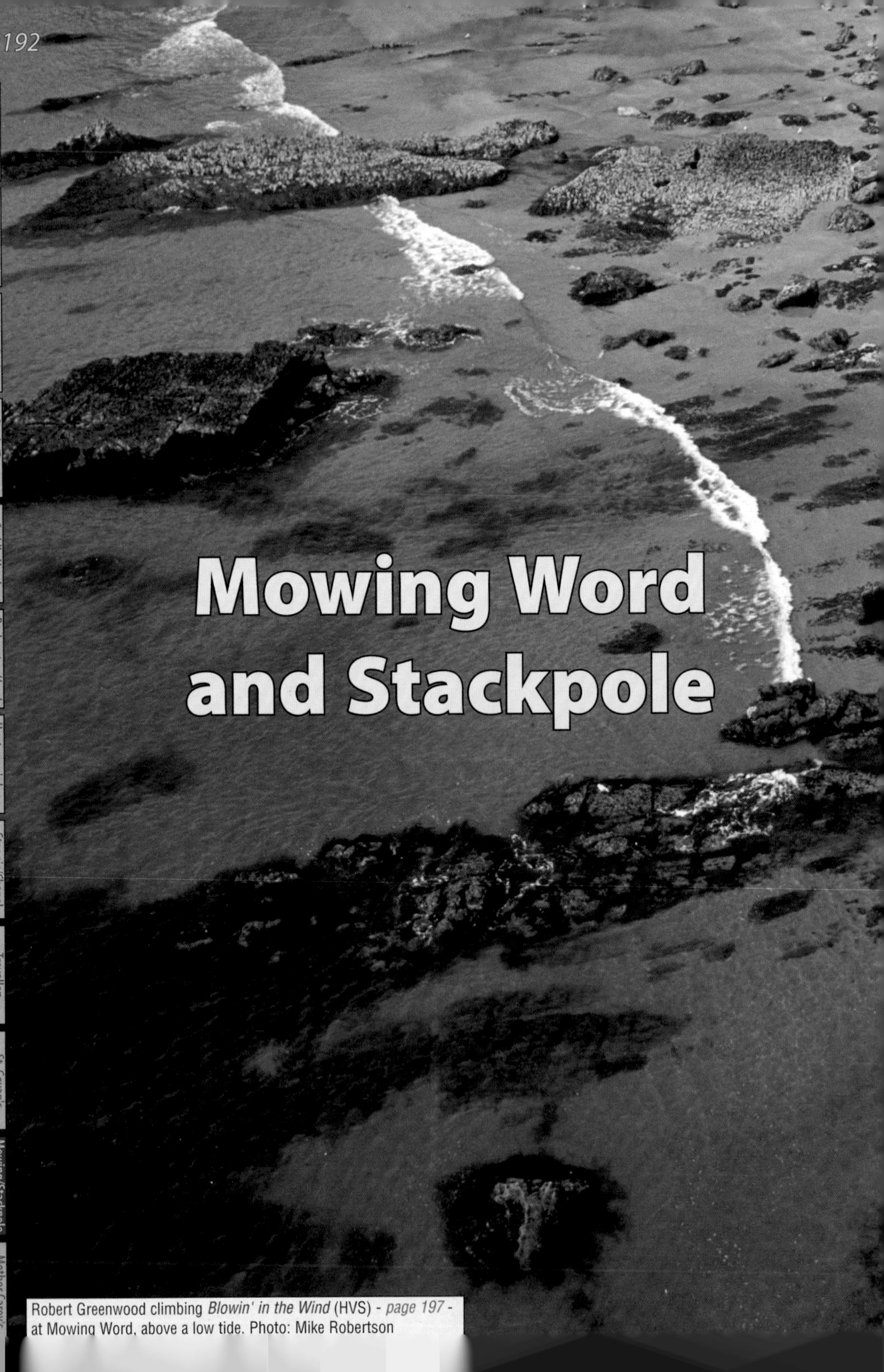

Robert Greenwood climbing *Blowin' in the Wind* (HVS) - *page 197* - at Mowing Word, above a low tide. Photo: Mike Robertson

	No star	1	2	3
Mod to S	-	-	-	-
HS to HVS	-	7	3	2
E1 to E3	-	4	9	4
E4 and up	-	-	6	-

Mowing Word is one of those spots which can elude climbers year after year - many is the time I've heard folk say "must get that one done tomorrow/next week/this season", only to reappear the following year with nothing bagged in the interim. That's bird-restricted crags for you. But maybe that's the attraction? … this means you'll never run out of routes to do - surely this is the epitome of paradise. In the meantime, devote your energy to getting started on such west-facing beauties as the amazing *Diedre Sud* (HS), the multi-extravaganza *Heart of Darkness* (HVS), *Snozwanger* (E1), *Flax of Dream* (E2) and the demanding *In One Door* (E5). And if that's not enough to drag you back time and time again … you are climbing too fast.

Access Restriction - Mowing Word has an agreed restriction because of nesting birds, no climbing from 1 March and 1 August each year. This includes all the routes in this guide except two on the East Face on page 200.

Conditions
Mowing Word can be windy and exposed although often this is far more pronounced on the clifftop than on the routes themselves. It doesn't suffer too badly from greasy starts since most of the routes avoid them by traversing in above the tide line. It faces west and receives afternoon and evening sun and is a delightful place to be in the evening when the whole cliff turns orange.

Approach
From Broad Haven car park - Drive through Bosherston and turn left just after the pub (signed Broad Haven) and drive to the car park at the road end (pay). Drop down to the beach and cross this (notice the good bouldering on the far side). Follow the coast path eastwards past the deep fords of Chance Encounter Zawn and Raming Hole, around onto the narrow headland of Mowing Word.

From Stackpole Quay car park - Drive to the tiny village of Stackpole and pick up signs for Stackpole Quay and the car park there (pay). Pick up the track which leads south west along the coast past Barafundle Bay and eventually on to Mowing Word and Stackpole Head.

Tides
Getting to the starts of the routes at Mowing Word can be as taxing as climbing them. The base of the cliff is very tidal and the area to the seaward side of *Diedre Sud* is never uncovered. For this reason most of the routes are reached by abseiling down *Diedre Sud* and traversing along the horizontal breaks above the high tide line. Belaying and keeping the ropes out of the water needs a bit of ingenuity.

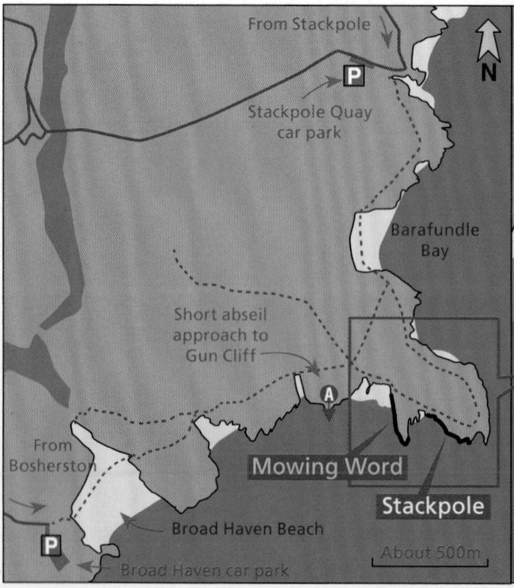

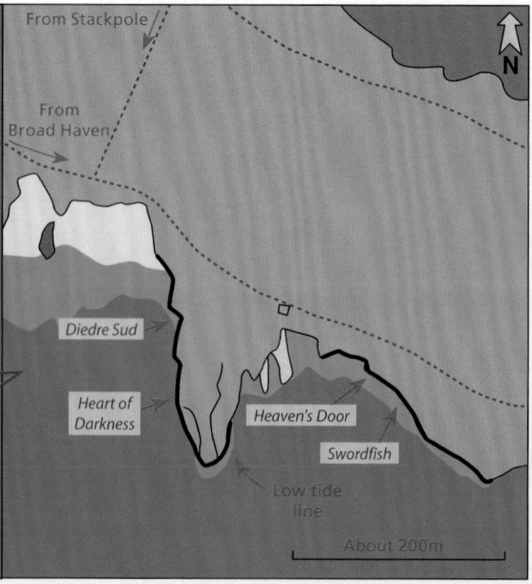

St. Davids
Flimston Bay
Mewsford
Castle/Rusty
Saddle Head
Bosherston Head
Huntsman's Leap
Stennis/Chapel
Trevallen
St. Govan's
Mowing/Stackpole
Mother Carey's

Libby Peter, belayed by Meilee Rafe, on *Snozwanger* (E1) - *page 197* - at Mowing Word. Photo: Mike Robertson

St. David's
Flimston Bay
Mewsford
Castle/Rusty
Saddle Head
Bosherston Head
Huntsman's Leap
Stennis/Chapel
Trevallen
St. Govan's
Mowing/Stackpole
Mother Carey's

Approach (Routes 1 to 3) - *Abseil to some small ledges in the centre of the face. The routes can be reached from the beach at very low tide, by abseiling down Diedre Sud.*

1 The Onion Eaters . . . . . . 2★ **E3 6a**
30m. A little gem with weird rock at the bottom and a fine finishing crack. From the ledge move leftwards to an open groove. Pull right around a small roof and move up to another roof. Pass this on the left and finish up a thin crack in the wall left of the corner.
FA. Roy Thomas 21.2.87

2 Crystal Grazer . . . . 1★ **E2 5c**
30m. Climb direct up the wall above on some large crystal-covered pockets to the break. Move slightly right then climb a steep corner above by its left wall. Pull around a small bulge into a wider finishing crack.
FA. Roy Thomas 4.87

3 Sea Goon . . . . 1★ **HVS 4c**
30m. Climb the right-hand side of the wall by a shallow groove, to a ledge on the right. Continue up the corner above.
FA. John Harwood 1975

Approach and Tides (other routes) - *From mid-to-high tide, start from a hanging belay on the line of horizontal breaks which run along the bottom of the face, above the high tide line. This is reached by abseiling down Diedre Sud and solo traversing along the break (only Diff but don't fall off).*
At low tide various ledges and blocks at the base of the cliff are uncovered which are also reached by abseil.

4 Seaside Salamander . . . 2★ **(E5 6b)**
35m. Sustained climbing and a wicked crux move high up, unfortunately it is a bit escapable. The old peg may not now be trustyworthy. Just left of the centre of the wall below two holes above the traverse line. Gain the left-hand one and move up above to gain a flake on the left. Follow this back rightwards to a break then move left and climb the numerous breaks above to a roof. Make a tricky move above to another roof, step right and make a series of very technical moves to gain the wall above. Move left then back right to finish.
FA. Gary Gibson 21.2.87

5 All at Sea . . . . 2★ **E5 6a**
35m. A better route than its left-hand neighbour. Start below a slim right-facing corner which is just above the right-hand of two holes above the juggy traverse line. Climb the corner to the break. Continue straight up the wall above, past some breaks and a crystal pocket, to the roof. Pull over then step right to gain a flake. Climb the flake for 5m then swing left to a rest. Continue up a small groove above to finish.
FA. Gary Gibson 20.2.87

6 Crises. . . . . 2★ **E3 6a**
35m. Follow *All at Sea* to the break, then trend right across the wall to a square-cut hole below the roof. Pull over with great difficulty (a stopper move for some) then move right to gain a long finishing crack which is still tiring.
FA. Nipper Harrison 6.8.83

7 Tie Me to the Tyburn Tree 2★ **(E4 6a)**
35m. An eliminate but with good climbing but it is probably not climbed in its current state due to the peg being old - maybe E5? Start below and left of two prominent right-facing corners. Climb straight up and over a slim W-shaped roof (crucial old peg). Continue past another roof to the largest overhang. Pull over this then step right below another smaller roof. Climb this and a thin crack in the headwall above to finish.
FA. Gary Gibson 24.1.87

8 Widowmaker. . . . . 2★ **E3 5c**
35m. A fine companion route to *Chimes of Freedom*. Start below two prominent right-facing grooves below the main line of overhangs. Climb the easy lower wall to the base of the right-hand groove then make a difficult move up left into the smaller left-hand groove. Follow it to its top then step right below the roof and pull over steeply onto a hanging arete. Go through a gap in the roof above to reach a break. Traverse left beneath another overhang and pull up into a crack which is followed to the top.
FA. Nipper Harrison 7.77

No climbing
1 March to 1 August

Chimes of Freedom
This huge lump of a buttress is crossed by a series of juggy breaks and small roofs. All the routes up the main face and the right arete are excellent and popular, giving great climbing and positions.

9 Chimes of Freedom . . . . Top 50 **E2 5b**
35m. One of the classic routes of the area which follows the most substantial line on the face. Start beneath the larger of the two right-facing corners. Climb the wall into the corner and follow this to the roof. The roof can be passed on either side. Move back to gain the exposed continuation groove/crack which leads to the top.
FA. Pat Littlejohn 5.76

10 Stand by to Boogie 2 **E3 5c**
35m. An easy start leads to a good steep finish. Climb easily up the wall about 5m left of the arete, to the band of overhangs and step right to a ledge. Move up and leftwards into an open groove. Follow this until forced left into a crack which leads, over a couple of small roofs, to the top.
FA. Nipper Harrison 5.78

11 Blowin' in the Wind . . . . 2 **HVS 5a**
30m. A popular photogenic route up the left arete of the *Diedre Sud* corner. It can be split at a belay on the arete. Start from a hanging belay, below a short groove, in the lower left side of the arete. Climb the groove and slabby wall above to reach a ledge on the arete (possible belay). Climb the wall just right of the arete then pull up steeply to gain some cracks above. Follow these and the arete above to finish. *Photos on pages 192 and 201.*
FA. Nipper Harrison 5.76

12 Snozwanger 2 **E1 5b**
30m. This excellent route fills the gap between the arete and the corner of *Diedre Sud*. Start from the base of the corner and trend leftwards up the wall, to the break. (It is possible to take a belay on the left at the break). From the break continue straight up some cracks above to the top. *Photo on page 195.*
FA. John Harwood 10.75

Afternoon | 25 min | Tidal | Abseil in

No climbing
1 March to 1 August

Approach and Tides (Routes 13 to 18) - *From mid to high tide, start from a hanging belay at the base of Diedre Sud, or further right if it is busy. This is above high tide. At low tide you can abseil further to blocks which are revealed.*

13 Diedre Sud . . . . Top 50 ☐ HS 4a

30m. The long corner in the centre of the face is one of the classic climbs of its grade in Britain; it does get busy though. Climb the corner to a ledge at half-height (possible belay). Continue up the corner above, passing the small overhang on the left.
At low tide, an alternative and wonderful approach can be made across the bay by descending as for Gun Cliff (see map on page 194) which requires a short abseil from solid rings (possible to use and retrieve your climbing ropes if necessary). Once down the walk across to Mowing Word is spectacular and you can even go through the huge sea tunnel. You still need to traverse the breaks to get to the base of the groove.
FA. Colin Mortlock 30.5.67

14 The Right Wall . . . . 2 ☐ HVS 5a

35m. Start at the foot of *Diedre Sud*. Move 3m right then climb the wall for 6m and move up and left across a groove to a small ledge. Climb steeper rock above to a large ledge (possible belay). Follow slabs up right to some cracks. Climb these to finish.
FA. Colin Mortlock 8.67

15 New Morning. . . . . 2 ☐ E1 5b

This route is best known as a finish to *Heart of Darkness* but it does have a reasonable 1st pitch. Abseil to the base of *Diedre Sud*.
1) 5a, 20m. Traverse right for 5m then climb up steeply to reach a shallow corner. Follow it to a small ledge on the left. Continue over a bulge, and the groove above, to reach the line of breaks. Move up to another break and traverse right to belay on a ledge.
2) 5b, 18m. Move rightwards up a flake to gain the fine wide crack which leads to the top.
FA. Jim Perrin 11.8.71

16 Ice Breaker . . . . 1 ☐ E3 6a

A good route with a technical top pitch requiring commitment.
1) 5c, 20m. From *New Morning* move right to below a crack. Climb the crack to the breaks and a junction with *New Morning*.
2) 6a, 18m. Climb a thin crack, up the wall left of *New Morning*, to a break. Move up left into a scoop and climb this to the top.
FA. Gary Gibson 1.8.83

17 Razorbill. . . . . 1 ☐ VS 4c

A long route which makes the most of the rock between *Diedre Sud* and the big sea cave giving good positions for the grade. Start by abseiling to the base of *Diedre Sud*.
1) 4b, 20m. Traverse right then move up to a ledge beneath the big corner at the lower left-hand side of the sea cave.
2) 4b, 15m. Climb a slab on the left to an overhang at a break. Step left of this and climb straight up to a large ledge.
3) 4c, 18m. Climb a groove above the stance trending left to the base of some twin cracks. Climb the right-hand one of these.
FA. Lyn Noble, Colin Mortlock 5.7.67

18 Flax of Dream . . . . 2 ☐ E2 5a

A good route with some exposed climbing. Start by abseiling to the base of *Diedre Sud*.
1) 4b, 20m. Traverse right, as for *Razorbill*, to the ledge below the big corner and belay.
2) 5a, 35m. Climb the corner to the roof (possible belay). Traverse left under the roof then pull around and mantleshelf onto a ledge. Step back right to reach the base of a crack and climb this to the top.
FA. Jim Perrin 1.8.81

Access to the routes on this side of the cliff is a bit awkward because the base is never revealed in any tides and the low level traversing is not possible past the sea cave. The normal approach is to abseil from blocks, above a small grassy terrace, slightly below the main clifftop. This takes you to ledges beneath the face, just above the high tide line. Scramble left along ledges and breaks to another ledge just to the right of the sea cave. All of the rest of the routes start from this ledge.

19 Heart of Darkness . . . . 3 ☐ HVS 4c

One of the best HVS's in Britain. It is a bit like *Dream of White Horses* - no hard moves or bold bits, just mega holds and exposure. Best done in the afternoon to give the cave a chance to dry out. Start from the ledge, as described above.
1) 4c, 30m. Climb up the arete on the left to reach the line of breaks. Follow the breaks leftwards into the corner then step down. Continue traversing to a small ledge on the arete and belay.
2) 4c, 25m. Move left to a small corner then climb up to the belay ledge of *Razorbill*. Move left again then drop slightly down and follow the breaks into *Diedre Sud*.
3) 4a, 15m. Finish up *Diedre Sud*.
FA. Jim Perrin 13.8.71

⓴ Heart of Darkness/New Morning Top 50 **E1 5b**
The most popular way of finishing *Heart of Darkness* is to climb direct from the arete belay at the end of pitch 1 of *Heart of Darkness* to gain the crack of *New Morning*.

㉑ In One Door. 2 **E5 6a**
A good route. Start from the ledge of *Heart of Darkness*.
1) 6a, 25m. Follow *Heart of Darkness* along the traverse then climb up to a roof below a hanging corner. Pull into this then move left for 5m to a gripping belay below a crack.
2) 6a, 15m. Climb the crack to the top.
FA. Gary Gibson 7.9.85

㉒ In the Heat of the Night 2 **E5 6a**
35m. A direct finish to *In One Door* which is climbed in one long pitch. Follow *In One Door* to the top of the hanging corner, then climb a thin crack line into a shallow finishing groove.
FA. Gary Gibson 7.9.85

㉓ Sealhunt. 3 **E1 5b**
35m. This excellent climb for those who have just enjoyed *Heart of Darkness*. Follow *Heart of Darkness* to the traverse line then climb up until it is possible to move left into the bottomless corner above the big roof. Climb the exposed corner to the top.
FA. Bob Burns 4.76

Afternoon | 25 min | Abseil in

No climbing
1 March to 1 August

Diedre Sud

Mowing Word is best know for two classic routes - *Diedre Sud* and *Heart of Darkness*. These routes have become significant milestones for many climbers. They follow the most prominent features of the central section of Mowing Word. The other routes on this section also have plenty to offer.

㉔ Seal of Approval 1 **E3 5c**
35m. The best of several eliminates to the right of the corner of *Sealhunt*. Climb the wall slightly right of *Sealhunt* to a ledge below the corner. Move up and right to gain some thin cracks on the right-hand side of the right wall of the corner. Finish up the arete above.
FA. Gary Gibson 8.9.85

㉕ Culinary Delights. 1 **E2 5c**
35m. Great climbing in the upper groove. From the ledge on *Seal of Approval*, move rightwards along the break to gain the groove; follow this to the top.
FA. Gary Gibson 8.9.85

㉖ Black Cat 2 **E3 6a**
35m. A terrific line. Start from the ledge right of *Heart of Darkness*. Climb the corner crack, to gain a small ledge. Pull slightly rightwards to reach the roof, traverse left and pull over to enter a shallow groove - off you go!
FA. K.Robertson 2.8.81

The Curver

The southern end of Mowing Word has a few decent routes worth looking at.

Approach and Tides - Abseil down *Cormorant Flake* to ledges which are covered for a short while at high tide.

No climbing routes 27 to 32
1 March to 1 August

27 Seal . . . . 1 ☐ **VS 4c**
25m. This one gets better and better. Climb the lower, slabby breaks, then move out left, to climb the corner feature. Pull left to gain the steep upper crack, and follow this to the top.
FA. Lyn Noble 17.7.67

28 Cormorant Flake . . . . . . 1 ☐ **VS 4c**
25m. The deep chimney flake. The easy lower ground gets you into the recess. Follow the feature all the way to an upper cap-stone, which is passed with a little intuitive footwork.
FA. Jim Perrin 6.5.69

29 The Curver . . . . 2 ☐ **VS 4b**
25m. A tidy bit of climbing to the right of *Cormorant Flake*. Climb the lower juggy wall to a crack, and follow this, moving gradually leftwards to finish a few metres right of the previous route.
FA. Colin Mortlock 29.5.67

30 Nijinsky . . . . 1 ☐ **E1 5b**
25m. The wall just right of the upper section of *The Curver* provides some excellent climbing.
FA. Gary Gibson 7.9.85

31 The Beak . . . . 1 ☐ **VS 4c**
25m. This route is based upon the upper corner. Climb the lower wall to a good ledge, then trend across to gain the corner. Continue up the corner to the top.
FA. Colin Mortlock 5.7.67

32 The Razor's Edge . . . . 1 ☐ **HVS 5a**
This route follows the big groove in the middle of the south face.
1) 5a, 25m. Climb up to the groove and follow it to the roof. Swing right to belay on a ledge.
2) 5a, 10m. Climb the wall above to the top.
FA. Gary Gibson 7.9.85

The next two routes can be climbed throughout the year - there is no bird restriction on the East Face of Mowing Word.

33 Olive Branch . . . . 2 ☐ **E4 6a**
25m. The steep groove and cracks 10m left of *Charenton Crack*. Climb a groove to a rest below the cracks, then launch up them.
FA. Pat Littlejohn 14.5.82

34 Charenton Crack . . . 3 ☐ **E2 5b**
25m. A real struggle for most up the steep corner - well worth seeking out though.
FA. Jim Perrin 9.72

Mia Stacey on the popular *Blowin' in the Wind* (HVS) - *page 197* - at Mowing Word. Photo: Mike Hutton

	No star	1	2	3
Mod to S	-	-	-	-
HS to HVS	-	1	-	-
E1 to E3	-	4	4	5
E4 and up	-	1	5	3

What an incredible spot; just when you thought you were all done at Pembroke, and then you discover this place! The alluring, hanging grooves of Stackpole are home to some magnificent lines, such as *Silver Shadow* (E2), *Swordfish* (E3), the mega-traverse of *Plane Sailing* (E3), and the amazing arete of *Always the Sun* (E6), along with countless other quality classics. Yet it attracts fewer visitors than you'd imagine - this has almost certainly been a combination of bird restrictions, a tidal window that gives between 2 and 4 hours of play, and lack of a good crag shot. So we've deleted one issue right here - now go there in August with a tide timetable and keep that promise to yourself!
A word of warning though: away from the main three E2/3 routes, the crag sees little traffic, in fact many may well never have had a second ascent. Treat all the routes with respect and make sure you know what you are letting yourself in for before you commit yourself to the free-hanging abseil!

Access Restriction - Stackpole has an agreed restriction because of nesting birds, no climbing from 1 March and 1 August each year. This includes all the routes in this guide.

Approach See map on page 194

From Broad Haven car park - Drive through Bosherston and turn left just after the pub (signed Broad Haven) and continue to the car park (pay). Drop down to the beach and cross this. Follow the coast path eastwards past the deep fords of Chance Encounter Zawn and Raming Hole, around onto the narrow headland of Mowing Word. Stackpole is the broader headland further east.
From Stackpole Quay car park - Drive to the small village of Stackpole and pick up signs for Stackpole Quay and follow them to the parking (pay). Pick up the track which leads south west along the coast past Barafundle Bay and eventually on to Stackpole Head.

Tides

The tide time window, when the base is uncovered, varies from 2 hours to about 4 hours on big tides. The most usual approach is to make a spectacular abseil straight down the left-hand (looking out) side of the *Silver Shadow* groove. This can be easily identified by a large detached pinnacle at the top. Abseil down just to the right (looking out) of this pinnacle.
It is also possible to scramble down a blocky ridge (a bit loose) on the west (Mowing Word) side of the cliff to a narrow projecting platform. From here a harder, but much more solid, scramble leads down to a boulder beach and some amazing caves below the cliff.

Conditions

Stackpole is slightly more sheltered than Mowing Word. The starts here can be wet but they tend to be juggy as well. It faces south west and receives afternoon and evening sun.
It is worth noting that, unlike Mowing Word, Stackpole is VERY popular for the birds. After August 1 the place can be pretty smelly and unpleasant and it is worth waiting for a storm or two to clean it up a bit.

The lonely figure of Graham Parkes on *Heaven's Door* (E2) - *page 205* - at Stackpole. Photo: Chris Craggs.

St. David's
Flimston Bay
Mewsford
Castle/Rusty
Saddle Head
Bosherston Head
Huntsman's Leap
Stennis/Chapel
Trevallen
St. Govan's
Mowing/Stackpole
Mother Carey's

Heaven's Door

Stackpole is at its tallest on its imposing left-hand side. Two caves dominate, split by the striking arete of *Always the Sun* with the cracks of *Heaven's Door* to its right.
Approach - Make a spectacular 40m abseil down the left-hand (looking out) side of the *Silver Shadow* groove and scramble left along the boulders. It is also possible to scramble down the promontory to the right (looking out) of the crag and navigate along its base at low tide.

1 Salty Dog . . . . 2 stars E3 5c

35m. A great route, found on the left-hand pillar of the first decent section of cliff. Climb to the first overhang, pass this with gusto, and continue up the wide crack above. Press on to gain the faultline above, move left, and follow the groove above to exit.
FA. Nipper Harrison 1.8.81

2 The Whaler . . . . 2 stars E2 5b

An ancient classic; an excellent yet daunting prospect. A rockfall at the start makes the first pitch's grade a little uncertain.
Photo opposite.
1) 4c, 25m. Climb up the groove to the chimney above, and continue to an overhang, move left to belay in a slot cave (possible belay to reduce drag). Climb out and traverse leftwards, to gain the base of a small chimney. Move up to belay.
3) 5b, 20m. Move up to the big roof above, then traverse strenously leftwards until beneath a flared crack. Battle your way up this feature to reach a scoop; trend rightwards to finish.
FA. Pat Littlejohn, Chris King 3.5.78

3 Immortality . . . . 3 stars E5 6b

38m. Brilliant! Superb climbing throughout, but at the top of its grade. Climb the groove for some 9m, then move left, to climb the left wall up to the the overhang above. Pull over this, and move into a slight groove, peg runners. Make a series of hard moves rightwards to the arete, and dive up this to a good ledge. A diagonal line leftwards takes you to an airy finish.
FA. Gary Gibson 23.8.87

4 Neptune . . . . 1 star HVS 5a

35m. One of the original lines here, and still a terrific one. It takes the central line of grooves between the caves, in the centre of the wide buttress. Climb up to an overhang at around 11m, then move left onto a good ledge. Easier moves then gain the foot of a steep groove, which is followed to a bigger ledge on the right (possible belay). Climb the cracked groove above to a good exit.
FA. Gordon Smith 26.9.70

The long groove to the right, running the full height of the cliff is **Aphrodite, HVS 5a**. *It has never been given any stars though it looks pretty good.*

5 Always the Sun . 3 stars E7 6c

35m. The massive arete is simply stunning. The fixed gear is not crucial to maintain the E7 grade. Start below the arete and climb it to a crack on the left which leads to a break. Swing left then pull up with difficulty to gain some breaks. Continue above to another break, step right along it then pull up to a large flake. Move right and climb the arete, past 2 pegs, to a break. Make more hard moves to another break, and peg. Step left and move up then back right to finish.
FA. Gary Gibson 31.8.87

❻ Cruise to Hell . . . . . ⟨2⟩ 🗡🏔 ☐ **E5 6b**
35m. A steep route up the left-hand side of the wall. Climb
Second Shadow then pull up rightwards into a hanging groove.
Step right out of this to join *Heaven's Door* and climb this onto
a block on the left. Move left below the left-hand crack in the
headwall and climb this to the top.
FA. Nipper Harrison 9.10.82

❼ Heaven's Door . . . . ⟨3⟩ 🗡 ☐ **E3 5c**
A superb route which takes the right-hand of the two cracks on
the left side of the headwall. At high tide it is possible to abseil
straight to the stance and just do the top pitch which is very
atmospheric when the sea is in. Start at a rightwards facing corner
below the right-hand side of the headwall. *Photo page 202.*
1) 5a, 10m. Climb the corner to a ledge on the left (often wet).
2) 5c, 25m. Move up and left, on large holds, to a short arete.
Continue with difficulty to the right-hand crack and climb this.
FA. Pat Littlejohn 4.77

❽ Second Shadow . . . . ⟨1⟩ 🗡 ☐ **E5 6a**
This is a typical Stackpole route; a steep start, a traverse and a
well-positioned upper section. Start below a steep crack.
1) 6a, 30m. Gain the crack from the right and climb it to a break
4m below the main roof. Trend leftwards to a hanging arete
below a break in the roofs. Climb into the groove above and follow this to a ledge on the left.
2) 5a, 10m. Move across to the wide crack and finish up this.
FA. Nipper Harrison 2.8.81

❾ Iron Maiden . . . . . . ⟨2⟩ 🏔🗡 ☐ **E4 6a**
38m. This awesome route follows the crack in the left-hand side
of the huge roof. Climb the steep crack all the way to the roof then
launch out into upside-down-land and try to get yourself established in the chimney on the lip. Climb the chimney to a corner on
the left and follow this to a ledge. Finish more easily above.
FA. Pat Littlejohn 24.9.80

Chris Craggs and Jim Rubery on pitch 2 of the
neglected classic *The Whaler* (E2) - *opposite* -
at Stackpole. Photo: Craggs Collection.

St. David's
Flimston Bay
Mewsford
Castle/Rusty
Saddle Head
Bosherston Head
Huntsman's Leap
Stennis/Chapel
Trevallen
St. Govan's
Mowing/Stackpole

Swordfish

The vast central section of Stackpole is an awe-inspiring hunk of rock, undercut by caves below huge roofs and sharp aretes and grooves. Luckily it is crossed by some big juggy breaks at convenient intervals which allow a few routes to weave their way up here at a relatively friendly grade for such steep territory.

Approach - Make a spectacular 40m abseil down the left-hand (looking out) side of the *Silver Shadow* groove.

10 Swordfish . . . . Top 50 E3 5c

40m. One of the best E3s in Pembroke! It manages to cover some incredibly steep ground without really pulling over any roofs. The traverse is very pumpy and not a good one to fall off if you are seconding! Climb the corner, past a couple of bulges, to a line of breaks below a roof. Traverse left along the breaks to below the main corner. Pull up to a ledge on the left (possible belay) then climb a small corner above. Step right into the main corner and follow this all the way to the top.

FA. Pat Littlejohn 2.5.78

11 Plane Sailing 3 E3 5c

A massive trip across some wild rock formations which is guaranteed to get the blood pumping and the heart racing. Allow plenty of time and make sure you are a competent well-balanced team since escape after the tide has come in is tricky. The line continues on the topo on the previous page.

1) 5b, 15m. Climb *Swordfish* and belay at the base of its groove.
2) 5c, 25m. Climb up to the break then follow it leftwards to a ledge just right of *Heaven's Door*.
3) 5a, 20m. Step down then pull around the arete. Follow the break to the ledge of *Neptune*.
4) 5b, 25m. Reverse down the groove of *Neptune* to gain the juggy band, then traverse left to the slot stance on *The Whaler*.
5) 5b, 30m. Follow *The Whaler* but continue left along the upper break to a hanging belay on the arete.
6) 5b, 15m. Traverse the slab using a horizontal crack, then pull up into a groove which leads to the top.

FA. Pat Littlejohn, Steve Lewis 13.1.80
FA. (P5 and 6) Pat Littlejohn, Chris Pound 24.9.80

12 Hammerhead 2 E5 6a

40m. An exposed trip up the big arete between *Swordfish* and *Silver Shadow*. From the base of the groove on *Swordfish*, climb direct to a break, then traverse right to a thread on the arete. Climb the arete, using holds on the right, to a break (peg). Continue past two threads to a ledge and finish direct.

FA. Gary Gibson 3.9.87

13 Silver Shadow . . . . Top 50 E2 5b

40m. If Swordfish is one of the best E3s in Pembroke then this is one of the best E2s. Climb the corner to the roof, as for *Swordfish*. Traverse right along the breaks then move up to another roof. Traverse back left to a small ledge beneath two cracks. Climb these then bear right into the corner and follow it to a break. Using a hold on the right move up to a continuation corner to the right of a roof. Follow this to the top.

FA. Pat Littlejohn 2.5.78

14 Break of Dawn 2 E5 6b

40m. Another great route, which aims for the bottomless groove above the right side of the massive roof. Cimb the bold lower wall to a rest below the roof, then pull leftwards through the roof. Move back right, then climb up into the slim groove, following it all the way to the top.

FA. Gary Gibson 5.8.90

15 Leap Frog 1 E3 5c

40m. A good but cruxy line, essentially reaching and climbing the groove right of *Break of Dawn*. Start some 4m left of the blunt arete. Climb up and diagonally rightwards, to reach the arete where it gives way to the blank wall above, then make hard moves to gain some obvious flat holds above. Follow the excellent groove above to the top.

FA. Pat Littlejohn 28.10.78

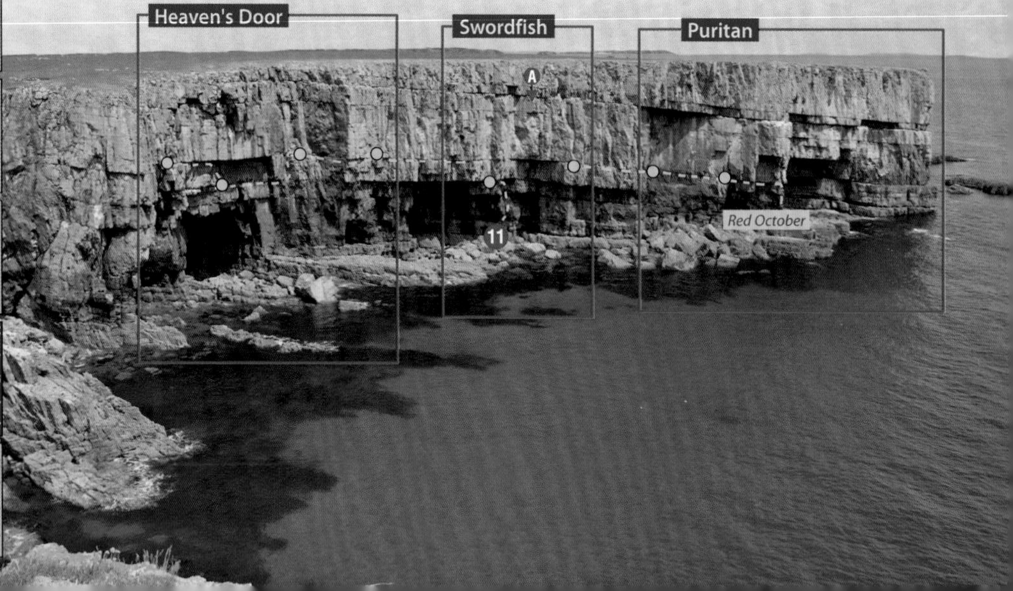

From mid morning
25 min
Tidal
Abseil in
A
Plane Sailing
11
12
13
Red October
High tide
14
15
10

Puritan

The far end of Stackpole is even wilder (if that were possible). The most noticable feature is a huge red wall left of another vast cave. Further right the wall is 'only vertical' but doesn't offer quite as much good climbing.
Approach and Tides - Abseil direct to tidal ledges at the base of the crag. A low tide is required for most routes although the ledge below *Stackpole Grooves* and *Condor* remains clear of the sea for much longer.

16 Oranges and Lemons 3 **E6 6c**
This superb piece of climbing tackles the centre of the burnt-orange wall, found under the huge upper roof stack.
1) 6c, 32m. Climb brown scoops to tiny ledges beneath a smooth wall, then move right and ascend twin cracks to a break. Tackle the bulge above, move left to the main crackline, and climb this to better holds in a break; move up and right to a nut/thread belay below the roofs.
2) 6b, 10m. Traverse rightwards, and crank through the roofs above to gain the groove left of *Puritan*. Follow this more easily to the top.
FA. Martin Crocker 30.8.87

17 Utter Anarchy . . 3 **E6 6c**
More exceptional climbing, doing battle with the smooth face to the right of *Oranges and Lemons*. Take plenty of microwires.
1) 6c, 30m. Climb a short crack, then move slightly left to pass a roof; gain the break, dive rightwards into a groove, and climb it to an obvious projecting hold. Stand on this, and climb up to another break, then move right and ascend a thin crack to gain the stance.
2) 6b, 10m. As for *Oranges and Lemons*.
FA. Martin Crocker 29.8.87

18 Puritan 3 **E2 5c**
40m. Magnificent! The original and best line here, venturing up the amazing crack/stepped feature on the right edge of the smooth orange wall - and all at an unlikely grade. Climb the steep lower section on good holds to gain a narrow groove, and overcome this to reach the main crackline above. Follow this, entering the shallow corner formed by the smooth wall on the left, and continue to the breakline above. Move 2m right, and climb the leftwards-slanting groove to the top.
Parliamentarian, E3 6a - The hanging crack to the right of *Puritan* is a good pitch but it shares much with *Puritan*.
FA. Pat Littlejohn 3.74. FA. (Parliamentarian) M.Kemball 30.8.83

From mid morning | 25 min | Tidal | Abseil in

⑲ Consolation . . . . ☆① ⚑ [ ] **E1 5b**
39m. The groove in the hanging arete is very well-positioned. Climb up the right wall of the arete for 5m, then edge leftwards into the groove. Follow this up the buttress to the main upper breakline, then climb the easy upper groove to the top.
FA. Ben Wintringham 2.8.81

⑳ Red October . . . . ☆② ⚑ 🕐 [ ] **E3 5b**
This is the lower section to *Plane Sailing* (previous page) the traverse across the left-hand side of the crag. As yet, there are no known ascents of the connection of these two into a single monster traverse but that would certainly be some route!
1) 5b, 20m. Start up *Consolation* to the first break. Traverse left along it to a belay in *Puritan*.
2) 5b, 20m. Continue across the orange wall to the corner.
3) 5b, 20m. More horizontal break dangling leads to *Leap Frog*.
4) 5b, 20m. Bale out up *Leap Frog*, or continue ....? (probably harder than E3).
FA. Paul Donnithorne, Alan Leary 19.8.94

㉑ Mrs Pearson's Fine Damson Jam
. . . . ☆① ⚑ [ ] **E3 5c**
40m. A great line. Follow *Consolation*, then pull past the small overhang to reach a good ledge. Carry on up the buttress to the upper breakline, and finish just to the right of *Consolation*.
FA. Gary Gibson 22.2.87

㉒ Honeypot . . . . ☆③ ⚑ ✊ [ ] **E5 6b**
38m. Sustained and strenuous. Climb the initial wall to a break, pull onto the face above, and up to an undercut. Continue up to a small ledge and a break, and ascend the wall above using pockets and a thin crack. The top wall is straightforward.
FA. Gary Gibson 22.2.87

The next two routes start from a ledge which is only covered during high tide. It can be reached direct by abseil from above.

㉓ Condor . . . . ☆① ⚑ [ ] **E3 5c**
Start from the left end of the ledge (or lower if the sea allows).
1) 5c, 17m. Climb the initial recess for 3m, then move left into the groove and follow it, trending a little rightwards, to gain a shallow groove. Follow this to a decent stance below the roof.
2) 5c, 15m. A leftwards traverse brings you to a good hold on the lip of the roof; climb up to a sloping ledge, and use a thin crack to head for the top.
FA. Nipper Harrison 3.77

㉔ Stackpole Grooves . . . . ☆② [ ] **HVS 5a**
Stackpole's first ever route. The first pitch drags you around to the South Face a little; the second pitch features the upper groove system on the West Face. It's also possible to climb the variation start at 5a, which gives a better balanced and higher quality route.
1) 4c, 18m. Climb the accommodating groove, to arrive at the halfway ledge, then traverse leftwards along the ledge system to gain the foot of the groovy second pitch.
2) 5a, 14m. The clean groove is followed all the way to a good exit.
1a) variation start 5a, 16m. Climb the lower corner, then the steep groove above, using the short slab on the left to gain the belay ledge above.
FA. Colin Mortlock 20.7.67

Leaning Tower Wall - *This feature is the southerly limit of this Stackpole menu. As with the main cliff, low tide conditions provide the key, and use of the huge boulder makes life slightly easier than it might otherwise have been.*

㉕ Adam Adamant . ☆③ ⚑ ✊ 🕐 💧 [ ] **E5 6b**
Ace. A crack(ing) first pitch is followed by the stonking arete above. Start from the huge boulder.
1) 6b, 15m. Step over to reach a tiny pod, and make hard moves to gain a vertical slot. Use this to span leftwards to a crack, and press on to gain a horizontal crack, then the ledge above.
2) 6a, 15m. Climb into the corner, then break out leftwards to climb the right side of the hanging arete - bold moves finally give you a slim finishing groove. Belay 10m back.
FA. Martin Crocker 20.9.87

St. David's | Flimston Bay | Mewsford | Castle/Rusty | Saddle Head | Bosherston Head | Huntsman's Leap | Stennis/Chapel | Trevallen | St. Govan's | Mowing/Stackpole | Mother Carey's

Alan James at the top of one of Mother Carey's lesser known gems, *Sunsmoke* (E2) - *page 217*. In the background Alison Martindale starts up *Brazen Buttress* (E2) - *page 219* - and in the sea a lost rope swirls around amongst the rocks. Photo: Mike Robertson

Mother Carey's

	No star	1 star	2 stars	3 stars
Mod to S	-	-	1	1
HS to HVS	1	1	3	1
E1 to E3	1	5	5	7
E4 and up	-	4	4	14

Mother Carey's Kitchen is one of Pembroke's best crags offering superb climbing in a great location, with routes from Severe to E7, and with few restrictions due to nesting birds or army shooting practice - in fact, mid-week in the first half of the year can leave it as the only major crag which is available to climb on!
It is often popularly known as '*Mother Scarys*' which is easy to appreciate as you heave up *Rock Idol*, or dangle from the Space Face, however, not everything here is steep and exposed, and the routes near *Crithmum* provide some of the best Severe and VS climbing along the whole coast.

Approach and Tides

Mother Carey's is situated on Lydstep Point, near Tenby. From Pembroke town, take the A4139 towards Tenby. After about 7 miles you reach the tiny village of Lydstep. On a bend in the road, about 50m before the Lydstep Tavern, turn right down a dirt track that looks like someone's driveway. After 250m the track bends to the left then turn immediately right up a steep track. This leads to a large grassy field on the clifftop. The cliffs can also be reached from Tenby by taking the A4139, which is signed to Manorbier and Pembroke, arriving at Lydstep village from the east. From the parking field, a path leads south east to some grassy knolls at the clifftop, the most prominent of these being the top of Brazen Buttress.
The approaches to the climbs at Mother Carey's are all affected by the tide to varying degrees.
Low tide approach - At dead low tide (springs only) walk down the promontory opposite the Space Face and scramble down underneath it onto the boulders below the faces.
Mid tide approach - For 4 hours at low tide, it is possible to scramble down the west ridge past an awkward rock step (about VDiff) to the bottom. Then make a juggy traverse under the west wall to reach the cliff base proper. Alternatively, abseil down the front face of Brazen Buttress from a big block.
High tide approach - In calm seas, you can abseil to various points beneath the wall: the cave at the bottom of *Strait Gate*, the ledges beneath *Crithmum*, the base of the left-hand through cave, a tiny ledge beneath *Herod*. Additionally, with a bit of rope trickery, the ledge beneath *Rock Idol* and the first belay of *Mother Night* can also be reached.
All the routes in Blind Bay are also accessible at high tide which is especially important if you are intending on soloing them.

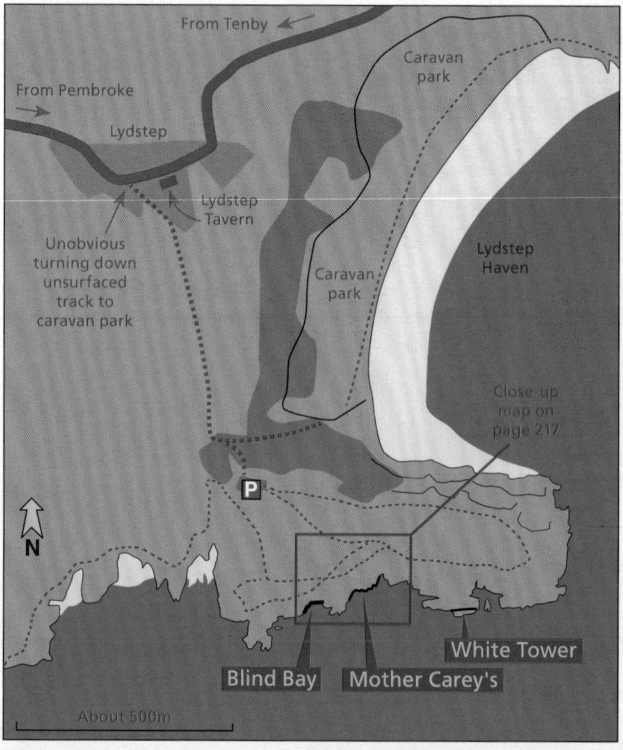

Conditions

Mother Carey's Kitchen faces roughly south although the Zeppelin Wall and the Space Face face east and only receive the morning sun. The square-cut corners give the cliff some shelter from westerly winds. The rock quality near the sea is solid, higher up there are some loose bits and it is another crag where the Pembroke *put an extra runner in for the top* maxim is worth remembering. The morning slime can linger, especially on the Space Face and in Blind Bay, and it is often slippery and wet inside the through-cave. In these conditions the routes in the through-cave are still climbable but it is best to keep away from the Space Face and the other hard routes.

Mick Ryan tackling *The Cracks* (Severe) - *page 217* - one of the great easier routes at Mother Carey's. Photo: Mike Robertson

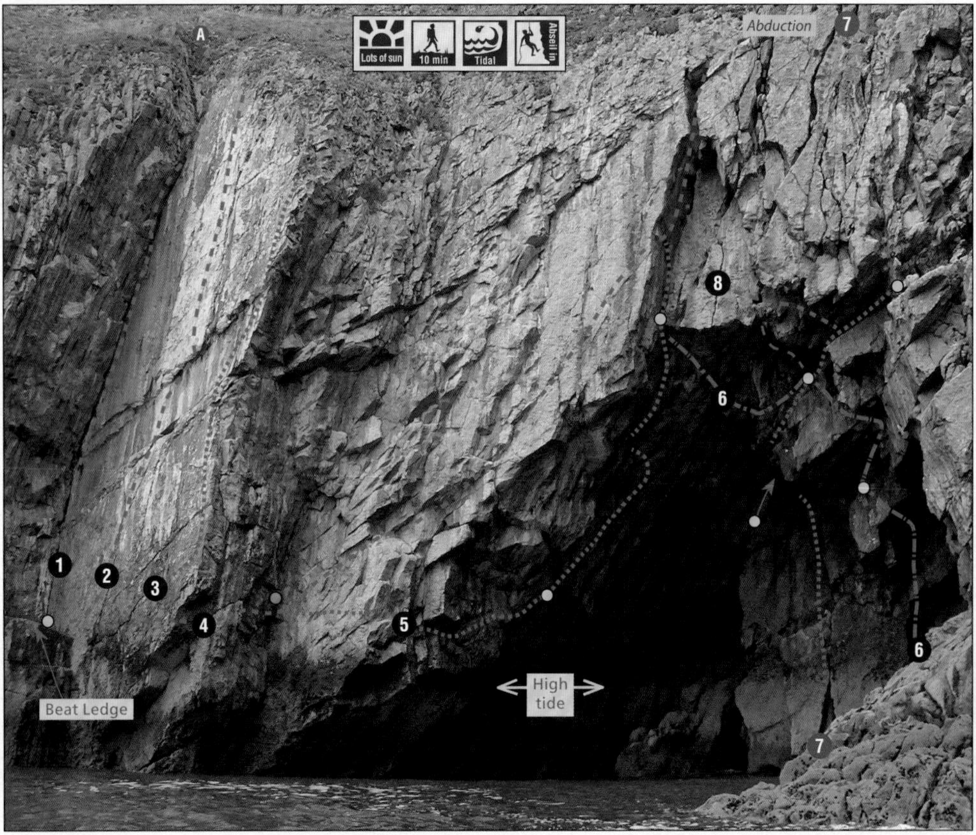

Blind Bay

This hidden bay contains some of the best hard routes in the area but most people don't even know it is there. The corner of *Beat Surrender* is superb, the expedition of *The One-eyed Man* is magnificent, and the atmospheric Alien Cave gives awesome routes for those keen to go bat-style.

Approach (see map on next page) - *Abseil into the Beat Ledge to access the first 5 routes; the ledge should be accessible in all but the very highest tides (or the craziest seas).*

1 Beat Surrender 3 E5 6b

24m. An absolute classic, taking on the towering corner above the ledge. High in the grade, but very well-protected. Climb the corner with increasing difficulty, then continue on, with more than a little use of the left sidewall, to the top.

FA. Andy Sharp 8.86

2 Aristocrat 1 E5 6b

26m. The crinkly low face leads to a pleasant crack. (**S3, 7a**).

FA. Andy Sharp 2.9.86

3 Toffee Nose. . . . 1 E5 6a

26m. Gain the technical lower arete via the diagonal seam, and follow the arete past a small overlap to the top. (**S3, 7a**).

FA. Julian Lines 1.9.2005

4 The One-eyed Man 3 E5 6a

36m. A stupendous expedition weaving across the entire crag to finish up the hanging corner above the Alien Cave. Can be split into 2 pitches, using the base of the groove. From the Beat Ledge, traverse steadily rightwards, keeping just above the cave lip, to gain the exposed arete. Take either of the two good cracks (the lower one is recommended) to swing into the welded-flowstone corner on the right, and continue up this to the top. (**S3, 7a**)

Photo opposite.

FA. Crispin Waddy 1991

5 The Abyss. . . 3 E7 6b

A brilliant, visionary line, tackling the massively overhanging left wall of the cave. The first ascent was soloed (**S3, 7b**) and it has yet to be led on gear.

1) 20m, 6b. From the Beat Ledge, follow *The One-eyed Man* across the lower face, then drop down and traverse into the cave, using the fingery hanging wall. Make a hard move into the inner cave, to belay on a slab beneath the hanging off-width.

2) 16m, 6b. Move up and rightwards into the hanging 45° off-width and follow this. Then swing left and take a series of jugs to reach a hanging tunnel for a well-earned rest. Drop out of the tunnel and move left on undercuts, to gain the lip of the cave. Move up the wall to reach the thread belay in the base of the corner.

3) 12m, 5b. Climb the superb welded-flowstone corner all the way to the top.

FA. Julian Lines (solo) 11.9.2005

St. David's
Flimston Bay
Mewsford
Castle/Rusty
Saddle Head
Bosherston Head
Huntsman's Leap
Stennis/Chapel
Trevallen
St. Govan's
Moving/Stackpole
Mother Carey's

Julian Lines soloing *The One-eyed Man* (E5) - *opposite* - in Blind Bay. Photo: Mike Robertson

Approach (see map on next page) - *For the following 3 routes, use a low tide to wade/boulder across to the ledges inside the cave itself - a low spring tide would be ideal. An alternative would be to traverse in from the right (looking in). Conditions are very important here - a steady breeze from the south should dry the cave out.*

6 The Anti Matterhorn

. . . . **E6 6b**

Steep, crazy climbing, tackling the cave at its very centre. Start on the right side of the pillar. (**S3, 7b**).

1) 13m, 6a. Climb the short groove, then up through two roofs, to belay on the left.

2) 10m, 6a. Traverse rightwards along a fault, then pull up and left to gain a hanging wall, belay at the top of this.

3) 10m, 6b. Climb leftwards and down slightly, to make a precarious bridge onto the horn; then get established on it, using a distant undercut. Follow a line of undercuts to gain the corner above, belaying on the thread as for *The Abyss*.

4) 12m, 5b. As for *The Abyss*.

FA. Andy Long, Crispin Waddy 1990's

7 Alien World/Blind Vision

. . . . **E3 5c**

The original line is better when combined with the alternative top pitch of *Blind Vision*. Start on boulders below the triangular niche.

1) 8m, 5a. Climb the niche/crack to a big ledge.

2) 12m, 5c. Climb easily up the corner, then continue up to threads below the roof. Move left, then rightwards over the roof. Belay in the back of the cave.

3) 10m, 5c. Drop down right into a bottomless groove. Traverse up and rightwards to belay in a niche (on *Anti-Matterhorn*).

4) 9m, 5c. Continue scrunging up and right, to belay on a big ledge.

5) 13m, 5a. Step up and left onto the cracked, hanging wall, and press on up the deep crack to the top.

FA. (AW) Clark Alston, Frank Ramsay 23.4.90
FA. (BV) Paul Donnithorne, 12.5.96

8 Alien World Direct **E4 6a**

20m. A fine finish from the cave belay at the end of pitch 3. Traverse up and right for 3m to a seat just inside the cave. Pull out over the overhang via a block and swing left to a good thread. Climb leftwards to gain the hanging corner of *The Abyss*.

Abduction Finish, E4 6a - From the same belay, pull directly around the roof to gain a big slot (a no-hands leg rest), then swing around the lip on big pockets to the thread. Climb direct to the steep wide crack above.

FA. Frank Ramsay, Dave Turnbull 30.6.90
FA. (Abduction) Julian Lines 3.9.2005

Lots of sun | 10 min | Tidal | Abseil in

Strait Gate

The left-hand side of the crag has a huge overhanging corner - *Rock Idol*. Left of the corner the cliff bulges for almost its entire length, to the right is a magnificent wall laced with cracks and with a prominent pod-shaped cave low down (*Strait Gate*). To the right of *Strait Gate* the cliff is covered in a mass of cracks and caves running up its full length which give a few classic lower grade routes.

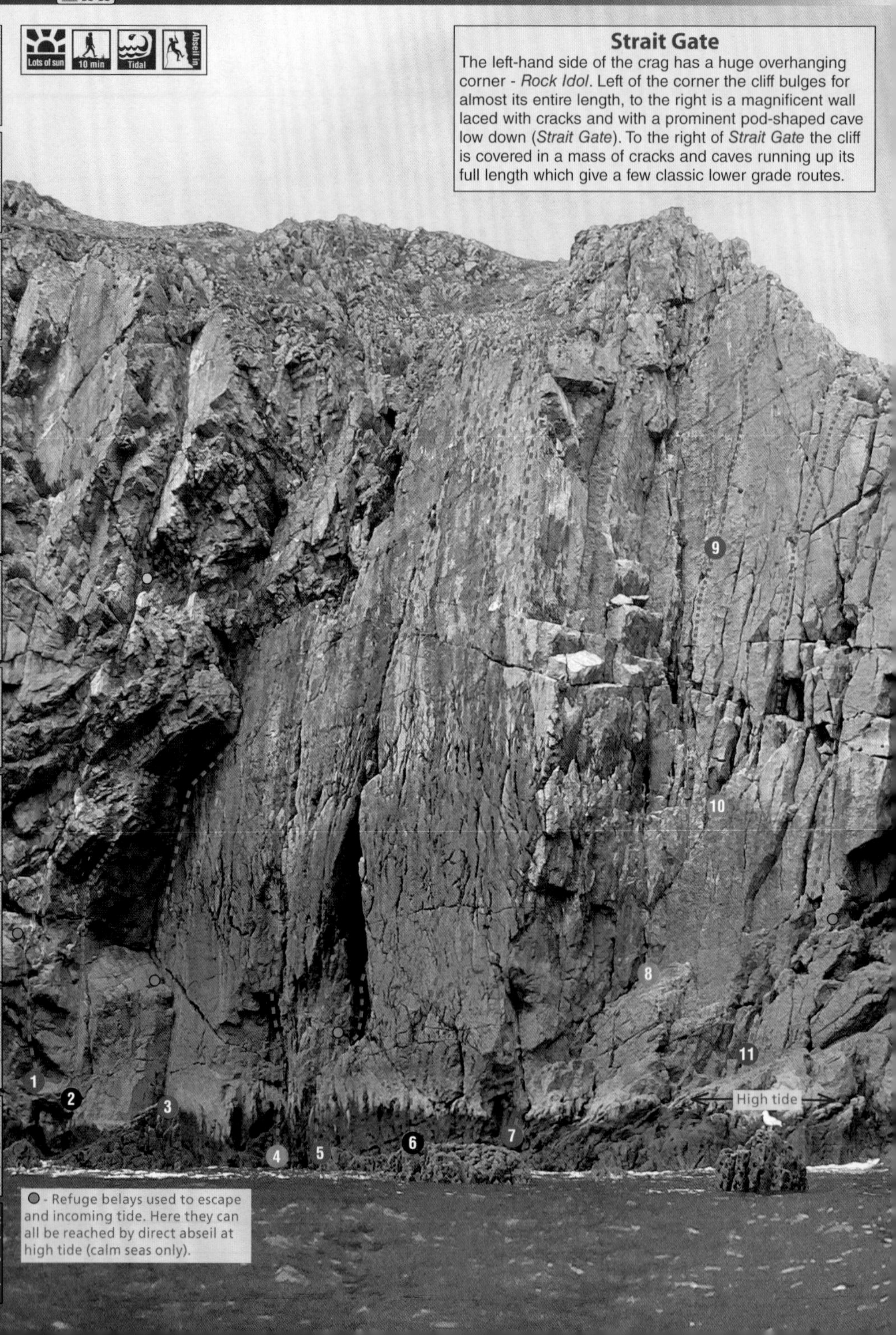

● - Refuge belays used to escape and incoming tide. Here they can all be reached by direct abseil at high tide (calm seas only).

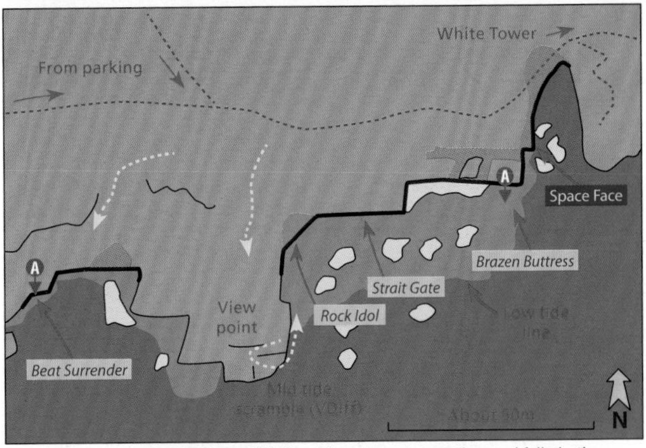

1 Zeppelin Top 50 ☐ **E3 5c**
A Pembroke classic which soars up and out over the sea with more buckets than a garden centre. It is usually done in one pitch but can be split at a small stance if the tide threatens. Start beneath a line of grooves 5m left of the corner.
1) 5c, 20m. Climb up to the base of the first groove and follow it to a bulge. Power around this then swing up and right to a jutting flake (hands-off rest possible!). Continue up cracks to a well-positioned stance.
2) 5b, 15m. Pull into the upper groove and follow it more easily to the top. Stake belay well back.
FA. Pat Littlejohn, Nipper Harrison 13.8.77

2 Hindenburg . . . . ★★★ ☐ **(E7 6c)**
35m. The wall between *Zeppelin* and the corner contains a similar route to *Zeppelin* but without all the jugs. The crucial peg on the first section has rotted and this bit hasn't been climbed in its new state, although reports are that it will still be E7. As an alternative it is possible to sample the wild upper wall at **E5 6b** by breaking right from *Zeppelin* on the shared ledge.
FA. Steve Monks 17.6.91

3 Rock Idol . . . . Top 50 ☐ **E1 5a**
35m. The best E1 in Britain? Probably! The line follows the huge corner all the way but on an angle of rock normally reserved for E5s. Start below the corner and climb up to the sloping ledge. Climb the right wall to an overhang. Move around this and continue to another bulge with a line of holds leading out right. Ignore these holds and pull over the daunting bulge above on some of the biggest holds in the universe. Continue straight up the crack and right-leaning groove above to ledges. Climb the crack above to the top, then stand back and beat your chest triumphantly!
FA. Pat Littlejohn 5.76

4 Joyous Gard . . . . ★★ ☐ **HVS 5a**
35m. The line of grooves and cracks between the corner and the cave of *Strait Gate*. Climb the grooves then move slightly right into the cracks. These lead steeply to a small groove on the right. Move up into a cave then climb the loose gully above to the top.
FA. Jim Perrin 30.8.70

5 The Strait Gate . . . . Top 50 ☐ **E1 5b**
35m. Another mega route with all the ingredients you come to expect from Pembroke - stunning lines, great climbing and bags of atmosphere! It is a hard E1 though so make sure you have a bit in reserve for the stiff finish. Climb into the cave (possible belay if the tide threatens and it can also be reached by abseil if the tide is in). Move up the chimney until it is possible to step onto the wall on the right. Climb back above into the cracks and follow these until they start to close. Make some hard moves straight up the wall to the top. It is possible to traverse left from where the crack closes into the finishing gully which is a bit easier - **HVS 5a**.
FA. Jim Perrin 26.8.70

6 Talk's Cheap . . . . ★ ☐ **E4 6b**
35m. This direct route up the wall between *Strait Gate* and the arete. Climb the wall, on some large sharp holds and cracks, to a break. Move up slightly rightwards to reach some good holds. Stand up on these, step left, and make hard moves up the wall above to the top.
FA. Gary Gibson 28.5.87

Rockfalls and Birds - *There have been a few rockfalls in the area between Wraith and Crithmum. Several routes have been destroyed and the remaining rock is still unstable in places. Take care when climbing these routes. The ledges are a popular bird nesting location. This only causes a problem on Crithmum as there is often a nest on the route.*

7 Wraith . . . . ★★ ☐ **E3 5c**
35m. A great climb but perhaps not as great as it once was, and it should be considered as high in the grade. Start below a small niche at the base of the arete. Climb into this then step left onto the wall which is followed easily to some large ledges. Climb the left-hand side of the arete above.
FA. Jim Perrin 9.72. When first climbed this was a fine jamming crack at HVS. A huge rockfall removed the right-hand side of the crack to turn it into the harder arete climb that it is today.

8 Crithmum . . . . ★ ☐ **VS 5a**
32m. Once an enjoyable and popular classic but it has suffered from rockfalls over the years. The route has now stabilised but is still a bit dirty and is also a popular nesting zone. Start beneath the corner and climb the right-hand groove and some cracks above it, to a ledge. Follow the corner above to its top.
FA. Colin Mortlock 20.8.69

9 Sunsmoke. . . . . ★★ ☐ **E2 5b**
32m. A superb crack in the wall right of *Crithmum* which is better now that *Crithmum* is further away! Climb *Crithmum* to the base of its upper corner then step up right into the crack. This gives sustained and interesting climbing with one tricky section. A gem! *Photo on page 210.*
FA. Gary Gibson 28.5.87. The original line started to the right and followed the wider cracks on the right in its upper section.

10 The Meridian. . . . . ★★ ☐ **VS 4c**
30m. A good route which takes a line up the cracked wall starting as for *Crithmum*. Move up a crack, trend rightwards out of *Crithmum*, to a square-cut niche in the centre of the wall. Follow the twin cracks above to the top.
FA. Jim Perrin 23.12.68

11 The Cracks . . . . ★★ ☐ **Sev**
30m. The wall just left of the through cave. Climb cracks in the wall to a triangular niche (historical belay). Move right out of this and follow more cracks to the top. *Photo on page 213.*
FA. Lyn Noble 31.12.68

St. David's
Flimston Bay
Mewsford
Castle/Rusty
Saddle Head
Bosherston Head
Huntsman's Leap
Stennis/Chapel
Trevallen
St. Govan's
Mowing/Stackpole
Mother Carey's

12 Threadneedle Street. . . . . . . Top 50 **Sev**

A brilliant and highly entertaining route that gets you into some spectacular situations. It is probably best to do it in the three short pitches to avoid rope drag and the route is a bit harder when wet (which it often is). Start by scrambling through the upper through-cave dropping down and heading left to the very back of the chimney. *Photo opposite.*

1) 12m. Climb the chimney mainly on the left wall, to a stance.
2) 15m. Traverse out and left along a massive juggy hand-rail, to the mouth of the cave. Pull up then step left to a triangular niche.
3) 10m. Move right out of the niche and climb a crack to a short corner and the top. This is the top of *The Cracks*.

FA. Richard Crewe 25.3.78

13 Karma Waters 1 **E1 5b**

25m. A route which bisects the traverse of *Threadneedle Street*. Climb the steep wall on the left-hand side of the through cave and pull up above into the wide crack sprouting from its top left corner which leads to the top.

FA. Dave Viggers 4.92

14 Eight Gauge . . . . HVS 5a

25m. Start on the right-hand side of the through cave. Climb the pillar on the front edge then step right onto a ramp. Pull onto the wall above and climb to the top right corner of the through cave. Finish up the wide crack which is a bit vegetated.

FA. Colin Mortlock 20.3.69

Brazen Buttress

The centre of Mother Carey's is dominated by the tall tower of Brazen Buttress. Around the tower are a series of caves and pillars composed of some great fissured rock. This wall has some of the best easier routes around, plus a couple of 'big tick' E2s.

15 Narrow Carriage . . . 1 **E1 5c**
25m. Start as for *Eight Gauge*. Make one move up then branch leftwards up a faint groove. Climb the easy slab above to the top corner of the through cave. Pull up then step left out of the chimney of *Eight Gauge*, above the roofs. Follow the wall above past a protruding pedestal.
FA. Paul Donnithorne 4.92

16 Tempest 2 **E1 5c**
28m. A good route which uses the start of *Eight Gauge* to gain the fine crack to the left of *Brazen Buttress*. Climb the pillar on the front right-hand side of the through cave, then step right onto a ramp (as for *Eight Gauge*). Follow the ramp to a crack in the smooth wall. Climb the crack and another crack on the right until the wall blanks out above a jug. Make a tricky move up and left to easier ground.
FA. Nipper Harrison 25.3.78

17 Whirlwind 1 **E1 5c**
30m. This hybrid starts and finishes on other routes but there is some good independent climbing, and it should be of interest to those looking for something new on this wall. Start up *Brazen Buttress* then traverse up and left across the wall to the right-hand side of the pedestal. Climb direct up a crack above to join *Tempest* at its crux and finish up this. It originally finished left of *Tempest* but this is very artificial. The original start up the arch is worth about **E3 5c** and combining this with the direct finish to *Brazen* makes a decent and balanced **E3 5c** combination.
FA. Paul Donnithorne 30.8.91. Via the direct start through the arch. The version here was done while checking for the guide.

18 Brazen Buttress . Top 50 **E2 5b**
35m. A superb and popular route. Start beneath a left-facing groove in the middle of the south face of the buttress. Climb over a small roof into the groove and follow this to the top of the big pedestal (possible belay if the sea is threatening). Climb up and left past a deep crack to gain a rising crackline. Follow this and at its end climb direct to the top. *Photo on page 210.*
Direct Finish, E3 5c. Direct from half way up the crackline.
FA. Pat Littlejohn 4.76

19 Herod 2 **E2 5b**
35m. The arete of *Brazen Buttress* gives a magnificently-positioned pitch which has set many a camera clicking. Start beneath the arete. Climb up the left-hand side to gain a crack. Follow this to some ledges on the arete (possible thread belay if the sea is threatening). Climb the left-hand side of the arete then move onto the arete proper. Follow this to the top.
FA. Pat Littlejohn 5.75

20 Heroes 1 **E2 5b**
35m. An eliminate with some good climbing. Start as for *Herod* but move onto the wall on the left until forced back into *Herod* - all a bit pointless, but now things improve. Step left from the top of the crack and climb the wall and cracks direct to the top.
FA. Nipper Harrison 13.8.77

Mike Robertson swinging from the world's biggest jug-rail on *Threadneedle Street* (Severe) - *opposite* - at Mother Carey's. Photo: Mick Ryan

Star Gate

The deep cleft behind Brazen Buttress is home to some of the most bizarre and wild adventures in Pembroke. *Deep Space* and *Star Gate* stand out but to be honest, they are all good. The one factor than can spoil your ascent is if the cave itself is too wet and slimy, so try and aim for dry days with a light breeze.

Approach and Tides - Abseil down *Brazen Buttress* and scramble around into the cave which is filled for a short while at high tide.

1 Inner Space. . . . . 3 ☐ HVS 4c
This amazing route follows the inside of the through cave to the lip, eventually popping out onto *Deep Space*. Start at the left-hand side of the landward wall of the through cave.
1) 4c, 35m. Climb easily up the wall to a large blocky ledge and walk rightwards along this. Move up until you are level with the top roof of the cave and then pull around into a chimneying position. Back and foot to the chockstone near the lip. Wild!
2) 4b, 10m. Squeeze through above a second chockstone (also wild) and climb the corner crack above to the top.
FA. M.Harris, C.Powell 18.4.81

2 Galaxy . . . . 2 ☐ E3 5c
An often-slimy experience up the landward wall. If it is dry, then it is a stunning and unusual addition to the Mother Carey's repertoire. Take lots of slings for the threads. Start inside the through cave, on the back landward wall, 6m left of *Deep Space*.
1) 5c, 20m. Climb up cracks and pockets to a lump. Move right on big holds then climb to the roof. Pull around this with difficulty, then belay in the chimney.
2) 4c, 15m. Continue up rightwards towards the boulder choke and squeeze through the hole and finish as for *Inner Space*.
FA. Paul Donnithorne, Emma Alsford 30.8.91

3 Deep Space. . . . . Top 50 ☐ E2 5b
This magnificent route which gives entertaining climbing in a weird situation. Unfortunately the first pitch can be a bit slimy since it is buried in the through cave but the second pitch is superb. If there are birds nesting in the cave then consider doing it in one long pitch. Start beneath the left-hand of two grooves at the right-hand side of the back wall of the cave. *Photo this page.*
1) 5b, 20m. Climb to a ledge then move left onto the wall. Move up to gain a rightwards rising line which is followed to a good flake. Continue up and right (thread runner) until level with a hole on the right. Step down and gain the hole from below.
2) 5a, 20m. Pull out left then swing around the roof to gain a chimneying position above. Bridge up the outside edge above (or climb the right wall) and continue up the corner to the top.
The Fresh Air Finish, E2 5b. Climb straight over the roof above the cave and move right to the hanging arete. Pull onto this on its left and continue up the wall above in an amazing position.
FA. Pat Littlejohn, Dave Garner 5.75. FA. (FAF) Pat Littlejohn 1.12.77

4 Star Gate . . . . Top 50 ☐ E3 5c
No climbing 1 March to 1 August because of nesting birds.
40m. A seminal route in many climber's careers; as your arms become tired, the holds just get bigger and bigger! Start below the groove as for *Deep Space*. Climb the groove, which is surprisingly technical and slabby, until a line of jugs leads out right to another groove. Follow this, with most of the Atlantic Ocean beneath you, then move right into an easier finishing crack.
Warp Gate, E5 6b - The version described in Extreme Rock is actually the best line on the crag but is seldom climbed. It starts up *Warp Factor* and continues up *Star Gate*. Solid E5!
FA. Pat Littlejohn, Nipper Harrison 3.77. FA. (WG) Kim Carrigan

5 Warp Factor . . . 2 ☐ E5 6b
No climbing 1 March to 1 August because of nesting birds.
The first of the hard routes has a steep start which is often a bit too wet. Start on a block below the groove right of *Star Gate*.
1) 6b, 15m. Step off a block and climb the groove to a bulge. Cross this and step right above the bulge into a corner. Follow this to a thread and swing around the arete to a small stance.
2) 5c, 20m. Pull out right above the stance and climb the bulge and wall above to some good holds on the left. Move up then step right into a cave. Finish leftwards up *Star Gate*.
FA. Pat Littlejohn 31.7.77

Fiona Fullwood on the belay of *Deep Space* (E2) - *opposite* - at Mother Carey's. Photo: Jon Fullwood

The Space Face

This well-named hunk of rock has some of the best and steepest hard routes in Pembroke. Believe it or not, the wall actually feels even steeper than it looks!

Approaches and Tides

Very low tide - Walk to the boulders underneath it.
Mid tide - Traverse rightwards from below *Warp Factor*.
High tide - Abseil from the stake down the open groove which is the top of *Hyperspace*, to the ledge on *Mother Night*. You will need to place about three bits of gear to pull you slightly leftwards and in. Your second can then abseil down and remove the bits of gear.

6 Hyperspace 3 E4 6a

No climbing 1 March to 1 August because of nesting birds.
This route makes the most of the Space Face by taking an intricate diagonal line across it. Start on a block.
1) 6a, 15m. Move diagonally right to a bulge. Pull through this then swing left (direct to here is much harder) then press on up the jugs above to a short groove leading to a small ledge.
2) 5c, 10m. Move up to some juggy pockets which lead rightwards, past some threads, to the stance of *Mother Night*.
3) 5c, 20m. Pull out right from the stance to below an open groove. Traverse right across the blank wall to a good pocket. Follow the crackline above, moving right around the bulge at the top.
FA. Pat Littlejohn 6.5.79

No climbing route 6
1 March to 1 August

7 Fireball XL5 . . . (3) **E6 6b**

30m. A mega direct route up the wall left of all the threads. Climb up a vague bulging arete to a good slot. Continue straight up to two threads on the left. Move left (possible belay) then pull back right through the bulge into a shallow groove. Climb boldly up the groove to reach good holds at its top. Step right and finish up a diagonal crack in the loose upper wall. *Photo this page.*
FA. Gary Gibson 28.5.87

8 Just Klingon . . . . . . (3) **E5 6a**

30m. Classic steep climbing past loads of threads - about 7a+ but check the threads first! Start 10m left of the *Mother Night* ledge. Climb up then move right around the first bulge to a thread in a diagonal slab. Climb up the overlaps leftwards to the traverse line of *Hyper Space*. Pull up above and follow the line of threads, keeping left of the short groove, to the upper break. Either finish straight up the wall, or as for *Mother Night*.
FA. Gary Gibson 28.4.91

9 Mother Night . . . . . . (3) **E4 6a**

The central route on the wall provides a magnificent challenge. Get yourself onto a tiny ledge, just left of the big cave, either from below or above; or start from lower at low tide.
1) 6a, 15m. Climb up left from the ledge to a small roof. Make a very hard move around this to a tiring undercut above. Pull up left (also hard) into another groove then climb up over the overlaps to reach a good stance at the base of a steep corner.
2) 5c, 15m. Climb the corner then traverse left to a monster thread on the very nose of the buttress (you'll see what I mean when you get there!). Step left and climb the wall to the top.
FA. Pat Littlejohn 7.4.78

10 Zoony . . . . (2) **E5 6b**

30m. Yet another steep and hard route. Start as from the ledge of *Mother Night*. After pulling around the first roof, make a hard move up onto a hanging ramp above. Climb this delicately to a rest at its top. Pull up above then make a hard move to a good side-pull at the base of an open groove. Climb the groove on flake holds and pull rightwards around the top bulge.
FA. Gary Gibson 12.7.87

11 Unconscious . . . . . . (2) **E6 6c**

30m. A desperate direct line which reaches the last section of *Hyperspace* from below. Start from the *Mother Night* ledge. Climb rightwards onto the hanging slab then pull straight up the wickedly steep rock above. Move left onto a hanging ramp and climb this rightwards to a roof. Pull straight over to reach the large pocket on *Hyperspace*. Finish as for this.
FA. Gary Gibson 24.3.89

12 Tiger Tiger . . . . (3) **E5 6b**

30m. A stunning route which makes the most of the right-hand side of the wall. Take a lot of small cams. Start from the ledge on *Mother Night*. Move out right to a large overhung, sloping ledge. Leave this rightwards into a steep groove which is followed to a good hold on its left-hand side. Pull up into a corner above and follow a crack up right to a roof. Move back leftwards up a crackline then climb the wall above to the top, finishing just left of a block.
FA. Pat Littlejohn 18.7.79

13 The Laughing Hygena (3) **E6 6c**

35m. If you thought that the other routes on this wall were steep then take a look at this one! It is a direct start to *Tiger Tiger* which requires a very low spring tide and dry conditions. If these two criteria are satisfied, start in the cave right of the face, below a thread in the middle of nowhere. Step off a boulder and climb an overhanging crack to some overhanging pockets. Pull up above to join *Tiger Tiger* at its good hold.
FA. George Smith 4.94

Seán Villanueva cruising *Fireball XL5* (E6) - *above* - on the Space Face at Mother Carey's. Photo: Patrick Daniel

St. David's | Flimston Bay | Mewsford | Castle/Rusty | Saddle Head | Bosherston Head | Huntsman's Leap | Stennis/Chapel | Trevallen | St. Govan's | Mowing/Stackpole | Mother Carey's

1 Sackless . . . . ☐ **E1 5b**
16m. This short route follows the left-hand crack. Climb past the hole and continue up the crack, gradually moving leftwards to finish on the wobbly left arete - a square notch provides the belay.
FA. S.Ferguson 13.4.87

2 Petit Blanc . . . . 1 ☐ **E2 5c**
18m. Some good, tricky climbing. It takes the discontinuous crack line just to the right of *Sackless*.
FA. Steve Lewis 1984

3 Dog Nobbler . . . . . . 1 ☐ **E4 6b**
25m. The lower rising breakline across the face provides some great and pumpy entertainment - and there is one hard move, too. Finish in *Sea Groove*; either up it or down it, depending on where your gear is.
FA. Andy Gronowski 6.83

4 Killer White. . . . 2 ☐ **E6 6b**
22m. The first of the 'white' desperates; just superb. Sustained climbing all the way. Cross *Dog Nobbler*, and continue up the technical wall above, to the upper break. Trend leftwards to finish.
FA. Tony Mitchell 24.9.85

5 White Heat . . . . 3 ☐ **E5 6b**
25m. The strongest line on the wall, and one of the best the Tower has to offer. The route takes the left-hand, full-height crack all the way to the top. The climbing will tire your feet and test your resolve; staying power is essential! Don't expect a hard crux move, but don't expect any rests either.
FA. Pete Whillance 9.4.80

6 The Great White 3 ☐ **E7 6c**
30m. Arguably THE hard wall climb of its era. It's a mighty route, with a weighty reputation - and one which sees very few ascents even today, despite being featured on the cover of a famous hardback rock climbing book, and having no dodgy fixed gear.
It follows the soaring right-hand crack, which rather inconveniently peters out above the traverse of *Dog Nobbler*. The section above constitutes the crux; your aim is to press on to the next breakline, where the climbing becomes just a tad easier...
FA. Ron Fawcett 7.82

Lots of sun | 15 min

The White Tower

Grand, shapely and classic - Pembroke wall climbing at its very best. Yet it's much less trafficked than its close neighbour - this is because, darn it, the best routes are also the hardest ones! The White Tower is home to the incredible wall climb of *White Heat*, and the infamous testpiece *The Great White*. The best 'easy' is undoubtedly the lengthy *Sea Groove*, which flanks the right edge of the Tower.

Approach - From the gearing up point at Mother Carey's, follow the coast path eastwards. This leads up a slope to a level area beneath two towers (NOTE: from a distance, this looks like an innocuous grassy headland). Walk through a col between the two towers, and scramble easily down a wide ramp to ledges below. These lead back leftwards (looking out) to gain ledges at the base of the Tower.

Tides - The routes can all be approached at high tide - as long as the sea isn't wild. If you're approaching *Sea Groove* at high tide, the best method is to scramble around from the col/rear of the Tower on the various grassy terraces.

7 Sea Groove 2 **VS 4b**

38m. This fine little expedition follows the huge groove found in the eastern edge of the Tower. A great line, terrific positions - and at an amenable grade. Split it at one third height or lead the route in one almighty pitch. Reach it either via the front of the Tower, or, at high tide or in rough seas, use the descending terraces at the back of the Tower to reach it. To retreat from the finishing ridge, scramble across the very top of the Tower and then down directly to the access col.

FA. J.Rees-Jones, John Cleare 3.67

Meilee Rafe and Libby Peter climbing *Sea Groove* (VS) - *this page* - The White Tower. Photo: Mike Robertson

Rock Around the Block (E3) a traverse of the block at Trevallen best attempted at high tide. Photo: Ian Parnell

Mike Weeks tackles the sensationally-positioned *Undertone* (E5) - *page 92* - Rusty Walls. Photo: Ian Parnell

Jack Geldard sprinting on *The Fine Art of Surfacing* (E6) - *page 99* - in Hollow Caves Bay. Photo: Dave Pickford

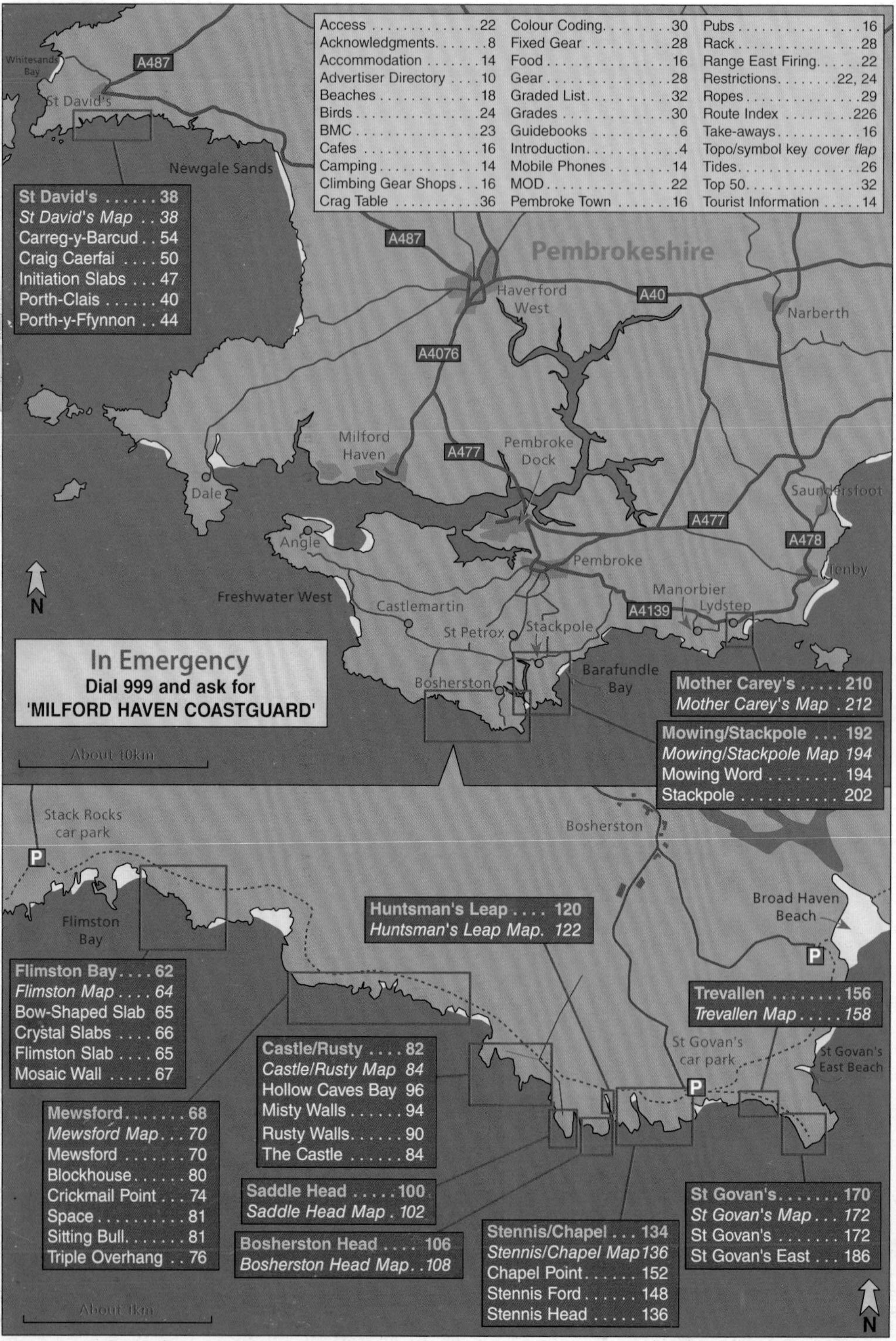

Whitesands Bay
A487
St David's
Newgale Sands
St David's 38
St David's Map .. 38
Carreg-y-Barcud .. 54
Craig Caerfai 50
Initiation Slabs ... 47
Porth-Clais 40
Porth-y-Ffynnon .. 44
A487
Pembrokeshire
Haverford West
A40
Narberth
A4076
Milford Haven
A477
Pembroke Dock
Dale
Saundersfoot
A477
A478
Angle
Pembroke
Tenby
N
Freshwater West
Castlemartin
Manorbier
A4139
Lydstep
St Petrox
Stackpole
Barafundle Bay
Bosherston
In Emergency
Dial 999 and ask for
'MILFORD HAVEN COASTGUARD'
About 10km
Mother Carey's 210
Mother Carey's Map . 212
Mowing/Stackpole ... 192
Mowing/Stackpole Map 194
Mowing Word 194
Stackpole 202
Stack Rocks car park
P
Bosherston
Flimston Bay
Huntsman's Leap 120
Huntsman's Leap Map. 122
Broad Haven Beach
P
Flimston Bay.... 62
Flimston Map 64
Bow-Shaped Slab 65
Crystal Slabs 66
Flimston Slab 65
Mosaic Wall 67
Trevallen 156
Trevallen Map 158
Castle/Rusty 82
Castle/Rusty Map 84
Hollow Caves Bay 96
Misty Walls 94
Rusty Walls...... 90
The Castle 84
St Govan's car park
P
St Govan's East Beach
Mewsford....... 68
Mewsford Map... 70
Mewsford 70
Blockhouse...... 80
Crickmail Point ... 74
Space 81
Sitting Bull....... 81
Triple Overhang .. 76
Saddle Head 100
Saddle Head Map . 102
Bosherston Head 106
Bosherston Head Map..108
Stennis/Chapel ... 134
Stennis/Chapel Map 136
Chapel Point...... 152
Stennis Ford 148
Stennis Head 136
St Govan's....... 170
St Govan's Map ... 172
St Govan's 172
St Govan's East ... 186
About 1km
N